International Environmental Law and Policy Series

Environmental Pollution Control
An Introduction to Principles and Practice of Administration

Series General Editor

Stanley P. Johnson

Advisory Editor

Günther Handl

Other titles in the series

The Environmental Policy of the European Communities, S. P. Johnson
and G. Corcelle
(ISBN 1–85333–225–9)
Transferring Hazardous Technologies and Substances, G. Handl and R. E. Lutz
(ISBN 0–86010–704–3)
Understanding US and European Environmental Law: A Practitioner's Guide, T.
T. Smith and P. Kromarek
(ISBN 1–85333–305–0)
*Air Pollution Control in the European Community: Implementation of the EC
Directives in the Twelve Member States*, G. Bennett (ed.)
(ISBN 1–85333–567–3)
International Responsibility for Environmental Harm, F. Francioni and
T. Scovazzi (eds.)
(ISBN 1–85333–579–7)
International Law and Global Climate Change, R. Churchill and
D. Freestone (eds.)
(ISBN 1–85333–629–7)
Environmental Protection and International Law, W. Lang, H. Neuhold and
K. Zemanek (eds.)
(ISBN 1–85333–611–4)
International Legal Problems of the Environmental Protection of the Baltic Sea,
M. Fitzmaurice
(ISBN 0–7923–1402–6)
The Antarctic Environment and International Law, J. Verhoeven, P. Sands,
M. Bruce (eds.)
(ISBN 1–85333–630–0)
Basic Documents of International Environmental Law, H. Hohmann (ed.)
(ISBN 1–85333–628–9)
*The Earth Summit: The United Nations Conference on Environment and
Development (UNCED)*, S. P. Johnson
(ISBN 1–85333–784–6)

(Please order by ISBN or title)

International Environmental Law and Policy Series

Environmental Pollution Control
An Introduction to Principles and Practice of Administration

J. McLoughlin

E. G. Bellinger

Graham & Trotman/Martinus Nijhoff
Members of the Wolters Kluwer Academic Publishers Group
LONDON/DORDRECHT/BOSTON

Graham & Trotman Limited
Sterling House
66 Wilton Road
London SWIV IDE
UK

Kluwer Academic Publishers Group
101 Philip Drive
Assinippi Park
Norwell, MA 02061
USA

First published in 1993

British Library Cataloguing in Publication Data
McLoughlin, J. Brian
  Environmental Pollution Control:
  Introduction to Principles and Practice
  of Administration. — (International
  Environmental Law & Policy Series)
  I. Title II. Bellinger, E. G. III. Series
  341.7623

ISBN 1–85333–577–0   Series ISBN 1–85333–275–5

Library of Congress Cataloguing-in-Publication Data
McLoughlin, James, LL.M.
    Environmental pollution control : an introduction to principles
and practice of administration / J. McLoughlin, E.G. Bellinger.
      p.   cm. — (International environmental law and policy series)
    Includes index.
    ISBN 1–85333–577–0
    1. Pollution. 2. Pollution–Law and legislation. 3. Liability
for environmental damages. I. Bellinger, E. G. II. Title.
III. Series.
TD174.M42   1993
363.73–dc20

                                                          92-38322
                                                          CIP

Typeset in Times by Expo Holdings Sdn Bhd, Kuala Lumpur, Malaysia
Printed and bound in Great Britain by Hartnolls Ltd, Bodmin, Cornwall

Contents

Preface

In both eastern Europe and developing countries, people are seeking effective ways of controlling environmental pollution. If their ambitions are to be fulfilled, that control must go hand in hand with economic development. They look to Europe, the United States and to other developed countries which have already tackled their problems.

This book is written largely with those people in mind. For that reason, it does not concentrate on any particular system of control or the control laws of any particular country. It is also not based on any particular philosophy or political beliefs.

It is an introductory book. It aims to introduce the reader to the problems of pollution control and the various ways in which those problems can be tackled. In seeking out the various ways, it does not advocate the adoption of any ready made system. The authors' experience in environmental consultancy has emphasised the mistake of trying to adopt a ready made system from elsewhere. A system is far better built on an existing institutional structure and an existing legal system. To do otherwise creates many problems.

We must add that the book deals with the control of pollution. It does not cover those measures taken with a view to ensuring that further development does not lead to undue degradation of the environment. They may be in the form of land use planning controls, or economic or fiscal measures.

In writing the book the authors have had in mind the administrator or future administrator. Too often a civil servant experienced in other branches of government is thrust into the administration of pollution control, having had little direct experience of the breadth of its problems, and sometimes unaware of the breadth of related tasks in the wider field of environmental management.

The book may also be of help to any politician likewise thrust into an office with responsibility for pollution control, and who seeks quickly to acquire a reasonably comprehensive body of background knowledge, and some introduction to the ways in which the problems have already been tackled in other countries.

Finally, it may be of help to students, and even those already involved in the executive work of control, by giving a broad overview of the subject.

We wish to thank John Butlin for writing the section on economic and fiscal controls, and Catherine Redgwell for her chapter on international obligations.

Our examples of laws and techniques have come from various jurisdictions. Wherever possible we have consulted lawyers from those jurisdictions. If any errors remain they are, of course, our responsibility. Those examples are included, however, merely to show some of the techniques which may be used, therefore it is not vital that they should be completely up to date.

We hope that the book will be useful in giving an introduction to the wide spectrum of pollution problems, and to some of the methods used in tackling them.

J. McLoughlin   E. G. Bellinger
J. McLoughlin and Associates   School of Biological Sciences
Tel: United Kingdom 05394 41759   University of Manchester
Fax: United Kingdom 05394 41709

Chapter I

Environmental Pollution

1. ENVIRONMENTAL CHANGE

1.1 Causes of environment change

1.1.1 Changes in the environment occur frequently, and those changes are from a great variety of causes. Many of them, including major changes which can affect the whole planet, come from natural events. Over the estimated 4,500 million years of the earth's existence as such, there have been several changes in its polarity. The cause is as yet unknown. There was another change which led to the extinction of the dinosaurs, and again the cause is unknown. Single events such as volcanoes can cause permanent changes in topography, such as the explosive eruption of Krakatoa in 1883, which demolished a large part of an island, the eruption off the coast of Iceland in 1963 which created the new island of Surtsey. More recently, man has witnessed the explosive eruption of Mount St. Helens, which flattened a wide area of forest and encircled the earth with a girdle of dust, and provided glorious sunsets even in other continents. There have been, and are continuing to be more gradual changes such as the desertification of large parts of Africa. The Sahara was once covered with vegetation. There are also many continuous changes on a much smaller scale, such as the natural ageing of a lake as its waters gradually become eutrophic.

1.1.2 Changes can also be caused by plants and animals. All living organisms produce waste products. Green vegetation produces oxygen, with beneficial effects for man. In its early years, the atmosphere of the earth was composed largely of methane, ammonia and water vapour, with no free oxygen. The advent of green, photosynthetic plants which release oxygen as a by-product of their processes led to a gradual, but dramatic change in the atmosphere, allowing life as we know it today.

Many wastes produced by animals can be detrimental to man, but are often present in amounts which can be degraded and rendered harmless by other environmental processes. When groups of animals, particularly humans, congregate in very large numbers, environmental processes may not in the short term, have the capacity to remove or degrade all the wastes produced.

Many changes are caused by the activities of animals. Beavers can reduce a lake-side forest area to what looks to us to be devastation. Goats introduced to an island can reduce the vegetation by their voracious, non-selective appetites, and introduced predatory mammals can wipe out whole populations of ground dwelling birds.

Man is pre-eminent amongst the animals for causing major changes to the environment in recent times. The human race has undergone a massive increase in population, particularly during the last century, and on a global scale that increase is still continuing. In areas of high population man's natural wastes alone have caused serious pollution. But most of all his agricultural and industrial activities have wrought great changes over large areas. Even his recreational activities have left their mark. Over-population, of course, brings with it many adverse consequences, of which pollution is only one. Over population, in terms of both size and distribution, is a problem which in some circumstances can solve itself, but which one day may call for serious conscious management.

1.1.3   The great majority of these changes are temporary, and natural processes return the environment to its former state. In some cases, however, the effects of a pollutant can cause changes which do not manifest themselves immediately. It may be even years before the adverse effect is felt, and long lasting damage may have been done before any action has been taken.[1] In other cases, where a self regulatory mechanism which has hitherto maintained a balance in nature has been upset, the changes can be apparently irreversible. Such changes give the greatest cause for concern.

1.2. Changes and consequent damage

1.2.1   Hitherto the word 'changes' has been used. Whether or not such changes are being considered to cause 'damage'[2] is a matter for subjective judgement.[3] For the beaver referred to above the changes he wrought were probably to him beneficial. Even the Mount St. Helens explosion and the dust it raised, as noted above, caused beautiful sunsets in some areas, which were greatly admired, while the dust was at such an altitude it caused little or no harm to anyone. Man's own pollution of the atmosphere can have similar effects. In the northeast of England, air pollution used to bring colourful sunsets, as a songwriter wrote:

> And the air pollution turns your collar grey, but oh the sunsets Geordie lad – they take your breath away!

1.2.2   Noting what changes have occurred is only the first step in determining whether or not they are 'polluting'. The next step is to see whether or not man's interests have been effected.[3]

That may be regarded as too narrow a view. Although it is accepted that man has the means of affecting the whole process of terrestrial change and development, that does not mean that he is called upon to act as God. He has neither omniscience nor omnipotence, and in some areas his record suggests that he is a notorious

---

[1]See Figure I, page 8.
[2]See section 3 for the meaning of 'pollution damage' as used in this volume.
[3]See 2.3.4(f) on the subjective nature of pollution.

bungler. He has not yet been able to manage his own social affairs, which suggests that he should not be let loose on wholesale environmental management. 'Sufficient unto the day is the evil thereof,'[4] and the evil is so often man's ill-controlled and perhaps unwitting interference with the environment. In the present rudimentary state of his knowledge and competence, it is sufficient to ask him to keep to a minimum his interference with environmental conditions, and especially with the self-regulatory systems which have served the planet for so long.

1.2.3 This volume is therefore concerned with man's task of controlling his own pollution. One criterion at least he can appreciate – that of his own interests. Those who still protest that is too narrow a view may find some satisfaction in the fact that man is now beginning to recognise that his own interests encompass a naturally stable environment, and as wide a variety of habitats and proliferation of species as his presence in the natural community will permit. The volume is also limited to the examination of legal and administrative measures to that end. Man's laws, regulations and administrative measures govern only man, although, as noted below, they can , nonetheless affect beneficially the common environment with its fauna and flora.

Ever since at least Roman times, the law has been concerned with persons and their interests. Indeed, the Romans defined a 'person' as someone with rights and duties at law,[5] and the law is designed to enforce and protect those rights and enforce those duties. Neither an inanimate object nor an animal can have rights or duties in law, because it cannot assert its rights in the courts, nor can the courts enforce the performance of its duties.

In recent years it has been claimed by some that lakes, rivers and mountains should have rights. In law that is an impossibility – the law can act only on behalf of persons against persons. If lakes and mountains are to be protected, it is man's activities which must be curtailed, or action required of man to conserve them. What such activities and actions will be, will inevitably be decided by man – and equally inevitably in his own interests.

Likewise much has been said in recent years of 'animal rights'. The law does not attempt to take any direct action either on behalf of or against an animal.[6] The law can and does protect animals and other parts of the natural world by controlling the actions of man. It may also require man to take action to conserve nature, or even to take action for the improvement of the physical environment .[7]

The paragraphs above refer to man's 'own interests' and 'action to conserve nature'. At the very basis of this book lies the idea that it is in man's own interests to conserve large parts of the environment in their natural states, with great varieties of habitats and great proliferations of species, and that those interests lie heavily in the balance when man is making his decisions on future action and future development.

[4]Gospel according to St. Matthew Chapter 6 verse 34.

[5]A slave in ancient Rome had no rights, nor any duties which were enforceable against him by process of law. He was therefore regarded in Roman law as a chattel rather than a person.

[6]A dog was once produced in a French court to face a man accused of ill-treating it. The dog is said to have leapt at the man's throat. In terms of law, that was simply material evidence to support a finding of guilt, or liability in French law according to whatever obligations the law imposed on him. In England, a local government by-law provided that 'It is an offence for any dog to foul the pavement'. No-one ever put a dog in the dock and asked it to plead 'guilty' or 'not guilty'.

[7]The English Town and Country Planning Act 1990, at Section 31(2) provides that a local authority structure plan shall include in its policy and general proposals 'measures for the improvement of the physical environment'.

2. SCOPE OF THE TERM 'POLLUTION CONTROL'

2.1 'Pollution control' distinguished from other related terms

2.1.1 The scope of the term 'pollution control' must first be determined for the purposes of this volume. Except where otherwise stated, the term will have the same scope also in all other books in this series.

2.1.2 Terms such as 'environmental management', 'environmental protection' and 'pollution control' have no established meanings which are the same in all circumstances. Their meanings will vary with the expressed intentions of those who use them, otherwise they will vary with the contexts in which they appear.

For the purpose of this series, subject to any contrary indication, the terms will be used to mean the following:

Environmental management. Plans made and actions taken to control the environment in which people live. They may cover both the natural and the man-made environment. The term includes plans and actions to change the natural environment by measures such as the diversion of rivers, creation of artificial lakes, planting of forests, and the cultivation of artificial gardens. Included also are measure taken to prevent natural changes such as desertification, and restoration of former natural conditions as by reforestation.

Environmental protection. Actions taken to protect the natural environment from changes due to man's activities. This includes the protection of sensitive areas from actions such as farming practices which change the character of those areas, and the protection of national parks from erosion by visitors who come merely to enjoy the amenity.

Control of pollution. This refers to action taken to prevent or reduce 'pollution' as defined in 2.3.3. It will be noted that 'pollution' is there defined to cover only the results of man's activities, and only effects which are adverse to man's interests. It will be noted also that the term relates to the physical environment, including the amenity it offers. Normally, the pollution control authorities do not concern themselves with the preservation of visual amenity. That is left to the land use planning authorities, who have greater expertise and more appropriate powers. Where the loss of amenity, however, is caused by physical pollution, the pollution control authorities may be called upon to take action.

Control of pollution must also be distinguished from conservation. The latter relates simply to what we already have, whether it is natural or man made, even though it may bring no benefit to man except, for example, to satisfy his interest in the history of his own culture.

2.2 Arbitrary limitations on the scope of this study

2.2.1 Pollution of the environment in the workplace

Pollution of the environment in a place of work is within the scope of the term 'pollution' as defined at 2.3.2. Moreover, its effects can be very serious to people who work there, or who even just enter that place for other purposes.

Controls over such pollution, however, lie in restraints on the employer, duties owed by the employer to his employees and to others who have reason to enter that place, duties owed by employees to their fellow workers and to others, and in measures to protect people by way of protective clothing, protective creams, ear protectors and the like. It therefore forms a separate, and in some jurisdictions a highly developed, branch of law.

Controls over pollution in the workplace will therefore not be considered in this series, except where they have particular relevance to the matter under discussion.

2.2.2 Pollution of the home environment

Within the limits of its resources, every household controls its own environment inside its home. In many jurisdictions, it is assisted by public authorities in various ways.

(a) Land use planning and pollution controls seek to reduce pollution of the physical environment of the area, so as to help householders to maintain a clean and quiet environment in their homes.
(b) The imposition of building standards helps to eliminate or reduce the intrusion of pollution into the home. Building standards sometimes go further, laying down requirements for sound attenuation by interior walls, and for ventilation.

This series is concerned with the population control elements of (a), i.e. pollution of the common environment which may intrude into the home. It is also concerned in some cases with measures to prevent or reduce such intrusion, such as grants for noise insulation near airports.[8]

2.2.3 At policy level, all those matters merge, and may be dealt with by the same body of policy makers. At the level of implementation, however, they will be matters for such authorities as may be determined by the legislators or the government, which for the various purposes may be pollution control authorities, or others such as those concerned with land use planning or building.

Only to the extent that pollution control authorities are involved, or with advantage could be involved, are those matters dealt with in this series.

2.3 Definitions of 'pollution'

2.3.1 There have been many definitions of 'pollution' published by different public authorities for different purposes. Some are restricted to pollution of particular parts of the environment, such as the definitions of 'pollution of the marine environment'. They will be examined in subsequent volumes relating to those parts. Here attention is centred on definitions of general application.

2.3.2 Some years ago, the Environmental Pollution Panel of the US President's Science Advisory Committee advised the President on the meaning of 'pollution' in the following terms.

---

[8]Those matters will be dealt with in the volume in this series dealing with noise.

Environmental pollution is the unfavorable alteration of our surroundings, wholly or largely as a by product of man's actions, through direct or indirect effects of changes in energy patterns, radiation levels, chemical and physical constitution and abundances of organisms. These changes may affect man directly, and through supplies of his water and of other agricultural and biological products, his physical objects or possessions, or his opportunities for recreation and appreciation of nature.

This was offered as an explanation rather than a definition, but it does draw attention to most of the essential elements of pollution. See also chapter VIII, section 4.

2.3.3 Definition of pollution for the purposes of this book

For the purpose of this book, except where otherwise stated, 'pollution' shall mean:

The introduction by a person into any part of the common environment, of waste matter or surplus energy, which so changes, or will change, the environment as to affect adversely, directly or indirectly, the opportunity of people to use or enjoy it.

2.3.4   The following notes to the definition may help on the understanding of the characteristics of pollution as thus defined.

(a) *The introduction by a person*
     This limits pollution to the consequences of the activities of people. There may be degradation of the environment from natural causes, as noted at 1.1.1, e.g. from the natural ageing of a lake, or from the effects of a volcano, but the wording of the definition excludes degradation from such causes.
(b) *into any part of the environment*
     Matter may be moved from one part of the environment, where it has no adverse effect, to another where it has, e.g. the deposit on land of colliery waste taken from underground.
(c) *surplus energy*
     Sound may be in the form of music. If it is too loud, or radiated more widely than necessary, it may be properly regarded as surplus energy. Where it has effects regarded as adverse by some people, it may properly be regarded by them as pollution.
(d) *or will change*
     This is included so that the interests of future generations can be taken into account.
(e) *directly or indirectly*
     There may be a direct effect, such as an effect on a person's health of gases released into the atmosphere. There may be an indirect effect, such as an effect on fish spawning grounds of a chemical released into water. That may reduce the numbers of edible fish available, or kill members of an endangered species of scientific interest by migration of pollutants through a food chain.
(f) *to affect adversely*
     What is adverse to the interests of one person may be beneficial to those of another. The criterion is entirely subjective. A sediment discharge to settle on the sea-bed may drive away benthic species such as crabs and lobsters, a loss for some fishermen; but it may attract free swimming flat fish, a profit for others. Likewise, some forms of popular music may be an exciting and delightful sound to one person, but a noise nuisance to another.

(g) *opportunity of people to use and enjoy it*

Controls are applied to protect the interests of humans in the environment. The term 'environment' is usually used to include its fauna and flora. Effects on those plants and animals, in so far as the effects are adverse to man's interests, can be regarded as pollution. That applies whether his interests are commercial as with herring, scientific as with certain rare species, or merely aesthetic as with animals such as the cheetah. No-one seeks to protect malaria carrying mosquitoes or dangerous bacteria. Many animals which adversely affect people's interests are declared to be pests, and killing is encouraged.

3. POLLUTION DAMAGE

3.1 The nature of pollution damage

3.1.1 When a substance is discharged into the environment it may have an adverse effect.[9] Some effects are obvious, such as the destruction of fruit crops by an ethylene discharge from a chemical factory. Others may be less obvious, and take many years to show themselves, e.g. the effects of low levels of radioactivity on the incidence of leukaemia in certain areas. The important question about these effects is whether or not they result in damage to any of man's interests, remembering that man's interest range from the welfare of himself and his community, the welfare of other and even distant peoples, present amenity, recreation, scientific interest, and the welfare and all the corresponding interests of future generations. The altruistic nature of man must be accepted, even though it may be difficult to analyse. It must be remembered also that such welfare and other interests depend on having a varied and thriving environment.

3.1.2 In considering the control of pollution, it is therefore necessary to distinguish between damage or injury which can be regarded as pollution, and that which cannot.

For example, if a farmer has a field of turnips, and that field is exposed to a very high concentration of sulphur dioxide, there could be two possible consequences, dependent on when the pollution occurred. If the exposure occurred only an hour or two before harvesting, the leaves or other aerial parts of the plant would be badly injured, but the root crop would be unaffected and the crop yield undiminished. Hence there would be no economic loss, and no damage to man's interests would occur. Therefore there wold be no pollution damage. If, however, the exposure to the toxin occurred a month or more before harvesting, the aerial parts of the plant would be so injured as to prevent full development of the root crop, hence there would have been economic loss, and pollution damage would have occurred. Both examples assume that the aerial parts of the plant would not have been made use of in this case.

Environmental biologists tend to refer to the first of those consequences merely as 'injury', and the second as 'damage'. The essence of the distinction is that the second consequence was an adverse effect on man's interest in the crop, and therefore was a form of pollution.

There can even be cases in which there has been no injury to a plant or animal,

---

[9]See 2.3.4(f).

so far as present day methods of examination can detect, yet an adverse effect on man's interest in it. Oil residues in the sea can taint the flesh of fish living there, but apparently the fish themselves are unaffected. To commercial fishermen on the other hand, it is no longer marketable, and therefore of no value.

3.2 Long and short-term pollution damage

3.2.1 The kinds of damage done may also be classified according to whether their effects are immediate, long-term or even delayed, and according to rates of recovery. The immediate and long-term effects are illustrated with reference to water in Figure I. Delay in effects may be due to the time taken for a pollutant to travel through the food chain or along some critical pathway to reach a sensitive receptor. It may also be due to a rate of emission into the environment which exceeds the rate of decay, thus resulting in a slow accumulation.

Rates of decay are measured in terms of 'half life' – the period of time taken for a pollutant's effects to be reduced by one half. It may become important to reduce the rate of emission into the environment to ensure that the cumulative effects of discharges do not reach an unacceptable level. For example, krypton 85 is released into the atmosphere from some nuclear processes. Its half life is 10.8 years. It had been calculated that with emissions from various sources, a critical concentration would be reached by the year 2000. Because of that, British Nuclear Fuels at its

Figure I   Time Scales Storm Runoff Water Quality Problems

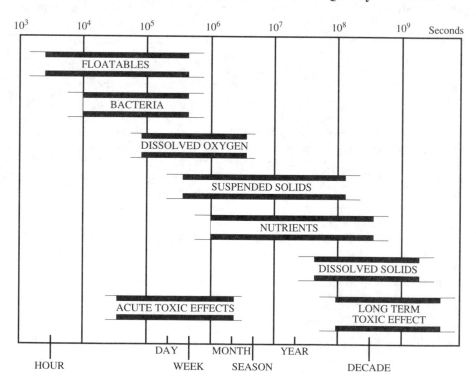

Sellafield installation stores the krypton it produces for a period of about ten years – equivalent to one half life. The release of radioactive tritium into the hydrosphere still presents a similar problem.

3.3   Indirect pollution damage

Thus 'pollution damage' is a term used for all adverse effects on man, his artifacts and his interests in the environment. It includes both short term impacts caused by acute pollutant exposure, and long term exposure leading to chronic effects.

3.3.1   Pollution damage does not occur only when an organism or structure is directly exposed to a pollutant. When that does occur it is termed direct or primary damage. If a toxin on the other hand, is passed through a food chain and another organism is affected, indirect damage may occur to the consumer organism higher up the food chain, as in the case of peregrine falcons which were affected by pesticides used on crops. Indirect damage may also occur to families or relatives of a person affected by a pollutant. Such a person may suffer death, depriving the family of support and causing severe economic loss.

In addition, further indirect damage may be done also to wide ranges of people. If the owner of a business is made ill for a long period by environmental pollution, and the business fails, not only members of the family could be affected. Employees could be adversely affected, and even the state could suffer, losing income tax revenue from the business and it employees and having to pay unemployment benefit. If a hotel on the coast is closed due to massive oil pollution, suppliers, people providing services, and other dependent businesses may be affected.

3.3.2   In any legal system, it would be unusual for all such people to be awarded compensation. The courts will not award compensation for damage they consider too remote a consequence. That does not mean, however, that an administrator considering the possible effects of a pollutant should not take them into account, or a person making an environmental impact assessment should ignore them. For them, such consequences, even though remote, are pertinent considerations.

Other problems of remote consequences can arise. For example, when the *Torrey Canyon* foundered on the rocks off the Scilly Isles, large quantities of oil escaped and drifted up the English Channel. They approached the French fishing grounds but did not reach them. Nevertheless, the sales of fish in the Paris fish markets dropped by 50 per cent. It could be argued that the customers' reaction was a reasonable precaution, or a reaction which could have been expected. That raises the question of whether the fishmongers suffered pollution damage.

Compensation for pollution damage is discussed more fully in Chapter V.

4.   OBJECTIVES OF POLLUTION CONTROL

4.1   Elimination and reduction of pollution

4.1.1   First it must be noted that the elimination of pollution does not necessarily mean the elimination of all discharges and deposits. Interpreted in accordance with the definition at 2.3.3, pollution does not occur unless there has been or will be an adverse effect, and that does not follow from all discharges. For example in the past, and in some areas today, discharges of domestic sewage have been used to promote growth in fish ponds, and some deposits of inert waste materials form useful landfill.

4.1.2   Give sufficient resources, it is possible to minimise most forms of pollution today. The outstanding exceptions are the various forms of accidental pollution. It is not possible to eliminate risk entirely. This has been shown in the history of nuclear installations. It is apparent elsewhere. In exploratory drillings into the sea-bed in search for oil, it has been calculated that even when the operator is using the best available techniques and using all due care, there will be on average a 'blow out' about once in every 500 drillings.[10]

Even where the elimination of pollution is technically possible, it is not necessarily economically feasible. The cost of eliminating pollution from all domestic sewage would be so high in most areas that the process would be financially unacceptable in political terms. The cost of eliminating pollution from industrial discharges would in some cases be so high and so damaging to the industry concerned, and to employment opportunities therein, that again the process would be unacceptable.

4.1.3   Once the decision has been made to accept some pollution for the sake of economy and the creation of material wealth, the community is confronted with the need for a second decision – how much pollution is to be accepted? One or two simple examples will illustrate this point.

Any community of people must decide the extent to which it will treat it sewage before discharge. A very high standard of treatment may eliminate or almost eliminate pollution, but it is possible that many householders would be unwilling to make their proportionate contribution to the cost.

In industry, cleaner processes and less polluting products are beginning to make a substantial contribution to environmental protection. The development and adoption of clean technology is discussed in Chapter III at 8.4.6 to 8.4.13 Unfortunately, such advances may be largely offset by the increasing kinds and quantities of highly toxic wastes now being produced. Technological advances are not entirely solving the problem. In many areas decisions still have to be made on what degree of pollution to tolerate in order that industry will no be unduly burdened with the cost of waste treatment and waste disposal. Many a polluted river could be cleaned substantially in a relatively short period of time, but at considerable cost, and with considerable damage to local industry and employment opportunities.

Unless appropriate machinery is provided for the making of those decisions, pollution control will be haphazard and at the mercy of political and social interests which have not been properly co-ordinated to produce a balanced policy.[11]

4.1.4   The problem is many sided. An attempt has been made by an economist, R.G. Ridker, in the *Economic Costs Of Air Pollution* (Praeger, London) to provide a graph which could be used in reaching a decision on the level of pollution which may be regarded as the optimum in terms of overall cost, including the cost of

[10]Note that this raises implications for compensation provisions. See Chapter V at 4.3.
[11]For example see Chapter V at 6.4.4.

Figure II : Ridker Graph

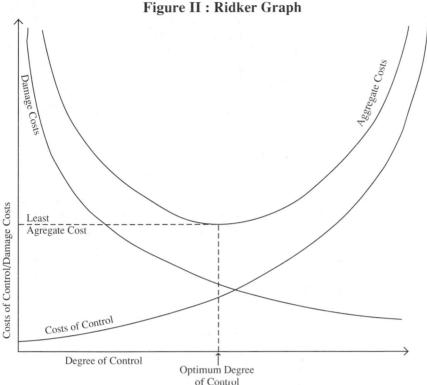

damage done as well as the cost of control, in any particular circumstances. It is shown in Figure II.

The curves shown in the diagram are hypothetical, but represent the kinds of curves found in many cases, in which the amount of damage done decreases rapidly in the earlier stages of control, but less rapidly as further controls are applied. It may be relatively easy to reduce the concentration of a pollutant in a discharge from 15 to 10 parts per million, but very difficult and costly to reduce it from 2 to 1. Conversely, costs rise more steeply as the degree of control applied increases.

For any point on the degree of control axis, a combined cost of control measures and resultant damage can be calculated by a simple addition. Those combined costs can be represented as a graph which forms a curve.[12] The lowest point of the curve thus represents the lowest point of combined costs, and a vertical dropped from the point can show on the horizontal axis the optimum degree of control in terms of the aggregate of effects on the community.

4.1.5   The graph can be a useful tool in decision making, but its limitations must be noted.

(a) The first is that for some forms of damage there can be no satisfactory eva-
     luation in monetary terms. The shortening of human life is one. If a boy of ten
     years of age contracts leukaemia from radioactive discharges, and the medical

---

[12]See Figure II. The curves are approximations. For some pollutants they will not be regular curves.

prognosis is that he is unlikely to live for more than another three to five years, no amount of money can be adequate compensation, neither to him nor to his parents. Many other less dramatic examples could be found, where a sum of money would likewise be inadequate compensation, e.g. of lives shortened by chemical pollution of the atmosphere.

Even when a reasonable estimate of adequate compensation seems to be possible, the figures will vary with different people and different circumstances. A wealthy man would pay more for a quieter environment than would a poor man – the compensation he would regard as sufficient for a noise nuisance would therefore be higher.

A study of air pollution, carried out by a research team at Harwell in the United Kingdom, produced results relevant to this problem, and interesting in at least one other respect. The team tried to discover the value that people put on clean air, and chose an area which was to become a 'smoke control area'. Before the smoke control order was made, they asked people to put a monetary value on clean air. A few years later, when the order had been made and had been in effect for some time, they returned to ask the same people a second time. The values given on that second occasion were significantly higher than on the first. Having experienced a clean atmosphere, they valued it the more. That brings a hopeful message to those people who claim that pollution control is worthwhile.

The main point for our present purposes, however, is that without a reasonably accurate evaluation of damage, the Ridker graph cannot give useful results.

(b) The second limitation is that the graph can give an estimate of the optimum degree of pollution only in terms of costs to the community as a whole. But the community includes groups of people, and individuals, who pay the costs of control in different proportions, and suffer pollution damage to different degrees.

Bentham's criterion of 'the greatest good for the greatest number' is inappropriate where a minority of people bear an unfair share of the burdens, in order to sustain a greater good for the majority. By the same reasoning, the Ridker graph falls short of being a reliable guide in that it does not take account of the inequitable distribution of benefits and burdens. It deals only in aggregates for the community as a whole, and further highly complex analysis would be needed to give results which were just to minority groups and individuals.

The error that comes from ignoring that limitation can be seen also in the minority report in the Third Report of the Royal Commission on Environmental Pollution, in the United Kingdom. That minority report advocated a system of charges for the disposal of wastes into rivers and tidal waters,[13] and at paragraph 2 supported the use of such charges with the words

> pollution should be reduced to the point where the costs of doing so are covered by the benefits from the reduction of pollution.[14]

[13]For a discussion on such systems see Chapter III at sections 5 and 8.8.

[14]Quoted from paragraph 20 of the First Report of the Royal Commission on Environmental Pollution, of the United Kingdom.

The minority report then goes on to say

> For example, society as a whole would lose if, say, £2 were to be spent to eliminate a
> further unit of pollution that had imposed £1 of damage on society.

It will again be noted, that that is expressed in terms of society as a whole, and
in those terms is undoubtedly true. But in the large majority of cases the money
is spent by the discharger, and the damage suffered by another person. That
other person may legitimately reply

> However much it may cost the discharger, he must not do damage to me or my
> property. I am not to bear the burden in order that he can save money, even if that
> saving is regarded as a saving to society as a whole.

Even if the £1 were paid as compensation, that would not necessarily provide a
satisfactory answer. Many people, such as couples living contentedly in a
carefully chosen home bought for retirement, do not want monetary compensation – they want a clean environment.

Clearly, the computation and comparison of aggregates is not enough. What
is needed is a scheme of control which takes into account minority and
individual interests. Those matters will be considered in the next chapter.

(c) To these must be added other limitations. The use of the graph does not take
into account loss or damage which may affect future generations, which many
people today feel is an important consideration. Nor does it take into account
international obligations. Many of the pollutants now released cross international boundaries. responsibility for trans-frontier pollution is recognised, and
is dealt with in many treaties, both global and regional. This is too complex a
matter to be dealt with here, but more will be said about it in Chapter VII.

4.2   Formulation of pollution policies

4.2.1   The task of deciding how much pollution a community might reasonably be
expected to accept is highly complex. It must take into account many factors,
including many conflicting interests. Those factors include:

- costs imposed on members of the community, e.g. by sewerage and sewage
  disposal charges, by the use of smokeless fuels for domestic heating, by noise
  reduction;
- costs imposed on industry, agriculture and public authorities by the reduction,
  treatment and control of discharges and deposits;
- effects of those costs on industry and agriculture;
- effects on employment opportunities;
- damage effects of pollution, suffered by the community as a whole, and by
  minority groups and individuals, including effects on
  amenity and the quality of life,
  natural beauty,
  places of scientific, geophysical, cultural and historic interest,
  opportunities for recreation,
  amount and diversity of wildlife;

–   adverse effects for future generations.
–   international obligations.[15]

The list, of course, is not complete.

It must be borne in mind also that even where interests do not conflict, many people put different values on such things, and therefore give different weight than do others to the same factors.

4.2.2   To this task is added the complication that the weight to be given to many of the factors will vary according to circumstances. In times of economic stress or national crisis, there may be justification for relaxing standards, or relaxing controls over some industry of overriding national importance, allowing of course for any possible long term harm. Flexibility in a system of control is necessary for those purposes.

4.2.3   It will be seen from the above that the task is essentially a political one. An appropriate authority must make the decision after having been informed of all factors and all interests, and after taking into account all available expert advice.

The choice of such authority, and its composition and the procedure it will follow, will depend on the political philosophy of the state concerned, its constitution, and the general pattern of its administrative structures. Administrative structures will be examined in the next chapter.

4.3   Immediate purposes of a system of pollution control

4.3.1   It may be useful at this stage to set out, in the light of what has been said above, what may legitimately be regarded as the purposes of any system of pollution control.

4.3.2   Those purposes will include:
(a) To encourage the reduction of waste.

The first step in the reduction of waste is the adoption of 'clean techniques', and the conservation of energy, so that less is discharged as waste substances or surplus energy, in either case with less polluting effects.

Private enterprise will not adopt a new technique unless it can find a commercial advantage in doing so. This is not stated as an adverse criticism of those involved. Most private enterprises are marriages between capital and expertise. The shareholder provides the capital on the understanding that those who direct and manage the enterprise, within the scope of its agreed objects, and within any legal restrictions imposed, will earn profits as high as possible. The directors and managers therefore owe an overriding duty to the firm, and hence to the shareholders, to maximise the returns on capital. Any spending which does not do that, directly or indirectly, would be a breach of their duty.[16]

Some firms do try to avoid bad publicity, and try to present a 'green' image. They are usually those which sell goods to the public under the firm's own name. They can reasonably claim that indirectly, money spent on cleaner tech-

[15]See Chapter VIII.
[16]See Chapter III at 8.4.2, and note also the comments at 8.4.3.

niques, attendant 'green' publicity, and an advertised reduction of polluting effects, benefits the shareholders.

To some extent, improvements in techniques can be encouraged by the imposition of standards based on 'best available technology' and 'best practicable means'; and that can be re-enforced by a power to expressly require their adoption.[17] On the other hand, the standard of good oilfield practice',widely used in the oil production industry, while it may require newer or smaller firms to keep pace with technological development, does permit the industry as a whole to set the standard. To that extent it is more a form of acquiescence than a form of control.[18]

(b) To encourage in any process, the recycling or re-use of substances, even the principal product, e.g. newspapers.

To the extent that an industrial plant is discharging to the environment substances that could be re-used or put to another purpose, the use of that plant may be regarded as uneconomic.

The word 'uneconomic' is here used as meaning not economic for the community as a whole. That takes into account many costs which do not appear in the books of account of the firm concerned.

For example, a firm producing metal ingots of iron or aluminium can either recycle metal from scrap, or extract ore to produce new metal. On the firm's books of account, the latter may be cheaper, but there are costs to the community as a whole which do not appear on those books. Such costs, which may be called 'social costs', or 'external costs', take into account

–   provision of land as sites for the disposal of the unused scrap, and loss at least for a time of alternative uses of that land;
–   despoilation of land from which the fresh ore is extracted, with loss of that land for other uses, and loss of amenity;
–   in some cases, a further significant depletion of valuable natural resources.

When those costs are taken into account, recycling may be found to be the more economic from the point of view of the community.

It is relevant to note also, that the people who suffer the loss of countryside and high amenity are not necessarily the people who benefit from the finished product. Even if they are, they may be suffering a disproportionate share of the damage, and hence paying a disproportionate share of the cost.

Land use planning control, of course, may here play one of its many sided roles by restricting further mining.

The production of paper provides a comparable example.

(c) To determine the level of pollution which will be environmentally acceptable in any particular place.[19] As a matter of policy, special protection may be given to places of very high amenity such as the areas of national parks.

(d) To enforce the necessary measures to eliminate or reduce pollution to that level.

(e) To protect the interests of the public, of minorities, and of individuals.

The control of environmental pollution is essentially a means of protecting the public and its interests. The controls adopted must therefore be geared to

[17]See Chapter III at 8.4.9 and 8.4.10.
[18]See Chapter III at last paragraph of 8.4.17.
[19]See 4.1.3 *et seq.*

the uses the public make of their physical environment. That will include breathing the air, drinking the water, following recreational pursuits such as sailing, swimming and fishing, enjoying amenity and taking an interest in nature, wildlife and the community's cultural heritage. The protection of those things is an essential purpose of pollution control. To this may be added the protection of the physical environment for the sake of future generations.

The protection of the interests of minorities and individuals may be achieved by two separate means. The first by taking their interests into account when setting environmental objectives or standards, and then properly enforcing the controls which will achieve those objectives or standards. The first step involves the grant of rights to make representations and objections: the second is normally done by criminal sanctions, imposed through the criminal courts. The second is by awarding compensation for damage already done, and imposing injunctions to prevent future damage. Those remedies are normally provided by the civil courts.

The criminal sanctions will be discussed in general terms in Chapter III at 8 and in Chapter IV. They will also be examined in more detail in relation to different forms of pollution in later volumes.

The civil remedies, and their relationship to criminal sanctions, are discussed in general terms in Chapters V and VI.

(f) To protect the environment for the benefit of future generations.
     For that purpose, there is something to be learned from the philosophies of older pre-industrial communities, such as those of the American Indian tribes. There is also much to be said for the idea that all land is held on trust for the community, including future generations.

     It is relevant here to note also the principle set out in the Sharia, the Islamic law.

> The Sharia .... gives priority to human welfare over human liberty. Muslims as well as non-Muslims living in a Muslim state are bound not to exploit common resources to their own advantage, destroy good producing land, and ruin the potential harvest or encroach upon neighbours land. Since a man in Islam is not merely an economic animal, each person's equal right to life, and to a decent level of living, has priority over the so called economic liberty.[20]

4.4   Protection for the polluter

4.4.1   There is justification also in regarding pollution control laws as protection for the polluter. Industry, for example, even with re-use and recycling, inevitably produces some waste, and it must be permitted to dispose of that waste. In any country, however, with basic environmental protection laws, or even merely laws protecting the public against nuisances, the free disposal of waste meets legal barriers. In many instances, therefore, permission is needed for the disposal of that waste, even though it may cause some degradation of the environment or some nuisance or inconvenience to the public. Such permissions have often been categorised as 'licences to pollute'

---

[20]Abdur Rahman I. Doi, *Sharia: the Islamic Law*, Ta Ha Publishers, London. UK 1984, p.9.

The purpose of pollution control in those circumstances is to permit the disposal, subject to controls which ensure that the least harmful method is used. That can mean protecting the disposer against at least some of the existing laws.

4.4.2 That is less likely to happen in a country such as England, where the basic rule is that a person may do anything which is not prohibited by law. Even there, however, there are laws on private and public nuisance, and rights concerning river waters, which present restraints on many forms of disposal. Consequently, there has long been legal protection for polluters. Any entity, such as a local authority or a nationally owned enterprise, which has a statutory power to do some specified act such as the disposal of waste, is protected against legal actions for damage caused to others, if that damage was an inevitable result of performing the authorised act. Provided that authority or enterprise took reasonable care, taking into account all technical means and scientific knowledge, it has a good defence, usually referred to as a 'defence of statutory authority'.[21]

The laws which protect the polluter may be placed into three broad classes.

4.4.3 Falling within the first class are those consents, authorisations or permits which merely protect a person against criminal liability which he would otherwise incur. Examples can be found in many countries.

In England, under the Water Act 1991, a person may receive from the National Rivers Authority a consent to discharge liquid waste into a river. That consent protects him from criminal penalties under the Act itself, and also under various other prescribed statutes,[22] but does not give him any defence against a civil action brought at common law by a riparian owner.

In Germany, a licence may be granted for an installation which emits discharges to the air. Other public law regulations do not then prevent the establishment or operation of the installation. If, however, pollution damage is suffered by any person from such an installation, which is established and operated in accordance with that licence, he can claim compensation if the polluting effects are considered unreasonable.[23]

In France, under the Law of 9 July 1976 relating to classified installations, any person wishing to establish an installation which produces inconveniences resulting from noise or vibration, must comply with the requirements of that law. Subject to rights of public participation in the authorisation process, and a right of appeal to an administrative court, the person can then establish and operate the installation. A person suffering disturbance, however, from noise therefrom which is an "abnormal neighbourhood inconvenience," may be awarded compensation. The courts can also grant an injunction to close down the installation, but are very loath to do so.[24]

Where adequate precautions against undue pollution are included, and there are no restrictions or limitations on the rights of redress of individuals, there can be no reasonable objection to such legislation – it is merely a co-ordination of those controls which are enforced by criminal penalties.

[21]See *Manchester Corporation* v *Farnworth* [1930] AC 171.
[22]See Water Act 1991 s.88(1).
[23]See Dr. Salzwedel, *Law and Practice of Pollution Control in the Federal Republic of Germany*, at 2.1.2.1 and 2.1.8.5. See also BGHZ 48, 98, 54, 384, and 14 BlmSchG.
[24]See M. Despax and W. Coulet, *Law and Practice of Pollution Control in France* at 8.1.5.1.1 and 8.1.5.2.3. See also Cass. Civ. 29 March 1962, Bull. Civ II, No.365, p.258; Cass. Civ. 2nd, 28 April 1971, Bull. Civ, No.162, p.113.

4.4.4 The second class of legislative controls is one in which ordinary civil rights of redress are replaced by rights which are more restricted or limited.

Two examples may be given, and since they are both the products of international conventions, they may be given as implemented in one state party to the conventions.

The United Kingdom Nuclear Installations Act 1965 provides for controls over nuclear installations. It also provides for compensation to be granted to any person who has suffered injury or damage from an occurrence involving nuclear matter, or from the emission of ionising radiations. That liability is more strict than that at common law, but the aggregate of compensation payments which may be awarded from one occurrence or one breach of duty is subject to statutory maxima. The Act also provides that no other liability shall be incurred by any person by reason of that injury or damage.[25]

Members of the public are thereby granted an advantage as a result of the strict liability, in being able to succeed more easily in obtaining compensation. On the other hand, as a result of the limitation on the measure of damages, they stand a real chance of receiving only inadequate compensation, and lose any right to sue the owner at common law, and any right to sue other persons who might have been involved in that breach of duty.

The United Kingdom Merchant Shipping (Oil Pollution) Act 1971 at Section 1 provides that if an occurrence involving a ship carrying a cargo of persistent oil in bulk results in the discharge or escape of any such oil from that ship, the owner shall be liable for any consequent damage, and for the cost of any measures reasonably taken for preventing or reducing such damage after the occurrence. Again liability is strict, and subject to certain exceptions. If the occurrence was without the actual fault or privity of the owner, his liability is subject to a statutory maximum of 133 special drawing rights[26] per ton of the vessels tonnage, or to an overall maximum of 14 million special drawing rights, whichever is the lower. The Act further provides that, whether or not the owner is made liable under Section 1, he shall not be made liable otherwise than under that section, nor shall any servant or agent of his, nor any salvor, be made liable.

Again, members of the public are given the benefit of strict liability, although in some cases that may not be an advantage over the common law. On the other hand again, they can be placed at some disadvantage in the following ways.

(a) Limitation of liability is imposed.
(b) Plaintiffs are restricted to actions under Section 1, and therefore in all claims are subject to the statutory limitations.

The French, also parties to the convention,[27] were faced with this restriction after the occurrence involving the *Amoco Cadiz*, which spilled vast quantities of crude

---

[25]See S.12(1)(b). See also Convention on Civil Liability for Nuclear Damage (Vienna 1963) at Arts. II 5 and V.

[26]'Special Drawing Rights' are explained in the Agreement of the International Monetary Fund, Articles XV *et seq* second amendment, adopted 24 March 1976. On 30 Jan. 1992 1SDR equalled US$1.39921. The Merchant Shipping Act 1988, at Schedule 4, paragraph 4, gives a higher maximum based on the 1984 Protocol to the International Convention on Civil Liability for Oil Pollution Damage. Neither paragraph 4 of the Schedule nor the 1984 Protocol, however, are likely to be brought into force.

[27]The International Convention on Civil Liability for Oil Pollution Damage (Brussels 1969), as amended by the Protocol of 1976.

oil on to the French coast near Brest. Full compensation for that damage far exceeded the limited compensation under the convention.[28]

In this class of cases, the protection given to the polluter may permit him to carry on his operations without the risk of very heavy liability, but in so doing it can encroach unfairly on rights the public would otherwise enjoy. (For further discussion on this see Chapter V.)

4.4.5 In cases falling within the third class, no new rights are given in the legislation, but there is an exclusion of existing rights. This does not mean that the exclusion cannot necessarily be justified.

The United Kingdom Civil Aviation Act 1982, at Section 76(1), provides that

> No action shall lie in respect of trespass or in respect of nuisance, by reason only of the flight of an aircraft over any property at a height above the ground which, having regard to wind, weather and all the circumstances of the case is reasonable, or in the ordinary incidents of such flight, so long as [there has been compliance with certain orders and statutory provisions].

Section 77(2) provides that

> No action shall lie in respect of nuisance by reason only of the noise and vibration caused by an aircraft on an aerodrome to which this subsection applies by virtue of an Air Navigation Order, so long as the provisions of any such order are complied with.

The reasoning behind these pieces of legislation is that the ordinary rules of common law trespass and nuisance had developed before the advent of air transport, and that if they now applied to aircraft the development of air transport would be seriously inhibited. Parliament appears to have considered that in the new circumstances, it is better that the Secretary of State makes regulations which achieve a fair balance between the interests of the public in a quiet environment on the one hand, and the advantage of civil air transport on the other. That necessarily means restricting the rights to sue at common law for trespass and nuisance. The achievement of the balance clearly involves difficult political decisions, for the balance of interests of members of the public vary from one set of persons to another.

In some cases also, the effect of the restriction can go beyond its original purpose. In *Bernstein* v *Skyviews & General Ltd*[29] the defendants had flown over and taken photographs of the plaintiff's country house, with the intention of offering the photographs for sale to him. He was a prominent member of society, with good reason to fear terrorist attacks. He demanded that all the negatives and prints be handed over to him or destroyed. The defendants did neither. In the case which ensued, the defendants succeeded partly on the ground that the Civil Aviation Act 1949, later replaced by the 1982 Act, protected the defendants from liability in trespass.

A further illustration arises from the United Kingdom Fuel (Lead Content of Petrol) Regulations 1976.[30] These provided that the maximum permitted amount of lead per litre of petrol should be: for the period 30 November 1976 to 31 December

---

[28]The French succeeded in circumventing the restrictions by suing the oil company in the US courts. They first succeeded in principle in a Chicago court, the measure of damages to be determined at a subsequent hearing. The Chicago court decision has twice been affirmed in the appeal courts.

[29][1977] 2 All ER 902.

[30]Now superseded by the Motor Fuel (Lead Content of Petrol) Regulations 1981.

1977, 0.50 grams; and after 1 January 1978, 0.45 grams. The BP and Shell oil companies complied with those regulations.

In 1978, actions were brought on behalf of Fidel Budden, aged two years, and Merlyn Albery-Speyer, also aged two years,[31] on the ground that those infants had suffered injury from ingesting lead derived from exhausts of cars using petrol from those oil companies. They claimed on the basis of negligence and nuisance. The oil companies applied to have the claims struck out, as showing no cause of action in law.

The court decided in favour of the oil companies. It noted that they had done what was expressly permitted by the regulations. It also said that it was difficult to believe that different standards should be, or would be, applied for fixing criminal and civil liabilities.

The decision is open to criticism. Different standards are certainly applied in England for criminal and civil liabilities both for air and for water pollution. Furthermore, compliance with a permit to discharge to water renders a person free from criminal conviction,[32] but not from civil liability. The same applies to some forms of air pollution.

To many people, the proposition that compliance with a permit, or even a statutory standard, frees the discharger from all civil responsibilities to members of the public is unacceptable.[33] They would consider that protection for the polluter had gone too far.

[31]*Budden v BP Oil and Shell Oil, Albery-Speyer v BP Oil and Shell Oil* (1980) 124 SJ, [1980] JPL 586.
[32]Water Act 1991 s.88(1).
[33]Contrast the laws referred to in 4.4.3 above.

Chapter II

Systems of Administration

1. NECESSARY ELEMENTS OF A SYSTEM OF CONTROL

1.1 Any complete system of pollution control will include at least four elements.

(a) Formulation of pollution policies.
(b) Administration of the scheme of control.
(c) Enforcement of controls.[1]
(d) Research and the gathering of information necessary to any progressive system of control. The kind of research, however, needed for the purpose of policy making, is in many cases different from that needed for administration and enforcement. This function is dealt with under 3.2 and 4.1.2(d).

1.2 The need for policy control

1.2.1 The statements in Chapter I at 4.1.2 and 4.1.3 explain the need for policy decisions as a necessary part of any system of pollution control. It is submitted further that all pollution controls are based on policy decisions. They may range from decisions made for compelling reasons of public health, through decisions made on the basis of quantification of risk, to those based on a simple choice between protection of amenity and an increase in material wealth.

It must be remembered also that pollution control is only one of many and diverse functions of government, and must be properly co-ordinated with the others if the government's overall policy is not to be torn with internal conflicts.

1.2.2 Initially, the policy decisions on environmental management will make it possible to develop a coherent system of pollution control. To the extent that those policies are well founded, they will form a justification for the administrative decisions that flow from them.

Furthermore, in all but the smallest states, there are likely to be regional and local bodies exercising control functions independently. A national policy is

---

[1]The justification for separating this from general administration is given in 4.1 *et seq*.

necessary if consistency is to be achieved throughout the jurisdiction. The mechanism by which it may be achieved, e.g. appellate jurisdictions, ministerial directions and guidelines will be discussed later.[2]

1.2.3   Another reason why policy control is needed is that, as noted in Chapter I at 4.2.2., the weight to be given to various factors in determining the strictness of control to be applied usually varies. It varies first with the political philosophy of the party in power, and often later because of changed circumstances.

The first is normally a legitimate exercise of political will.

The second may be a proper reaction to that change in circumstances. It may be a national emergency in which the manufacturing output of some particular industry must be increased, or food production increased. Alternatively, some particular industry which is vital to the national economy may be in difficulties. In such circumstances, it is a matter of policy whether and to what extent pollution controls are to be relaxed.

Conversely, scientific research may reveal pollution damage which was previously unsuspected, as with damage to the ozone layer, or which was not previously proved to the satisfaction of governments, as with acid rain. Unfortunately, the standard of proof required for that satisfaction appears to vary directly with the cost of control measures which would be needed. Again, policy decisions on whether, and to what extent, stricter controls are to be applied must be made.

There may also be new international conventions to which the government has become a party, which impose new obligations, or in the case of EEC countries, new European directives.

Finally, some major incident may occur, or an emergency may arise requiring decisions which fall outside the ambit of established law or policy.[3]

2. SYSTEMS OF CONTROL

2.1   The systems of administration and policy control will reflect the political philosophy of the party in power. The systems may also be constrained by the constitution of the state.

It is not an aim of this book to discuss the merits of different political philosophies, nor the different forms of constitution. Most of the examples of pollution control given in this volume derive from countries with some form of democratic government. Even in those states with more authoritarian regimes, however, good administration demands some degree of consultation, even if amongst a restricted class of people. The problems of control are therefore examined on the basis that at least some forms of consultative procedures will be needed.

---

[2]See section 9 below, and Chapter III at 6.1 to 6.2.

[3]An example of this occurred in the United Kingdom in 1967. An oil tanker, the *Torrey Canyon*, foundered on rocks just outside UK territorial limits, and was spilling large quantities of oil. A decision was made by the UK authorities to destroy the vessel, setting fire to the oil, even though the propriety of that act at international law was in doubt. The incident led to the making of the International Convention relating to Intervention on the High Seas in Cases of Oil Pollution Casualties, Brussels 1969, and to the passing in the United Kingdom of S.12 of the Prevention of Oil Pollution Act 1971. A further example may be taken from Cyprus, where in 1987 large transformers were imported as scrap. When the importer opened them he found a substantial quantity of polychlorinated biphenols, which he emptied into a ditch. Cyprus had at that time no law expressly governing such circumstances.

2.2 The discussion in the remainder of this chapter is based on the three tier system of control: policy making, administration and enforcement .

3. THE POLICY MAKERS

3.1 Formulation of policy

The policy maker will be the executive government. That could range from an absolute ruler to a cabinet of ministers responsible to an elected assembly.

Whatever the form of government, however, it will be essential to a balanced system of control to have at least:

(a) A procedure for consultation with, within and between departments of government who stand to be affected, beneficially or adversely, by any new or changed forms of control.
(b) Expert advice available, and the development of an adequate data base. At this level, it is also advisable to apply integrated pollution control, whereby all options are considered.[4]
(c) A procedure whereby unforeseen major emergencies and other matters of grave public concern can be referred to the highest authority for decision.[5]
(d) It is necessary also for the policy makers to have powers to ensure the implementation of the agreed policies.

3.2 Research

For the formulation of sound polices, research is needed into such matters as:

– population and its distribution;
– land use;
– developments and proposed developments in industry, agriculture, etc;
– new forms of pollution, new sources of pollution and pollution trands.

Such research may be commissioned by the policy makers, or done or commissioned by the administrators. Some may be done by or on behalf of independent 'watch dogs'.

4. THE ADMINISTRATION

4.1 The functions of the administration

4.1.1 For the purposes of this study, the administration of pollution control is considered separately from enforcement. There is a clear distinction between the two kinds of work, and in some areas an even clearer distinction between the personnel involved.

---

[4]See 9.3 below.
[5]Informal procedures are often too uncertain or too slow.

4.1.2   The principal functions of the administration will normally be:

(a) Direct supervision of actions taken to implement the established pollution control policy.
(b) The determination of:
     – quality objectives;
     – discharge standards;
     – consents, authorisations and approvals;
     – product standards;
     and such other determinations as are necessary for the operation of the particular system of control adopted.
(c) In some systems, where administration and enforcement are carried out by different bodies, the administrative authority is given the task of ensuring that quality objectives are at all times maintained. In order to do that, they will have to engage in, or commission, environmental monitoring.
(d) Normally, they will be given the task of conducting, or promoting, research into such matters as:
     –   sources of pollution;
     –   nature and extent of pollution damage;
     –   methods of technical control, including pre-discharge treatment and risk reduction;
     –   cleaner production methods and less polluting substances,
         (much of this research can be done by such bodies as industry associations, or even individual firms. Whether or not that research may be subsidised is a policy decision for the government. Even if there is no subsidy, other forms of encouragement may be used).
     –   methods of legal, administrative or fiscal control.

Whatever body or bodies conduct those forms of administration, considerable resources of expertise will be needed. They will usually be centrally based bodies, but may have departments in particular regions, e.g. where a particular industry or form of agriculture is practised.

4.2   Integration of pollution controls

4.2.1 It is advantageous for an administrative structure to cover all forms of pollution, so that they can be integrated into a single system, under which the 'best environmental option' for the disposal of any particular kind or quantity of waste can be chosen. This kind of integration is discussed at 9.3.

5. ENFORCEMENT PROCESS

Enforcement is discussed more generally in Chapter IV.

5.1   The enforcement process involves at least the following:

(a) Detection
     This is simply the process of detecting when a pollution offence has been or is being committed. In some cases, action must be taken if an unlawful act has

not yet been done, but is likely to be committed. The United Kingdom Control of Pollution Act 1974, at Section 58, provides that

> Where a local authority is satisfied that a noise amounting to a nuisance exists, or is likely to occur or recur . . the local authority shall serve an abatement notice.

It is submitted that in any case, an enforcement officer will serve a useful purpose of he anticipates a possible offence, and warns and advises a potential polluter. Good enforcement involves giving guidance as well as promoting prosecutions.

(b) Exercise of a discretion

Only in rare cases is prosecution obligatory. The task of an enforcement authority is to ensure, so far as it can, compliance with the relevant law. That can often be achieved, in the case of a person ignorant of the law or the means of compliance, by guidance, and in other cases by warnings. It is only in cases in which such methods are likely to be ineffective that prosecution is justified. For that reason, an enforcement authority is normally given a discretion whether or not to prosecute. That discretion may be exercised by the officer on the spot, a senior officer, or the authority itself.

(c) Collection of evidence

Once an officer has decided that a prosecution may be brought, he must proceed to collect sufficient evidence for that purpose.

That part of the task varies with different legal systems. In common law countries the evidence must be sufficient to establish proof 'beyond reasonable doubt'. Note that proof in law does not mean establishing a fact with absolute certainty, but in presenting evidence sufficient to satisfy the court in accordance with the standard of proof required, and in accordance with all the rules of evidence which are binding on that court.[6]

5.2 It is apparent that the officer must have some legal knowledge, combined in some cases with technical knowledge and expertise.

Even in such a seemingly simple matter as taking a sample of water, some degree of expertise is necessary. There have been cases where the discharger's staff have watched with quiet amusement while an enforcement officer has taken a sample of river water, knowing that their discharge is carried in a current alongside the opposite bank. In other cases the defence advocate has been pleased to learn that the enforcement officer, taking a sample of sea water for bacteriological analysis, has failed to keep it in an appropriately cooled container, leaving the organisms to joyfully reproduce in the summer sunshine. Other forms of pollution, such as those by pesticides or radioactivity, or even pollution of the atmosphere, call for much higher degrees of expertise.

5.3 Laboratory analyses of samples, however, may be done separately from the remainder of the administrative and enforcement processes. In that case it would be necessary for the laboratories to be approved as having personnel with adequate levels of expertise and the right equipment available.

It is submitted that there is no need for analysis by an independent laboratory, so long as there are adequate safeguards for the discharger. In the United Kingdom law on the pollution of inland waters, that safeguard lies in a provision that

[6]See 5.2 and 5.3.

evidence of analysis of a sample of a discharge will not be admissible in legal proceedings relating to that discharge, unless the sample has been divided into three parts – one part given to the discharger, a second sealed and set aside for future comparison if necessary, the third taken by the enforcement authority.[7]

5.4   A further consideration in the appointment of enforcement officers is their regular presence 'on the ground'. Officers who frequently visit the sites of possible infringements, regularly, or more usefully irregularly, are more likely than others to detect occasional as well as systematic offences. That is important where evidence of the offence is transient, and will disappear before a further visit can be arranged, e.g. noise emissions, or where the offender himself may disappear, as with fly tipping. The frequent appearance of such officers may itself discourage potential offenders. In some circumstances it may also enable the authority to carry out regular sampling as part of an early warning system.[8]

Thus every police officer may be instructed to detect and report unlawful noise emissions from motor vehicles, and emissions of dark smoke from diesel engined vehicles. If an instrument to measure the emission is needed, he may be empowered to detain the vehicle and send a request by radio to the nearest testing station. Alternatively, he may serve a notice on the driver requiring him to take the vehicle to the testing station within a specified period.[9]

5.5   Conversely, where a high degree of expertise is needed for enforcement, e.g. for provisions on the disposal of radioactive waste, a central body may be both the administrative and enforcement authority, perhaps with its enforcement officers regionally based.

5.6   Hybrid arrangements

5.6.1   The problem of providing a high degree of technical and scientific expertise, with a continuing local presence and knowledge of local circumstances, may be solved in another way. Two such examples may be drawn from United Kingdom legislation.

5.6.2   The first is found in the Clean Air Act 1956. Under Section 3, no person may install a furnace in a building or any boiler or industrial plant attached to a building, unless it can be operated continuously without emitting smoke when burning a type of fuel it was designed to burn. A furnace installed in accordance with plans and specifications approved by the local authority will be deemed to have been installed in compliance with that requirement.

Local authority officers grant approval, but in doing so act in accordance with guidance given by a central laboratory within the Department of Trade and Industry. Legally, the local authority is the enforcement body, and exercises the discretionary powers; in practice, it acts as if it were an agent of the Department.

---

[7]Water Act 1991 s.209.

[8]Long term monitoring strategies will be dealt with in subsequent volumes on particular forms of pollution.

[9]See Chapter III at 8.7.2 below, particularly the last three paragraphs. Such procedures will be discussed in subsequent volumes on pollution of the atmosphere and pollution by noise.

5.6.3 The second example is the controls over the heights of chimneys. The local authority has the discretionary power to determine the height in each particular case, but acts in accordance with the Memorandum on Chimney Heights issued by the Department of the Environment, applying its guidelines to local conditions.[10] If further advice is needed, they usually consult officers of HMIP, who are also within the Department of the Environment.

5.7 Enforcement officers in the process of prosecution

5.7.1 Most legal systems provide safeguards against abuse of powers by prosecuting officers. In many of those, the enforcement officer will have no role to play. In the US, all prosecutions are brought by attorneys on behalf of the state, or in exceptional cases by the Attorney General or specially appointed prosecutor. In Scotland, they are brought by or on behalf of the Lord Advocate as the public prosecutor. In France, an examining magistrate, more properly called a *juge d'instruction*, takes all the evidence, and decides whether or not there shall be a prosecution.

5.7.2 In England an Wales there is the Crown Prosecution Service, which conducts all prosecutions instituted on behalf of a police authority, and certain other classes of prosecutions. It has not taken over the prosecution functions of local authorities and government departments.[11]

5.7.3 It has been the practice in England for various authorities, whether dealing with pollution control or other matters, to have their own officers present the simpler cases in the lower courts, thus avoiding expense, and saving the time of professional lawyers. The practice, however, can present some dangers.

5.7.4 A prosecutor is not there with the primary purpose of obtaining a conviction – he is there to see that justice is done. In order to do that, he must present the evidence objectively and fairly; and if he finds evidence which supports the case for the accused, he must take steps to ensure that that evidence is made available to the court.

An enforcement officer who has himself conducted the investigations into the alleged offence is therefore not necessarily the best person to present the case in court. In some cases, he will have warned the accused of illegal acts on previous occasions, in others he may have seen prosecutions against him fail because of lack of evidence, or even false evidence. He may be dealing with a 'known rogue' and be determined to 'nail him' at last. In any event, he will have expended time and energy in gathering evidence and preparing the case. In those circumstances he cannot bring to the presentation of the case the objectivity expected of a prosecutor.[12]

5.7.5 If enforcement officers are to be used for conducting prosecutions in simple cases, they should be senior officers who have not been involved in the investi-

---

[10]See Clean Air Acts 1956 s.10, and 1968 s.6.
[11]See Prosecution of Offences Act 1985 s.3.
[12]It is relevant to note that in Cyprus the powers of Government officers to conduct prosecutions have been strictly limited.

gations. Even then, they may show unwanted bias against those whom the department considers to be persistent offenders.

It is preferable also for those officers to be carefully selected, and instructed not only on the rules of procedure and evidence, but also on the codes of conduct to which professional prosecutors are expected to conform.

5.8   Improvement and prohibition notices

5.8.1   Improvement notices

In some jurisdictions use is made of notices requiring improvement of the methods used to control the discharge of pollutants, or used in other parts of the process.

The precursors of these forms of notices were apparently the abatement notices served under the United Kingdom Public Health Acts to secure the abatement of statutory nuisances. They could be issued by inspectors themselves, and could specify the steps which had to be taken to abate the nuisance. In later forms, as applied to environmental pollution, it is usually the authority itself which bears the responsibility for the issue of the notice.

Some improvement provisions empower the authority to lay down the steps which must be taken to secure the improvement. Others require the discharger to propose improvements, which will be subject to approval by the authority. (Examples are given in Appendix H.)

5.8.2   Prohibition and stop notices

Where there are arrangements or practices which could cause risks of serious injury or damage to health, or cause serious damage to the environment, a prohibition or stop notice may be used. That is a notice which requires the cessation of a process or part of a process.

The United Kingdom Health and Safety at Work etc Act 1974 at Section 22 empowered inspectors to issue prohibition notices. It is still in force so far as it relates to health and safety at work, but in its application to environmental protection has now been superseded by Section 14 of the Environmental Protection Act 1990. (The latter provision is set out in Appendix H. Provisions for orders of similar effect passed in Ontario and Mauritius are also set out in that Appendix.)

Great care must be taken in drafting such sections, and in the exercise of the powers. Cessation of a process can cause considerable financial loss to the firms receiving them. Where any such powers are granted, especially where the effects on production can be substantial, it is necessary to grant a right of appeal; otherwise there can be, at best, unjustified losses to the firm, and at worst an abuse of power and even corruption.

The danger to the inspectors and their authorities lies in the possibility of a successful appeal. For many orders, notice of appeal will suspend their operation. Where there are imminent risks of serious danger, however, it may be necessary to provide that there is no such suspension. If the process has thus been closed down, and the appeal succeeds, the firm may claim from the inspector or his authority, compensation for loss of profits, and that compensation could be considerable.

One safeguard against such danger is to include a provision for the protection of enforcing officers and agencies. That could provide that neither the inspector nor the authority may be found liable, either at criminal or civil law, for the affects of any statement or action made by them bona fide in the purported use of their powers. There is one school of thought that the authorities and their inspectors should be required to exercise their powers with care, and take responsibility for their actions. Where action may be needed to save life or protect persons from serious injury, however, such argument loses most if not all its force. (See also Chapter IV at 2.2.1.)

6. SAFEGUARDS FOR THE GENERAL PUBLIC

6.1 Information and consultation

6.1.1 The functions referred to above are all discharged on behalf of the state itself, even though some of the bodies may operate independently of government control. As part of their good administrative practices, some may inform the public of their policies and their work by means of reports published generally, and may also consult interested parties and the general public by means of consultation papers. Others may establish permanent consultative committees or councils on which sit government officers, members of non-governmental organisations (NGOs) and representatives of the public generally. Two examples are:

(a) Hong Kong Environmental Protection Committee

This is a committee on which sits representatives of government departments, industrial and other interested organisations, and persons representing the general public.

It provides a two way system of communication, but is used principally as a means of informing interested people of government policies and decisions.

(b) Cyprus Environmental Advisory Council

This council is chaired by the Minister of Agriculture and Natural Resources, who carries overall responsibility for environmental protection. Its members are from government departments with environmental responsibilities, NGOs, and other persons with special qualifications or experience in environmental matters.

Its functions are to advise the Council of Ministers on environmental matters and any serious conservation or environmental problems, to form a channel of communication between the Government and non-governmental environmental bodies, and to help the Minister keep the public informed on environmental matters.

In practice, the Government has used the Advisory Council more to inform the public than to receive advice.

6.1.2 Such organisations can be very successful in keeping special interest groups informed, e.g. conservation societies, societies for the protection of birds and other forms of wildlife. Representation of the general public, and dissemination of information to that public is often less satisfactory.

At best, well informed officers of NGOs can present arguments based on sound scientific knowledge, well prepared and well presented. At worst the meetings are used simply to explain and justify government policies and actions.

6.2   Public watchdog

6.2.1   Those committees and councils referred to above, however, are part of the Government's administrative structure. They largely reflect Government policy, and where factual reports are prepared there can be an emphasis, and even careful selection and presentation of facts, which favour the Government view. The NGOs are given an opportunity to present contradicting information and counter arguments, but often they do not have access to all the relevant facts.

The administrative and enforcement authorities may themselves be to some extent independent of government, as with the UK Health and Safety Executive in the field of health and safety at work, or may be independent government agencies with no operational or promotional responsibilities, such as the US Environmental Protection Agency. Those authorities themselves, however, may have an interest in withholding information, or presenting it in an unbalanced way. They may have their own deficiencies to hide, or their own policies to justify.

6.2.2   It is therefore submitted that there is always a need for an independent 'public watchdog'. That will be essentially a dog which barks but does not bite. It will be a body completely independent of government. It may be that the formal appointment of members must be by the Government, but independence can be secured if the Government can choose only from a list of persons submitted by independent organisations. The body will then be free to produce reports for general publication, with opinions conclusions and recommendations expressed freely, and as fully as the law permits. Some restraints on publication may be necessary, e.g. for purposes of national security, but the fewer there are of such restraints, the more able will be the watchdog to serve its purpose.

If, as is usual, the chairman and members are appointed by the government, its independence will not be complete. A person who is free to select the chairman and members of a committee can to a large extent determine its policies and the character of the decisions it will make.

That power, however, can be constrained. As noted above that can be done by requiring the relevant minister or ministers to select from lists of persons submitted by particular bodies. They may be interest groups such as conservation societies, or simply local authorities representing the general public of their areas.

It is submitted that, within limitations laid down on grounds such as those of national security and the protection of trade secrets, the ability of the watchdog to do an adequate job will be enhanced if it is empowered to require members of the government and other persons to give to them relevant information for which they ask, and if it has the power and the duty to publish reports.

6.2.3   The U.K. Royal Commission on Environmental Pollution may to some extent be regarded as a watchdog. The Government, however, is free to appoint to the Commission any person it thinks fit. Furthermore, although it has published reports regularly about annually, usually comprehensive reports on particular forms of pollution, it does not normally publish special reports on events or emergencies as they arise.[13]

Parliamentary committees can, and to a large extent do, serve this purpose, but

---

[13]For the terms of reference of the Royal Commission on Environmental Pollution see Appendix A at 4.2.

they contain politicians from the governing party as well as from the opposition. Moreover, their powers may be limited. The United Kingdom Select Committee on the Environment can compel the attendance of persons, including ministers and senior civil servants, but cannot compel them to answer questions.[14] Contrast that with the powers of the New Zealand Parliamentary Commissioner for the Environment.[15]

6.2.4 In any parliamentary democracy it is possible to have a Parliamentary Commissioner. He is a person appointed by Parliament, with a duty to enquire into, investigate and report on a specified field of government work, and that may be work on protection of the environment. His reports are to Parliament, to which he is responsible, but may also be published generally. Given that he has staff of sufficient expertise and competence, and adequate powers to obtain information, he can be a very effective watchdog on behalf of Parliament.

One danger is that he may be appointed by a majority of Parliament, which is also the party of Government, and which chooses a person unlikely to subject it to severe criticism. One way to avoid that is to provide that his appointment must be made, or simply approved, by the opposition. A similar precaution is taken in the United Kingdom with the Public Accounts Committee, a parliamentary committee appointed to examine and report on Government spending. By convention, its chairman is always a member of the opposition.

Appendix G gives an outline of the arrangements in New Zealand for a Parliamentary Commissioner for the Environment. The special protection he is given against dismissal or reduction of salary is a noteworthy precaution, similar to precautions taken to secure the independence of the judiciary.

6.2.5 The fact that there are relatively few such bodies stems from the reluctance of all governments to appoint committees, councils or public officers which may reveal facts and publish reports adverse to the government itself.

6.3 Freedom of information and public registers

6.3.1 Information may be made available to the public through registers. They are registers to be maintained, and which must contain specified classes of information, e.g. details of consents granted, results of monitoring of discharges. They must also be kept available for public inspection. A copy of a typical provision on registers is given in Appendix H.

Another method is to have a freedom of information law, under which members of the public have a right to specified classes of information. A copy of the relevant provisions of the United States Freedom of Information Act is given in Appendix H at paragraph 3. (See also Chapter VI at 2.2.4.)

The purpose of such provisions is to make available to individuals information on which they can take action to protect their own interests. Such provisions vary with different forms of pollution, and are therefore dealt with in the separate volumes of this series. For our present purposes it is sufficient to refer to one example, Section 190 of the UK Water Act 1991. The whole question of the right of members of the public to information is discussed more fully in Chapter VI at 2.

---

[14]See Appendix A at 4.1.
[15]See Appendix G at 2.3.2.

7. DEMOCRACY AND JUSTICE

7.1   Many countries rely on the democratic process to ensure that people are governed in their own interests. Representatives in an elected assembly can make known the needs and opinions of the people they represent. Where that is a legislative assembly, it legislates in accordance with the wishes of the majority.

It is notorious that the legislation protects the interests of the party in power. In England, when the hunting king and nobles held sway, it was a capital offence to kill a deer in another person's enclosed place. When agricultural interests were paramount, it was a capital offence to kill another man's sheep, and when the wealthy trading and manufacturing classes emerged, a capital offence to steal anything of more than £20 in value. The legislation of today may not be so outrageous, but still shows the same trend. With the growth of wealthy and influential shipping companies, came the laws which limited their liability for damage done by their ships, even when navigated negligently, except where that was with the actual fault or privity of the owner. More recently airlines have gained a similar right to limitation of liability, and the oil industry has pressed for similar protection. All those three limitations, moreover, are in accordance with worldwide international conventions.[16]

7.2   The counterpart to that is that the interests of minorities may not be given proper consideration. We need not look only at such extreme cases as that of the Kurds to see minorities oppressed. It happens on a smaller scale in many places. In one fruit growing area in England, many people are employed during the harvesting season, but left unemployed at other times of the year. A proposal to introduce industrial development into the area was rejected by the local council, which represented the interests of growers who would have lost their ready supply of labour during the harvesting season. In political terms at least, it is submitted that such conduct can be regarded as an abuse to power, being unjustifiable discrimination against one section of the community simply for the benefit of another. Likewise, in a large holiday resort, it can be difficult to persuade the local council to adopt a scheme which does not benefit the tourist industry.

To some extent there can be an imbalance in the protection of interests in some pollution control authorities today. Powerful interests may dominate the decisions of an authority, or in other ways swing the balance of advantage in their favour, leaving others to complain of being seriously disadvantaged. Under the UK Water Act 1973, Section 3(1), the water authorities controlling pollution had to have at least 51 per cent of their members appointed by local authorities, to represent the public interest. In the Water Act 1983, a new section was substituted for that provision, with no members to be appointed by local authorities – ministers appointed all members. Those ministers significantly increased the number of members from industry. In the years before that change, the quality of the river waters was gradually improving. After that change it deteriorated again. The evidence points to the deterioration being at least in part a result of the changes in membership. It could be argued, of course, that was a proper use of power, benefiting the community as a whole by securing economically viable industrial enterprises. That leads to the proposition that it is very important to secure a fair

---

[16]For further details concerning those limitations, see Chapter V at 7.3.

representation of interests on a control authority which is to be given discretionary powers.

Even then, the control authorities have difficult decisions to make. If guided by the Bentham criterion of 'the greatest good for the greatest number' they might easily benefit the majority, but throw an unfair share of the burden on a minority, and in many cases, monetary compensation is poor recompense. When land was compulsorily purchased for housing in the Manchester area, the day the purchase order was confirmed, the owner committed suicide.

When a democratic process can lead to oppression of minorities, it is clear that that form of democracy is not enough.

7.3 Some further safeguard is needed for the protection of minorities and individuals against possible abuse of power by those who dominate the control authority. There are several possibilities:

(a) There can be a right of appeal to a higher authority. That is usually to a minister, for valid reasons. Through his appellate authority he is able to exercise some degree of legitimate policy control. He is usually the one with the power to call for a public enquiry if the circumstances warrant it, or he may be empowered to appoint a commission of enquiry. He can also ensure that there is some consistency in the decisions of regional control authorities. Finally, appeal to him may be a useful safeguard against corruption.[17]

So far as the right of appeal is to safeguard against undue consideration for the interests of the majority, with a corresponding disregard of the interests of minorities, the minister will often be not the best person to hear the appeal. He will have a political duty to promote the interests of the majority which he may consider overriding, and he will possibly have been the person who appointed the members of the control authority − persons of whose views he doubtless approves.

One advantage of appeal to the minister, however, is that it can relate to the substance of the decision, as distinct from mere procedural or evidential irregularities.

(b) Alternatively there can be a right of appeal to an independent tribunal. That will normally relate to the substance of the decision, and is likely to be heard by a more impartial body, which is less likely to take political considerations into account.

The last point may sound to be an advantage, but it may be proper in the particular circumstances to take account of political reasons. Those reasons may concern the state of the economy, the state of some industry essential to economic welfare of that country, or they may concern national security. For those reasons, it is unlikely that appeals will be directed to an independent tribunal instead of the minister.

(c) There may be a narrower review, concerning only the procedure followed. That could be based on an application to a higher court for a 'judicial review', as in the United Kingdom.[18] The procedure does not relate to the substance of the decision, but to the correctness or the fairness of procedure followed, including a consideration of the rules of natural justice.

[17]See section 8 below.
[18]See Appendix A at 1.7.

(d) There may be a wider form of review based on the French concept of *détournement de pouvoir,* a ground which does not have to rely on the doctrine of ultra vires or on procedural irregularity. It may examine the motive for making the administrative decision, and quash the decision if that motive does not relate to any of the objectives for which the statutory power was given.

8. SAFEGUARDS AGAINST CORRUPTION

8.1 When decisions of considerable financial importance are to be made, there is always a danger of corruption. When the decisions are made through the exercise of discretionary powers, as they often are in pollution control, the danger is even greater. To get rid of those discretionary powers, however, would leave the system of control more rigid, and thus less able to take account of varied and sometimes changing circumstances. In many cases, therefore, it would be useful to seek other safeguards.

Whatever the country, those dangers are present, and safeguards are necessary.

8.2 A realistic, and reasonably effective, form of safeguard is to reduce the opportunities for corruption. For that purpose, any system involving the use of discretionary powers may usefully incorporate three characteristics.

(a) The exercise of discretionary power never to rest with one person. The more the responsibility is spread, the less will be the danger of corruption.
(b) In all cases, a right of appeal to be provided. That right of appeal, or the equivalent of appeal, to be extended to persons other than the applicant, being persons who might be adversely affected by the decision.
(c) Never to make a law which will not be regularly and consistently enforced. Otherwise it is possible to use a threat of enforcement or promise of non-enforcement as a means of securing a bribe, or as a means of achieving some other purpose which could not otherwise be achieved

The above is based on advice given by the Hong Kong International Commission against Corruption.

To these may be added one further safeguard.

(d) Publicity for all discretionary decisions to be compulsory, e.g. by way of registers open to public inspection. Any inconsistencies created by favourable treatment in particular cases will then be revealed.[19]

Those are a few simple rules. It must be added that methods of corruption are infinite in their variety. In one instance, of which the author had direct experience, the consultants were told by an officer of government, 'I am a hydrologist, and I can tell you that the site you have chosen is not suitable for waste disposal. If you insist on recommending that site, I shall tell my minister that it is unsuitable and persuade him to make regulations forbidding its use for that purpose. If, on the other hand, you engage me as a consultant hydrologist, I shall find a suitable site for you'.

[19]See, e.g., the UK Water Resources Act 1991 s.190.

9. INTEGRATED SYSTEMS OF CONTROL

9.1 Problems of co-ordination

9.1.1 The control of environmental pollution is closely associated with, and to a large extent dependent upon, land use planning controls. Conversely, conservation and the protection of wildlife are to a large extent dependent on the control of pollution.

To some extent, there is also association with the conservation of cultural heritage, which can be damaged where pollution controls are inadequate. An outstanding example is the damage already done by air pollution to sculptural works on the Acroplis, in Athens.

All this points to a need for links between pollution control and those other concerns. In some cases, as often with planning and pollution control, there is a need simply for a co-ordination of effort. Most obviously, planners may be asked to site polluting developments away from any which are sensitive to pollution, such as schools, hospitals, wildlife reserves, sites of archaeological interest, and areas valued because of their high amenity. Less obviously, planning and local environmental health authorities may co-operate to prevent local concentrations of pollution. That was done in Sheffield some years ago. The city of Sheffield lies in a valley, and pollution from local industry is sometimes trapped there by atmospheric inversion layers. It was agreed that further factory development should be allowed only on higher ground, and that the factory chimneys should be tall. This both gave them some initial altitude, and allowed them to develop sufficient up-draught for the emissions to break through the inversion layers, thus avoiding local concentrations.[20]

The need for co-operation with planners sometimes goes further. With noise, for example, judicious use of planning powers can often be the best form of pollution control, e.g. by careful siting of developments, conditions requiring noise insulated buildings, use of features such as natural depressions or road or rail cuttings to reduce noise nuisance. With other forms of pollution, planning is often the first step in pollution control. At best, planners can solve the problem, and in many other cases they can reduce it to manageable proportions. That may be done by refusing permission to site a factory at an unsuitable location, or by the use of planning conditions.[21]

For wildlife, in many places the loss of suitable habitat is the greatest danger. Co-operation with planning and pollutions control authorities is necessary in many cases if habitat is to be preserved.

Clearly there can be conflicts between those interests. Where they are the responsibilities of different ministries, the resolution of the conflict must lie in some form of inter-ministerial co-operation. That problem is not peculiar to pollution control, but ranges throughout governmental responsibilities.

---

[20]That, of course, is recognised today as a form of pollution control only in so far as it prevents high concentrations in local areas. It is now accepted that there is an obligation, in most cases at least, to seek stricter standards rather than mere dispersal. The merits or otherwise of high stack policies will be discussed in a later volume on pollution of the atmosphere.

[21]Planning controls are outlined briefly in Chapter III at 8.2. The relationship between land use planning and pollution will be discussed more fully in a subsequent volume on land use planning controls and pollution.

Within the field of environmental management there are conflicts – the interests of fishermen inevitably conflict with the interests many others who use inland waters for recreation, but they conflict only on how environmental management should be carried out. That calls for co-operation, and in some cases compromise.

9.1.2 There is therefore some advantage to be gained in placing responsibilities for those related matters in one ministry. Co-ordination is more easily achieved in a single ministry than by a ministerial committees. The need for a ministerial committee will always remain, however, for quite apart from the close relationships referred to above, decisions must be made on broader matters of policy in which environmental considerations are to be taken into account. That may be by a committee of ministers established informally at the behest of the Prime Minister, or by a more permanent or even statutory body comprising interested ministers.[22]

9.1.3 There can, of course, be other conflicts. There are often groups with special interests which conflict with environmental protection. They will be anxious to protect those interests and in many cases have special committees or even separate organisations to do so. For example, at national level the Confederation of British Industry has a special committee on environmental matters, which maintains close contact with the Government and puts the case for industry strongly and persuasively if necessary. At international level the oil industry has the Exploration and Production Forum, (E&P Forum), and at European level their organisation on the Conservation of Clean Air and Water in Europe (CONCAWE). The former is a particularly influential body, having a representative on the Marine Environment of Protection Committee of the International Maritime Organisation, and having a strong influence on the formulation of international treaties which affect oil companies.

Such pressure groups may be counterbalanced, at least in part, by voluntary organisations interested in the environment. Outside such international organisations such as Greenpeace and Friends of the Earth, however, few have the finance or expertise to match the work of the industrial organisations. The result is that in countries such as the United Kingdom, environmental legislation is distorted in favour of the latter. It is easier to establish a logical and evenly balanced system of environmental protection in a country in which such interests are less well developed and less well organised. For that reason it can be a mistake to follow closely the pattern of environmental protection in a highly industrialised country.

9.2 Framework law

9.2.1 One permanent arrangement is to have a single framework law. By 'framework law' is meant a law which establishes the institutional framework for all or most forms of environmental management. It may also lay down permanent

---

[22]As in Mauritius, where there is a National Environment Commission established under the Environmental Pollution Act. It is chaired by the Prime Minister, has the Minister of the Environment as vice-chairman, and as members the ministers responsible for: finance, economic planning, education, energy and water resources, tourism, youth and sports, agriculture, fisheries and natural resources, industry and industrial technology, labour and labour relations, health, and such other ministers as the Prime Minister may designate.

procedures to be followed, particularly those designed to provide for decisions where there is a conflict of interest to be resolved.

The principal advantage of such a law is that it puts on a statutory basis the institutions, the appointment of their members, their powers and duties, and often the procedures to be followed in their relationships with each other. None of those things can then be abandoned or changed without reference to the legislature. There may also be legal processes for compelling authorities to follow those procedures.

A period of trial for the operation of the law may be advisable, followed by amending legislation. Alternatively or in addition, the minister principally concerned may be empowered to make minor revisions, perhaps subject to the approval of the legislature.

Such a law gives some guarantee of stability. A single political party having then gained power cannot then easily make arbitrary changes for party political purposes. That stability can be of particular importance where procedures form the basis of safeguards for minorities and individuals. They can then neither be allowed to lapse nor be ignored without legal consequences, and, as noted above, cannot be changed without legislative sanction.

An even more compelling method of achieving stability is to embody some of the rights into the country's written constitution. They would then have the protection of any special procedures necessary for constitutional change. This possibility is discussed in Chapter VI at 1.2.3.

Finally, the act of making the law ensures that attention is paid to forging a properly integrated system, and to the relationship between its parts. The defect of many of the older bodies of environmental law is that they were made piecemeal over a long period of time, further provisions being added as new dangers were appreciated, often without sufficient consideration given to the relationship between the parts, or the cohesion of the system as a whole.

9.2.2 The decision whether or not to have a framework law will depend on the circumstances in each particular case, including the constitution of the country, the existing administration, and the existing legal system.

In general, a comprehensive framework law will be a more feasible proposition in a smaller country, with a less complex system of environmental management, and a less well developed and diversified economy.

9.3   Integrated pollution control

9.3.1 Whether or not there is a framework law, within the field of pollution control itself there is always a strong case for an integrated system of control. That is one in which all forms of control are administered by a single authority.

9.3.2 The principal case for integration is that it enables the control authority to choose the best environmental option for the disposal of waste, whatever its form.

Such options arise whenever a particular kind of waste may be discharged into two or more environmental media. For example, a substance may be discharged into inland waters, deposited at sea, incinerated thus discharging most of it to the atmosphere, or sent for disposal by burial or landfill. Different consequences flow from disposing of it into those different parts of the environment. In choosing the best option, account must be taken of the persistence of the various wastes, the probable patterns of transformation, migration, dispersal, and concentrations in different parts of the environment or its biota, and in some circumstances the possibility of synergistic effects. The costs of disposal and the impact of those costs on industry may also have to be taken into account.

In less straightforward cases, pollutants can migrate to cause damage in other media. For example, sulphur dioxide released into the atmosphere may form a weak solution of sulphuric acid to pollute the waters of lakes and rivers. Leachates from landfill may pollute waters. Substances such as pesticides entering the food chain may affect the survival of predatory birds or marine mammals, and viruses and bacteria may migrate in the drifting silts of coastal waters to infect bathers.

Furthermore, it must always be remembered that in many circumstances recycling or the finding of a further but different use is an option.

If there are separate, non-integrated authorities, each responsible for a different receiving medium, or different disposal area, each will have a duty to protect its own part of the environment. In some cases it even may be willing to accept waste simply because it can thus raise more money to finance its operations. An integrated authority, on the other hand, can choose the method and place of disposal which will cause the least environmental damage, or the least damage taking into account the cost of disposal and the possible effects on the industrial or agricultural enterprise disposing of that waste.

If no means are established to check that the best environmental option is chosen, the choice is left in the first place to the person seeking to dispose of the waste, and in the second to the separate authorities to whom application is made, who will simply take their own interests into account. Having a single integrated authority is the most obvious way of providing that means, although in larger jurisdictions that authority may necessarily be split into departments, and there is a danger that each will act as if it were a separate authority.

Not only is there a need for such decisions to be made if pollution damage is to be kept to a minimum, but much research needs to be done on damage effects, transformation, migration, dispersal and concentration of pollutants. The research may be limited in its scope, for example to a particular area such as one estuary. On the other hand, it may be more general in its scope, having implications for more than one environmental medium. In the latter case, it is more likely that an integrated authority would commission such research.

A further advantage with an integrated control authority is that there is a single financial regime, under which the authority can impartially examine the most effective use of available funds. An integrated set of accounts can provide a good guide for the future allocation of available funds, and a single integrated authority is best able to make such allocation.

10.   SYSTEM OF INTERNAL DEPARTMENTAL CONTROLS

10.1   There are some systems of law in which a ministry which promotes a particular activity, also controls any pollution therefrom. Such a system is used in the United Kingdom.[23] The Ministry of Agriculture, Fisheries and Food promotes agricultural production, but also exercises controls over the use of pesticides for the

[23]For an outline of the UK system see Appendix A.

protection of consumers and the environment; and the Ministry of Transport promotes inland transport, including carriage by road, and at the same time controls
pollution from motor vehicles.

10.2   There are advantages in that system of control.

The administration of controls is carried out by people who have a close
knowledge of the needs and difficulties of those involved in the polluting or
potentially polluting activity. They are also familiar with the costs involved, in both
production and the various methods of protection, and the financial vulnerability of
those involved. Furthermore, they are fully aware of established trends and any
plans for future expansion or retraction or other changes – factors to be taken into
account when assessing the probable impact of those activities in the future.

Out of that close relationship, however, can arise corresponding disadvantages.

The most obvious is that there will be a conflict of interest within the ministry. In
the first of the examples given above, it will have a duty to promote agriculture, and
agricultural production can flourish with a generous use of pesticides. Yet, it also has
a duty to control the use of pesticides for the sake of health, safety and the environment, and that control will almost certainly involve limitations on types and quantities
of pesticides used. It may be said that, having an intimate knowledge of both sides of
the problem, together with a duty to maintain a balance between production and
protection, and being in direct contact with both the policy makers and the men in the
field, they are the persons best placed to discharge those functions. There is a real
danger, however, that the discussion will take place, and the decision on the best
balance will be made, behind the closed doors of the ministry. Moreover, the greatest
relevant expertise may not be in that ministry, e.g. expertise concerning effects on
human health. Conflicts and even professional jealousies between ministries are not
unknown, and the decision may be made without consulting those best able to advise.
Quite properly, the Ministry of Health claims to have a right to play a leading role in
making decisions in environmental matters which could have an effect on human
health, on the grounds that the protection and promotion of human health lies primarily
with them, and that they have the greatest expertise in such matters. The problems of
consultation and co-operation which thus arise are discussed more fully at 12.

Where there is a danger that decisions will be made within the confines of one
ministry, the need for Parliamentary committees or an independent public watchdog becomes even greater, if accountability of the government to the public is to be
maintained.

Even apart from public accountability, there is no guarantee that all interests are
properly and fully taken into account, and to that extent there can be no guarantee
of a properly balanced decision. This can be seen in a comparison between the
United States EPA and a UK ministry exercising both promotional and control
functions. In the former, an administrator or enforcement officer who states the
case or acts fairly, forcefully and vigorously thereby enhances his prospects of promotion.[24] In the UK, on the other hand, a young civil servant given the task on
controlling the use of pesticides, and who likewise acts vigorously in that cause,
might find himself reminded by an 'older hand' that the principal function of the
Ministry is to promote agriculture, not to 'kill it', and that any zealously applied
controls over the use of pesticides could damage his promotion prospects.

[24]Personal communication with officers of the EPA.

10.3   It may well be that constraints on resources will compel a country to adopt
that system of internal controls, but if the interests of the general public, and of
minorities, are to be protected, safeguards specially for that purpose must be
included.

Such safeguards have already been discussed at 6 above.

11.   CONTROL BY INDEPENDENT AUTHORITY

11.1   At the opposite end of the spectrum of the various types of control systems
lies that in which an authority exercises controls over all sources and forms of
pollution, entirely independently of any department of government which conducts
or promotes activities, whether they be industrial, agricultural or recreational. Such
an authority will have administrative functions, and possibly powers of enforcement, but will normally be subject to government directions on policy.

11.2 US Federal Environmental Protection Agency

11.2.1   The archetype of this kind of control authority is the Environmental
Protection Agency established by US federal legislation.

It is a federal agency which is independent of any federal 'executive agency', i.e.
any agency or department of government which has executive responsibilities
under the President. Its Administrator and Deputy Administrator are appointed by
the President, with the advice of the Senate. Its functions are set out in Appendix B,
where a full outline of the control system is given.

It will be noted that the Federal EPA establishes standards, but normally most of
those standards are maintained under schemes of control proposed and administered by each state. The Federal Agency exercises default powers where
necessary. The exceptions are the standards for pesticides and hazardous wastes,
which are from the outset enforced directly by the Federal Agency.

11.2.2 The principal advantage of this system is that decisions on standards and on
enforcement are made by a body independently of any interests in either conducting
or promoting activities which could give rise to pollution. There is thus no conflict
of interest within the Agency. If any conflicts do arise between the EPA and an
industry, or the executive department of government which promotes its interests,
that conflict is resolved by discussions between them, and the dispute and its
progress normally receives adequate publicity. In any event, the Freedom of
Information Act ensures that the public can inform itself. If the conflict cannot be
resolved by discussion, it is referred to the President for resolution.

Through both his powers of appointment and his power to resolve disputes, the
President exercises a large degree of policy control.

Under this system, there is therefore a body which has a duty to promote
environmental protection, and can see that the case for that protection is put single-
mindedly and openly. Furthermore, as noted at 10.2 above, the officer who pursues
that cause vigorously will tend to enhance his prospects of promotion.[24]

---

[24]Personal communication with officers of the EPA.

11.2.3 The principal disadvantage is the cost. An agency which can independently determine standards which are both acceptable and practicable must have considerable resources at its disposal. Either it has its own staff to carry out the necessary research, or it must commission others to do it, such as the National Physical Laboratory in the United States, or independent research bodies. If there are universities with departments of high competence in the country, it may commission work to be done there, with perhaps considerable advantage to the university and its academic standing internationally. Without full consultation with people with the relevant expertise and experience, however, mistakes can be made. In the past, some of the decisions on standards do not seem to have an adequate technical, scientific or medical basis. In its earlier days, the United States EPA set standards for vehicle emissions, with a right to claim exemption granted because smaller firms might not have the capacity to meet those standards. In the event, all the principal motor vehicle manufacturers claimed and obtained exemption.

The United Kingdom operates a similar system in the field of health and safety at work, with an independent commission and executive. The executive does work of high quality, but there are regular complaints that it is understaffed. Only wealthier countries with adequate research facilities can hope to operate such a system. To a large extent, an agency can use research findings from other countries, but those must be related to local conditions.

11.2.4 Another characteristic of the system, which could degenerate into a disadvantage, lies in the need for consultation regarding environmental decisions. Prior consultation is more difficult when standards are set, and perhaps consents granted, by an independent agency. The problems of consultation and co-operation, however, arise whatever system is chosen. They are therefore discussed separately below at 12.1.

12.   THE CHOICE BETWEEN THE TWO MAIN SYSTEMS

12.1 Co-operation between interested ministries

12.1.1 Whichever ministry, department or agency sets the quality objectives or standards, or grants consents to discharges, it has many interests to take into account, which range across the responsibilities of, or otherwise affect, many ministries. Consultation and co-operation is therefore needed. To give one example, standards or consents for discharges in to inland waters can affect water resources, the health of bathers, fisheries and shellfisheries, and if stringent can retard the development of new industries. In a small developing country the last may be of considerable importance.

12.1.2 A non-integrated system of control, however, does permit a procedure to be used by which all interested ministries and government departments can be consulted. A permanent co-ordinating committee can be established, on which all interested ministries may be represented. They will include all those with responsibilities for matters which may be adversely affected by discharges, e.g. public health, fisheries, agriculture, water supplies. Represented also will be the ministry responsible for industry, and any other ministry responsible for persons who may be adversely affected by strict controls.

Any decisions on quality objectives, standards, emissions or discharges will be brought before such a committee, or before sub-committees dealing with particular receiving media. Each ministry may be permitted to send different representatives to different meetings, so that persons with relevant qualifications and experience may be chosen.

There may even be a right of appeal, made through the relevant minister, on behalf of any department which objects to a decision. The appeal would be decided at inter-ministerial level, on the basis of advice given by a specially constituted panel of experts. Scientific, engineering and policy matters can thus be taken into account.

12.1.3 It would be possible to adapt that procedure to an integrated system of control, although even with an integrated authority, there will doubtless remain a need for consultation with interested government departments.

12.2 Balance of advantages

12.2.1 For a wealthy, highly industrialised country, the balance of advantage appears to lie in an integrated system.

12.2.2 Most obviously, a wealthy country can bear the cost of an independent agency, doing or commissioning research for its purposes.

12.2.3 Less obviously, there can be a long term advantage in such a country applying stringent controls. The research into, and development of, cleaner techniques of production is costly. It does, however, bring rewards. A country adopting them will not only provide its own industry with techniques which are more efficient when taking into account the treatment and disposal on any wastes produced, it will be able to export the intellectual property thus acquired, the necessary equipment it produces, and its consultancy services.

12.2.4 The adoption of cleaner techniques, and more effective methods of treating wastes, can have another effect. The change to new production processes is expensive, and the plant required can also be expensive and suitable more for a firm with a larger scale of production. Such changes, whether made under legal compulsion or through commercial necessity, can lead to a restructuring of an industry. Small firms will not be able to afford the change-over, or the new technical regime itself, and will have to merge, be taken over, or simply go out of business. Whether or not the commercial and social consequences will be left to have their harsh and immediate effects, or whether an easier adjustment will be managed, is a matter or policy for the government.

12.2.5 That kind of change to more stringent controls can be seen in the United Kingdom. Under the old Alkali Acts, for the control of emissions to the atmosphere from certain industrial processes, the 'best practicable means' had to be used to prevent the escape of noxious or offensive gases into the environment, or to mitigate their effects. The question which inevitably arose was whether the means must be practicable within that industry, or practicable for the particular firm under consideration. In practice, the working groups advising the Chief Alkali Inspector on the best practicable means made allowances for the smaller firms. Under the Environmental Protection Act 1991, HMIP, which took over from the Alkali

Inspectorate, requires that the 'best available techniques not entailing excessive cost' be used. A similar question arises – excessive in relation to the harm to be averted, or for the industry involved, or for the particular firm under consideration even though it be a small firm.

The answer given by the Chief Inspector of HMIP is that no allowances will be made for the smaller firms – if they cannot afford the techniques required of them, they should not be in the business.[25]

12.2.6 The governments of small, developing states are faced with different problems.

In the first place, they cannot afford the research and development needed to produce cleaner techniques of production and more effective treatment of wastes. They simply adopt, when they can afford to do so, those developed by the more advanced countries. Many of them are also in the process of promoting industrial development, both to supply their local needs and to provide more export potential. In those circumstances, highly expensive pollution control requirements could cripple a nascent industry, and as a matter of policy it might be decided to accept less stringent controls temporarily to permit the industry to establish itself. The procedure for co-operation outlined at 12.1.2 might then be found most suitable. For example, it might be agreed that it would be more advantageous for the short term to grant consent to an industrial discharge polluting shellfisheries, and to forbid the sale for human consumption of shellfish taken from a fishery down-stream, or require the cleansing by immersion in clean water for a specified period before sale, rather than impose consent conditions which would compel the industrial firm to close.

In such a country, the non-integrated system of control may not simply be the only type that the state could afford, but may be better suited to its circumstances.

13.   OTHER SYSTEMS OF CONTROL

13.1   There are many other systems of control which have features from both the above. Quite properly, the systems are adapted to the prevailing political philosophy of the particular country, the type of constitution, the existing administrative structures and existing legal systems. They are also chosen to match the needs of the country and the resources available. A few special features of those systems are noted here.

13.2 Sweden

13.2.1   The Swedes have adopted a system similar to that of the United Kingdom, with ministries responsible for certain activities also responsible for the control of pollution therefrom.

There are, however, two bodies partly independent of the government, which play key roles in the administration of controls. One is the National Swedish Environment Protection Board, which is the central administrative authority on environmental control. The other is the Franchise Board for Environmental

---

[25]Chief Inspector of HMIP, personal communication.

Protection, which grants permits for a wide range of discharges. In doing so it acts as an objective, independent judicial body, balancing the interests of the applicant against those of the general public, as represented by the Environment Protection Board. It must be noted, however, that the Protection Board has some overriding powers, e.g. its power to exempt from the need for a permit, and that the government itself has an appellate jurisdiction.[26]

13.2.2 Appendix C on the Swedish system, also refers to the Ombudsmen, a form of institution which originated in Sweden. It will be noted that some ombudsmen have been appointed otherwise than by the Government, for particular fields of work. None has been appointed in the field of environmental protection, but they have been referred to as an institution worthy of consideration.[27]

13.3 Denmark

13.3.1 The Danes have also adopted a system similar to that of the United Kingdom. There are two kinds of additional bodies in their system of particular interest.[28]

13.3.2 The first are the 'boards' established under ministries or directorates. They may be central bodies, with nationwide powers of administration, or local bodies with merely local powers. Their membership may be mixed, including politicians, experts and members of special interest groups.[29]

It is noteworthy also that the ministry or directorate to which the board is responsible, has over it only such powers as are granted by law.

13.3.3 The second body of interest is the Environmental Appeal Board. This hears appeals from various administrative decisions on environmental protection. It is a representative body, and its decisions are final on substantive matters. Appeal lies to the established higher courts, but only for infringement of administrative law.[30]

13.3.4 A further point of interest is that members of the Environmental Appeal Board are appointed by the Minister, but that some of those appointments can be made only on the recommendation of certain bodies, which are themselves independent of government, e.g. Federation of Danish Industries, Federation of Danish Agricultural Societies.

13.4 France

13.4.1 In the main, the French administration follows the common pattern, with one Ministry having principal responsibility for protection of the environment, and a co-ordinating role.

13.4.2 It has several interesting means of co-ordination.

[26]For an outline of the Swedish system see Appendix C. On this point note 3.5.2.
[27]See Appendix G on the extension of the powers of the New Zealand ombudsman.
[28]For an outline of the Danish system see Appendix D.
[29]See Appendix D at 3.1.(c).
[30]See Appendix D at 3.4, and cf. 7.3(c) above.

In addition to the usual interministerial committee, in this case the Interministerial Committee on the Quality of Life, there is a High Committee for the Environment. This is an advisory body at the highest level – in addition to high ranking officials, there are 20 other persons chosen by the Prime Minister. It can advise the Government not only on executive action and future legislation, but on matters of policy also.

Of interest also is the fact that on the one hand it has specialised agencies to advise on such matters as air quality and disposal of wastes nationwide, and on the other hand Interministerial Missions to advise on 'across the board' environmental conditions in particular areas.

The system of classified installations is also a feature worthy of note.

13.4.3 A summary of the French system is to be found in Appendix E.

Chapter III

Techniques of Control

1. PURPOSES OF CONTROL MEASURES

1.1   The immediate purposes of a system of control are set out in Chapter I at 4.3.[1] as;

(a)   to encourage the reduction of waste;
(b)   to determine the level of pollution that will be tolerated in any particular place;
(c)   to enforce the measures to eliminate or reduce pollution to that level;
(d)   to encourage the development and adoption of cleaner production techniques and more effective techniques of waste treatment and disposal;
(e)   to protect the interests of the public, of minorities and of individuals.

1.2   The measures outlined below are not necessarily designed to achieve all those purposes. Some may be parts of broader systems of control, under which the executive or even the legislature may take complementary measures, e.g. by way of regulations which revise the discharge standards, or controls over the import or use of certain dangerous substances.

To the extent that a system as a whole does not achieve all the purposes set out above, it may be regarded as unsatisfactory.

1.3   In deciding whether or not a system is effective, it must be remembered that in none of our laws do we achieve total enforcement. In most states, murder and theft have been crimes for centuries, yet murders are still committed, and theft in its many forms is still very common. The two criteria to be applied lie in answers to the following questions:

(a)   Is the law effective enough to justify the costs of enforcement, when weighed against the damage which may be caused to the community or its individual members?
(b)   Is it more cost effective than alternative systems available?

---

[1]Those purposes are dealt with there a little more fully.

2. OBJECTIVES AND STANDARDS

2.1   Before embarking on an examination of the various methods of control, there will be some advantage in discussing two alternatives which lie at the basis of controls – the use of environmental quality objectives, and discharge or emission standards.

2.2   Environmental quality objectives

2.2.1   When an authority is considering controls over discharges to a certain medium such as a stretch of water, it must first ask

(a) to what uses will that water be put, at present or in the future;
(b) will there be a transfer to any other medium, including any food chain, or any pathway to a sensitive receptor?

On the basis of the answers to those questions, the authority can decide what quality is to be maintained in the medium to which the discharge is immediately made. It will then be its objective to exercise its powers of control so as to maintain that level of quality.

So long as more than one person discharges into that medium, to use that quality level for enforcement purposes is impracticable. If the quality falls below the prescribed level, the question arises – which of the several dischargers is to be made responsible? There are many circumstances in which that question cannot be answered with both certainty and justice.

2.2.2   A satisfactory solution is to make the prescribed quality an 'environmental quality objective'. The authority then has that as an objective, and may be required to use its control powers so that quality level is achieved and maintained. It can do so by granting, to the various dischargers, consents calculated to do so. If any discharger exceeds his consent level, he may be made criminally liable.

It may be that the authority itself could be made liable if

(a) the consents it granted made it impossible to guarantee that the quality objective would be maintained;
(b) the quality objective had not been achieved or maintained because the authority had not properly used its control powers.

2.3   Discharge standards

Another method, used notably in the European Community, is to impose fixed discharge standards for particular pollutants, or particular pollutants from specified industries.[2]

This form of control was adopted under a Directive on Pollution caused by certain Dangerous Substances Discharged into the Aquatic Environment of the Community[3]

---

[2]The EEC uses such discharge standards, but permits a Member State to use EQOs as an alternative.

[3]Council Directive 76/464/EEC. The UK Government persuaded the Council to accept a system of control by quality objectives as an alternative. The two methods are compared in 2.4. For an explanation of that compromise see Johnson and Corcelle *Environmental Policy in the European Communities*, (Graham & Trotman, London, 1989), pp. 26, 68.

Under that Directive there is established a 'black list' of substances[4] for which emission standards have been, or are to be, fixed by 'daughter directives'. Those standards are expressed in such terms as milligrams per litre and grams per kilogram handled, or milligrams per litre of effluent and grams per tonne of production capacity.[5]

2.4 A comparison between the two methods shows the following.

2.4.1 Reliance on emission standards does not give greater certainty in protection than reliance on quality objectives. Even if emission standards used lay down maximum quantities to be emitted during any specified period, the effect on the receiving waters will vary according to the number of emission sources, and the characteristics of the waters into which they are discharged, as noted below. Furthermore, it is essential for proper control of the emission standards to be combined with a requirement for prior authorisation for a discharge.[6]

What it does ensure is that all industrial enterprises in the Member States using that method are put on an equal competitive basis so far as environmental precautions are concerned. Each one must comply with precisely the same environmental requirements concerning its discharges. The EEC is concerned to ensure that no Member State secures for its industries any unfair competitive advantage over the others.[7]

At the same time, it seeks to establish similar environmental conditions throughout its area. Therein lies a conflict. Some countries have long, slow flowing rivers, which suffer considerable deterioration in water quality in response to pollution discharges. In contrast, the United Kingdom has short, generally swift flowing, well oxygenated rivers, which soon reach the sea. They can receive a greater pollution load from discharges for the same degree of environmental degradation. Fixed emission standards can thus lead to varying environmental conditions. The same can result from the varying seasonal water flows of the same rivers.[8] EQOs could therefore be a more satisfactory form of agreed control where rivers flow through two or more jurisdictions.

The principal United Kingdom argument in the difference with other EEC Member States was that it should be free to make use of the natural capacity of its rivers to receive pollutants without consequential damage.

That argument breaks down, however, if applied only to the inland waters which immediately receive the discharges. Pollutants which are persistent may continue to

---

[4]In the terms of the Directive, 'List 1'.

[5]The Directive itself, at Art.5, requires that 'The emission standards laid down in the authorisations granted ...... shall determine: (a) the maximun concentration for the substance permissible in a discharge. In the case of dilution the limit value provided for in Art.6(1)(a) shall be divided by the dilution factor; (b) the maximum quantity of the substance permissible in the discharge. For quality objectives, see Article 6.2.

[6]Under Directive 76/464, a prior authorisation is needed. See Art.3.1.

[7]See the Treaty establishing the European Economic Community (Rome 1957), Art.101.

[8]The differences between maximum and minimum flows can be considerable, e.g.,

Seine at Paris	max 2,100 mgd	min 18 mgd
Elbe at Hamburg	3,600	145
Danube at Vienna	9,600	504
Thames at London (excluding effect of Thames Barrier)	300	1

do damage when they reach coastal waters or even waters beyond. The special problem of persistent pollutants was recognised by the EEC in Article 5.2. of Directive 76/464/EEC. That permitted Member States to apply more stringent emission standards, taking into account toxicity, persistence and bio-accumulation of substances.

The validity of the argument for relying on EQOs, therefore depends on the authorities taking into account the persistence of pollutants, any tendency to bio-accumulation, and the pathways of the pollutants through the wider environment.

2.4.2 A further argument in favour of emission standards is their simplicity of application. The standards are fixed centrally, and apply to all discharges.

In contrast, although EQOs for each part of the environment may be determined by a central authority, the discharge consents are often granted regionally, and vary from case to case. That carries two disadvantages:

(a) considerable expertise is needed in the regional authorities to determine fair and proper consents;
(b) there is opportunity for corruption, political bias, or undue emphasis on particular interests.

Adequate safeguards against corruption may be provided,[9] but in some countries, the difficulty of finding sufficient expertise cannot easily be overcome.

Where expertise is available, however, the use of EQOs enables the relevant authorities to give special protection to areas of high amenity by setting high quality objectives and discharge standards in order to achieve them. Admittedly, different emission standard could be applied to those areas, but they would have to be linked to the type and extent of development permitted there. With EQOs, the task is simpler.

2.4.3 The choice of method will therefore vary with the state concerned, its relationship geographically and politically with neighbouring states, and the physical characteristics of its natural environment.

2.4.4 Note also the use of immission standards and emission limit values in atmospheric pollution in Germany, outlined at 8.6.2 below, and in Appendix F.

3. PRODUCT STANDARDS AND PERFORMANCE STANDARDS

3.1 Product standards relate to the composition of a substance, or the design and construction of plant or a piece of equipment. Performance standards relate to the performance of plant or equipment, the manufacturer being left to choose the design or construction he wishes, provided the performance meets the required standard. The effects of the two are the same, therefore no distinction is made between them in this section, and for both the term 'product standard' is used.

---

[9]See Chapter II at section 8.

3.2   The use of product and performance standards

3.2.1   Product standards may be used where a substance, plant or equipment may cause pollution when it is used, and where that pollution may be controlled most easily by the use of requirements relating to the product itself. The state may then prohibit its import, production or use unless it conforms to the product standard laid down in legislation.

Such standards are used widely to control noise and gaseous emissions from motor vehicles, noise from machinery, the biodegradability of detergents, and the sulphur and lead content of petroleum fuels.

3.2.2   The use of product standards can have other purposes. The European Communities seek to achieve similar environmental standards throughout their area. That not only tends to achieve similar levels of environmental quality for all citizens of their Member States, but it prevents any Member State from giving its own industrial enterprises a competitive advantage by permitting the production of items which are made to lower standards, and are therefore less expensive to produce.

Moreover, for a regional community such as that in Europe, at the same time it avoids the erection of artificial barriers to trade. Where the same product standards are in force throughout the region, any detergent, fuel oil or motor vehicle can be imported into any of the Member States.

That, however, can bring a corresponding disadvantage. If artificial barriers to trade are to be avoided, Member States must not be permitted to set higher standards for the import and use of machinery, for that would create an artificial barrier to trade with other Member States.[10]

3.2.3   Performance standards are also used in international treaties. In the International Convention for the Prevention of Pollution from Ships 1973 (MARPOL) and its Protocol of 1978, Annex 1 contains Regulations for the Prevention of Pollution by Oil. Regulation 16 deals with 'Oil Discharge Monitoring and Control Systems, and Oily-Water Separating Equipment' for various classes of ships in terms of performance standards and approval of the design of systems and equipment by the administration established under the Convention.

3.3   Dumping of sub-standard products

The enforcement of product standards in one or more major producing countries may have effects in others. One effect may be beneficial, in that products made to the higher standards become available. A less beneficial effect can be that companies holding stocks of products which fail to meet its own authority's standards may try to sell them off in countries where no product standards are in force. If those countries wish to improve their own environmental standards, they will need to have laws to prevent such 'dumping'.

[10]See Directive 84/532/EEC on common provisions on noise from construction plant and equipment, at Art.19.

3.4   Criteria akin to product standards

There are also criteria, applied particularly to offshore installations, which are closely akin to product standards. Where an oil production platform is to be installed on the continental shelf of any state, that state usually requires that it must be certified by a competent certifying body, as 'safe and fit for that purpose'. That is done primarily for the purpose of ensuring the safety of personnel, and of the installation itself. It also prevents the massive oil pollution which could follow the collapse of the platform.

The state sometimes also lays down criteria to be used in the certification or other approval process.[11]

3.5   Standards of competence of operators and other personnel

In some jurisdictions there are also requirements that persons should not be appointed to certain posts, or given certain responsibilities, unless they have had satisfactory experience or have attended satisfactorily specified courses. Such requirements can be found in countries with offshore oil operations.

In the United Kingdom, an offshore installation manager must have the skill and competence suitable for the appointment.[12] The operator is required to send to the Secretary of State a notice of any such appointment setting out the man's qualifications and experience.[13] A drilling supervisor or driller must within the two previous years have been granted a certificate by the Petroleum Industry Training Board, or one of the equivalent certificates listed in the schedule to the Regulations.[14] Finally, under the Petroleum (Production) Regulations 1982, Clause 24 of the Model Clauses for licences states that

> The Minister may from time to time give to the licensee instructions in writing as to the training of persons employed or to be employed, whether by the licensee or any other person, in any activity which is related to the exercise of the rights granted by this licence.

Norway has more detailed requirements. Regulations relating to safe practices, issued by the Royal Decree of 25 March 1988, at Section 16 provide that

> The licensee shall ensure that all personnel involved in activities at the drill site have the necessary qualifications for proper and safe performance of the work they have been assigned. Training of employees shall take place to the extent necessary and under satisfactory supervision. The licensee shall further ensure that all persons present on the installation or participating in the operations have adequate training and practice in connection with emergency preparedness situations.

---

[11]See, e.g., *UK Offshore Installations: Guidance on Design and Construction*, and the Norwegian *Acts and Regulations for the Petroleum Industry 1992*, Vol.2.
[12]Mineral Workings (Offshore Operations) Act 1971 s.4 (1).
[13]Offshore Operators (Managers) Regulations 1972.
[14]Offshore Operations (Well Control) Regulations 1980.

More detailed requirement for qualifications of drilling personnel are contained in regulations issued by the Norwegian Petroleum Directorate on 22 February 1983.

3.6   Safety standards and precautions which can forestall pollution

3.6.1   Most industrialised nations impose on their industries standards and precautions which seek to ensure that major accidents which cause death or serious injuries to persons do not happen. Consequences of such accidents, such as the release of poisonous gases as at Seveso and Bhopal, are severe forms of pollution, which in turn can cause death or injury. Examples of such standards and precautions are to be found in:

United Kingdom
   Control of Major Accidents Hazards Regulations 1984 S.I.1902, 1985 S.I.2023, 1986 S.I.294, 1988 S.I.1462, 1990 S.I.2325
   Notification of Installations Handling Hazardous Substances Regulations 1982 S.I.1357
   Classification, Packaging and Labelling of Dangerous Substances Regulations 1984 S.I.1244, as amended 1986 S.I.1922 and 1988 S.I.766, 1989 S.I.2208, 1990 S.I.s 1255 and 1487
   Reporting of Injuries, Diseases and Dangerous Occurrences Regulations 1985 S.I.2023, 1989 S.I.1457
European Communities
   Council Directive 82/501/EEC on the major accident-hazards of certain industrial activities
   Council Directive 67/548/EEC as amended, see particularly the sixth amendment 79/831/EEC
   Commission Directive 79/831/EEC making provision for Community wide notification of new substances

As these are classified mainly as health and safety legislation, with safety of persons as the main objective, they are not dealt with in any detail here.

3.6.2   Any countries without technically advanced industries would be wise to adopt similar measures. Large companies which seek places to undertake such work, but which face severe restraints at home, sometimes look abroad for places where there are no such restraints, or where the restraints are more lax. That means that they will bring hazards which would not be tolerated elsewhere.

   What is needed in developing countries, as a precaution against such 'dumping' of hazardous operations, is not only a policy of self-protection, but also legislation which imposes comparable standards and precautions on such operations. What form that legislation will take depends on the existing legal system of the country concerned. It may take the form of consents to industrial development subject to appropriate conditions, or safety legislation comparable to that of the industrially developed countries.

   This danger has even extended to experimental work in genetic engineering. Within recent years, a United States company wished to experiment with genetically modified organisms to combat anthrax in cattle. In order to avoid restrictions imposed on such work in the United States, they started work in Argentina without informing the Government or the public there.

4. CLASSIFICATION OF CONTROLS

The classification used for this study of controls is:

(a) Economic and fiscal controls;
(b) Administrative controls;
(c) Legal controls – civil and criminal.

5. THE CONTRIBUTION OF ECONOMIC INSTRUMENTS TO ENVIRONMENTAL MANAGEMENT

5.1 Government intervention and environmental management

Any intervention in a market, or the means whereby a government intervenes in a market, may be thought of as the use of an economic instrument. Economic instruments under this definition, however, would cover almost all central authority interventions involving taxes, subsidies, loans, grants, accelerated depreciation or a plethora of other, similar, corrective mechanisms directed to alleviating environmental problems using some form of financial instrument.

Intervention may be thought of as either directed towards prices or quantities. In all but the most extreme market situation[15] intervention directed at one variable must influence the other (as well as prices and quantities in related markets). It is more usual to regard as economic instruments policies whose primary target is the price of a particular good or service. This can be achieved either directly, using taxes or subsidies directed at the producer or consumer, or indirectly, by subsidising or taxing products produced or purchases by producers or consumers.

Examples of direct taxes or subsidies would be of those of a higher rate of corporation tax for producers not using a certain proportion of recycled materials, or allowing consumers to set repair and maintenance expenditures on durable goods against their personal tax liability (to encourage greater longevity for consumer durables and automobiles). Examples of indirect instruments would be excise taxes imposed on packaging to reflect the full waste collection and disposal cost, or *ad valorem* or per unit subsidies placed on recycled materials.

Markets for certain goods do not work adequately because the goods are so-called 'public' goods (mainly because, by their nature, individuals cannot be excluded from enjoying benefits from them). Many environmental services are of this nature, and are therefore provided either directly by governments, or by governments and private enterprise together. In several countries, the provision of amenity services is achieved in this way. The provision of 'public' environmental goods and services may be thought of as the use of economic instruments.

Finally, markets may be seen not to operate due to lack of information, either on the part of producers or consumers. The success of waste exchanges in several countries exemplifies how government provision of information on the availability of waste materials can be instrumental in establishing markets that had not previously

---

[15]That is, where either demand or supply is totally unresponsive to price changes.

existed, by bringing together (or at least bringing to light the existence of) supplies of or the demands for secondary materials.

Unfortunately, the experience with waste exchanges also demonstrates one of the problems of intervening in markets, namely that such intervention is not simply for the time being but must be for a considerable length of time, in some instances permanently. The example from the United Kingdom in the late 1970s demonstrates this. During that decade, a waste exchange had been developed, with considerable foresight, by the UK Department of Trade and Industry's Warren Springs Laboratory. Unfortunately, in 1979, the exchange was required to be self-financing. Although in its history the exchange had a clearly positive ratio of benefits to costs, it collapsed very quickly thereafter.

In addition to policies whose prime target is an environmentally-based objective, there are other policies which, by their nature, have direct implications for environmental management or resource recovery. Two examples of the many available are: the tax treatment of virgin materials producers; and the demand by central authorities for goods and services (known in some countries as government procurement requirements). Any comprehensive evaluation of economic instruments ought to take into account at least the most obvious of these.

In summary, to delimit the scope of the discussion, we shall adopt the following useful, if rather broad, definition of an economic instrument:

> Any government policy which aims to influence the cost of providing or maintaining environmental goods or services; or aims to use government expenditure to supplement private production of goods and services; or aims to provide a means whereby markets can be created.
>
> A rather crude generalisation of this would include all policies, relating to environmental management, which involve the taxes, subsidies or other forms of government expenditure, as economic instruments. Policies which are directed solely towards quantities, and are implemented mainly by specific legislation, may be thought of as 'regulatory' (although they obviously have economic implications, as was noted above).

5.2   The role of economic instruments in environmental management policy

The role of economic instruments in environmental management policy can best be seen in the context of the policy process as a whole. Theil (1958)[16] has provided the general outline of steps in the policy process. He envisaged the policy process as one whereby general policy goals are achieved using economic instruments to affect (or 'impact on') particular or specific targets. For example, the general goals of reduced solid waste disposal and improved resource recovery can be achieved, *inter alia*, by a specific policy directed towards particular items entering the solid waste stream, such as beverage containers and packaging. The proposed US product charge legislation was a useful example (US EPA, 1977). As particular targets are approached through the operation of the economic instrument, so are the more general goals of improved environmental management and resource recovery

---

[16]H. Theil *Economic Analysis and Policy*, (North Holland, Amsterdam, 1958).

approached. Thus, economic instruments should not be viewed in isolation, as ends in themselves, but rather in the context of the targets which they are intended to achieve, that is, as a means to an end.

From the foregoing it is apparent that economic instruments need to be assessed in the light of possible policy targets which they might be used to achieve. To some extent this will reflect past experience, and to some extent it will reflect experience with similar economic instruments in different policy spheres.

5.3   Categories of economic instruments

The placing of policy instruments into categories will inevitably lead to the problem of particular instruments not fitting into any particular category, or of certain instruments being eligible for more than one category. It does, however, provide an organisational framework, and it is for this reason it is resorted to here.

There seem to be at least two eligible ways in which economic instruments used in environmental management can be categorised. One way is by that part of the environmental degradation toward which they are directed, that is: air, water noise, and solid waste. The major disadvantage here would be in the number of instruments which would overlap categories. The major alternative basis for categories is by the purpose for which economic instruments are intended: to internalise external environmental costs, to provide public environmental goods and services, to provide adjustment aid for increased resource recovery, or to assist in the establishment of secondary materials markets and trade in recovered materials, for example.

Whilst this second basis for grouping instruments will have overlaps they will be considerably less than in the first, and, it is felt, will assist in understanding the use of particular policy instruments and the circumstances under which their use has been found to be, or is most likely to be, effective.

5.4   Economic instruments: nature, purpose and potential

The various classes of economic instruments that constitute the range of instruments under review have been outlined above. They broadly represent policies to correct externalities, policies to complement the supply of environmental goods and services with strong 'public goods' attributes, and policies to encourage the establishment of markets, the costs of establishing which would otherwise be prohibitive in relation to the individual benefits that could be realised. Most attention has been directed to the first category of instruments, but this does not detract from the importance, in practice or potentially, of the other two classes of instruments.

5.5   Charges and environmental management

The use of economic instruments, as opposed to a regulatory approach, in environmental management among developed countries varies from the indirect provision of waste collection, to the direct charge for municipal waste collection (user charges), to a charge on specific categories of waste and further, to the payment of a bounty on the return of specific categories of solid waste to specific collection centres. These policies are mostly incentive-based.

5.5.1   User charges

A user charge is essentially a payment for discharge of a pollutant into environmental media based upon the approximate pollutant loading. This simple definition conceals a large number of possible permutations. The administrative issues notwithstanding, the important question is whether the amount of pollutant generated are at all sensitive to the charges levied.

Possible material characteristics to be considered as the basis for user charges include weight, volume, environmental hazard and problems of measuring these. The problem with mixtures of pollutants is that, in principle, the charge should be based upon the component pollutants. In practice, however, such an approach would be totally impractical. Any charge, however, gives an incentive to avoid the charge (even though this may only marginally detract from the pollution reducing effects of the charge).

Deciding upon the appropriate rate for the charge will also provide problems. The charge should theoretically cover the full marginal damage costs of the pollutants. However, work in the US raises a difficulty even at this stage. Attempts to estimate the cost curves for pollutant charges both by public and private authorities revealed atypical cost curves. If these estimates had been utilised in practice, unusual and economically perverse effects would have resulted.

5.6   Product charges[17]

The concept of including in the final cost of a good a charge to cover the collection and disposal of the discarded good, or of the associated packaging, and any pollution thereby generated, is obviously founded firmly on the 'polluter pays' principle. The product charge has been defined as:

> an excise tax on the material content of consumer products entering the solid waste stream.

The key points relating to the principle of the product charge are:

(1) the products to be included;
(2) provisions for exempting reclaimed and recycled materials used in the products or in the packaging;
(3) the extent to which such an indirect tax will be regressive, i.e. the extent to which the tax will fall more heavily on the shoulders of the poorer members of society.

In principle the product charge should cover all products entering the municipal waste stream from domestic consumption. In practice, however, it is felt, at least in the United States, that the administration of a product charge on all goods would be too complex and too costly, and that the charge should be directed at products which comprise a large proportion of the household solid waste generated. The proposal in that country was to impose the charge on paper products and non-paper packaging materials. These two categories together constitute an estimated 80 per

---

[17]Much of the information in the following section comes from the US Environmental Protection Act or other studies referenced here.

cent of the US solid waste stream. Of the possible bases for the charge, that based on weight seemed to be the most suitable. The charge should be set at marginal direct cost of collection and disposal and the charge should be imposed as near to the point of manufacture as possible, to reduce the number of points at which the charge should be collected, and where regular monitoring needs to be carried out. However, the concept of utilising a product charge has fallen from consideration in recent years in the US.

The recycled material content of goods and packaging is another problem associated with the product charge. The problem is essentially one of identifying the amount of material reclaimed from household solid waste that is included in the manufactured product, and of assessing the value of this. ('Prompt' industrial scrap should not be included in the recycling credit.) The imposition of the tax or charge near to the point of manufacture considerably reduces the problem of assessing the reclaimed material content of goods or packaging.

The question of whether this charge, like any other indirect tax may weigh more heavily on the poorer members of society, is a matter of concern. It is popularly believed that any indirect sales tax will be regressive. However, in discussing a similar issue, the author of a report on the subject came to the following conclusion:

> In analysing the effect of [a] new tax on the distribution of income, it is important to recall that a single component of the government budget constraint cannot be changed in isolation. If tax revenues are increased by the institution of a new ... tax, then there must be a counterpart change in government spending on goods and services or on transfer payments and subsidies, in monetary policy, in debt management policy, or in the levels of other tax revenues ... the important point is that the counterpart change could well take the form of alterations in other taxes so that the combined effect of the measures would be distributionally neutral. The significance of this point is that it provides an immediate answer to the common, but misleading, complaint that sales taxation of any kind is regressive, and therefore to be avoided. It is far from certain that (such a) tax ... would be regressive, but in any case any such effect could be offset. (Butlin and Sumner, 1978, p.50.)

A further concern about the product charge concept relates to the elasticity of demand for waste disposal services. If the elasticity proved to be low the effect of a product charge could be expected to be relatively insignificant in terms of its effect on pollutant emissions. (This applies, of course, to *all* direct economic instruments.)

5.7   Examples of the use of economic instruments in environmental management

The use of economic instruments for environmental purposes in the real world varies considerably depending upon the country concerned. It is perhaps in the United States that economic incentives have been used in practice more than any other country.

Among the most famous of the early applications of economic instruments for environmental purposes was the USEPA's 'bubble concept' under which the USEPA encouraged states in the late 1970s and early 1980s to allow increases in air pollution from one or more sources at a single plant as long as equivalent reductions in emissions were accomplished at other sources in the same plant. The 'bubble concept' simulates a marketable permit system in which one source in a plant 'purchases' a right to increase emissions by securing an offset reduction elsewhere in the plant.

The USEPA 'bubble concept' policy was limited in a number of ways. Among these were

(a) reductions in one class of pollutants could not be swapped for increases in another class of pollutants, particularly hazardous pollutants;
(b) all the pollution from an individual plant could not be discharged from one source in such a way that air quality standards were violated;
(c) the concept could not be used as an excuse to delay compliance with air quality standards.

In addition to the 'bubble concept' policy noted above, the USEPA also promoted a more ambitious use of economic incentives by means of its 'offset policy', which was a response to a problem arising from the Clean Air Act. Under the provisions of this Act, an increase in pollutant discharge in areas already failing to meet the primary air quality standards established under the Act was prohibited. In order to overcome this problem, USEPA proposed that new sources seeking to locate in areas where primary air quality standards were not being met, or existing industries wishing to include its pollutant loading in such areas, should be allowed to do so providing they obtained off-setting reductions in air pollution from existing sources.

In effect, the 'off-set policy' represented the first full marketable permit approach to air pollution control in the US, and has been followed by a number of others. For this reason it is worth considering further.

The 'off-set policy' worked as follows: where a new company with significant gaseous emissions wished to locate in an area where primary air quality standards as designated under the US Clean Air Act had not been met. The company would need to identify existing polluters and offer to compensate one or more of them for reducing the discharge of the pollutant(s) by the amount that the new firm would emit in the course of its activities. If the existing firm could reduce its discharges for less than the new firm is prepared to offer it accepted the offer and increased its bottom-line profitability at the same time. It is apparent that the new firm could not eliminate the pollutant(s) for less money than it offered others; if it could, it would act in this way, and not by off-set. Thus, the creation of a market for reductions in pollution ensures that emission reductions are undertaken by those who can most cheaply achieve it (always presuming that newcomers can identify them). In principle at least, the 'off-set policy' ensures that a given level of environmental quality be achieved and maintained at least social cost.

In September 1991, the European Commission published a proposal for a 'carbon tax'. In effect, this is a two-component tax:

(a) A uniform energy tax applied to all sources of energy except renewable energy;
(b) A tax graduated according to the carbon content of individual fuels; the tax would be imposed initially at a level of $1 per barrel of oil and would rise within ten years to $10 per barrel of oil.

As with other fiscal instruments, whether used for environmental purposes or otherwise, a key requirement would be for the tax to be 'fiscally neutral', that is it should neither increase nor decrease the level of tax revenue generated as a result of its implementation. In addition, there is a proposal to consider exemptions for energy-intensive sectors, including iron and steel, non-ferrous metals, paper, glass, chemicals and cement.

Although relatively new, the proposals for a tax which the date of publication are being developed by the European Commission, have generated a considerable amount of adverse action. This arises from industrialists who maintain that the imposition of a tax would make European industry 'uncompetitive' and a rather different viewpoint, is from environmental economists who state that the tax would need to be significantly larger to have any noticeable effect, as a demand for energy is highly inelastic, particularly in the short run. This implies that large changes in price will only bring about small consumption quantity responses.

The proposal by the European Commission to impose a carbon tax is an example of the growing recognition by regulatory authorities of the value of economic instruments in environmental management policy. Further discussion is of little value, however, as the proposal will almost certainly be changed radically before it becomes a fully fledged Community regulation or directive.

Considerable effort has been dedicated over a period of time to identify what are the marginal social costs of discharging pollutants into the environment.[18] The implication of this work is that, to ensure that the market adjustment achieved with the use of an economic instrument is appropriate, and the marginal damage cost of the pollution loading must be estimated in order to ensure that the tax or subsidy is pitched at the appropriate level. Among the approaches which have been used to estimate marginal damage costs (or the obverse, the marginal benefit of reducing pollution damage) are

(1) using the surrogate market approach which identifies a market in which goods or factors of production are bought and sold and observes that environmental benefits or costs are reflected in these markets. For example, it would argue that one aspect determining a value of a house in a middle class leafy suburb is the quality of the environment in which the house is situated.
(2) The experimental approach which attempts to place respondents to question-naires in such a position that they respond to questions concerning their willingness to pay for environmental quality in the way that they would if such a market existed.

Both the surrogate market approach and the experimental approach are so-called 'direct' valuation approaches. The other group of approaches, the so-called 'indirect approaches', include

(3) 'dose-response' approaches: these estimate, in a two-step manner, the effect between a 'dose' of pollution and the physical response from a change in the dosage. Following this, an attempt is made to identify the willingness to pay for such a change (usually a reduction) in the pollutant dosage.

---

[18]Much of this information emanates from the work of David Pearce. It is particularly accessible in D. Pearce Anil Markandaya and Edward B. Barbier, *Blue Print for a Green Economy* (Earthscan Publications, London, 1989).

A number of analytical techniques have been used to identify the marginal willingness to pay or marginal damage cost associated with changes in the level in pollutant emission in individual countries. Among those which have been widely publicised in the past are:

- Australia (aircraft noise)
- Canada (aircraft noise, air pollution)
- Germany (air pollution, water pollution and noise)
- The Netherlands (air pollution, noise pollution and water pollution)
- UK (aircraft noise)
- USA (aircraft noise, air pollution, water pollution).

Various OECD studies[19] have identified the use of water pollution charges in Canada, Finland, France, Germany, Japan, the Netherlands, the United Kingdom and the United States; studies on charges on gaseous and particulate emissions from France, the Netherlands, Norway, Sweden and the US; studies on noise pollution from a wide number of countries; and studies on the use of economic instruments in relation to solid waste from Australia, Canada, France, Germany, Norway and the UK.

In other words, among the major OECD countries, there has been considerable application in the experience of various forms of economic instruments to achieve improvements in environmental quality, the advantage of economic instruments over other, regulatory or quantity based environmental control systems being that they give increased flexibility, enhance adaptation to technical change and are *a priori* the least cost approach to environmental quality improvement.

5.8 Conclusions

While the use of economic instruments of various sorts as an instrument of environmental policy has expanded over the years, their use is not as prevalent as might have been expected from the virtues extolled by environmental economists in the late 1970s and the early 1980s. By way of conclusion, it is worth reflecting on the reasons why this may have come about.

It would appear that there are at least four reasons for the use of economic instruments in environmental management not being as popular as might have been expected. These are:

- further market imperfections;
- uncertainty of various sorts;
- problems of measurement;
- problems of political acceptability.

Each of these will be addressed in turn.

---

[19]For example, D.W. Pierce *Pollution Changes, an Assessment* (1976) and A. Markandya, *Environmental Policy Benefits; Monetary Evaluation* (1989).

5.8.1 Further market imperfections

Lancaster's Theory of the Second Best demonstrated that use of tax/subsidy remedies to correct market imperfections or externalities was appropriate where there was only one such imperfection or externality. In the event of there being more, the Theory of the Second Best demonstrates that it is not necessarily optimal to correct each externality on the basis of a partial equilibrium marginal social cost correction. In reality, we live in a '55th Best' world, and it has been argued on occasion that the application of marginal damage cost or marginal willingness to pay valuations or charges is not necessarily even the least cost way of remedying the relevant environmental problem.

5.8.2 Uncertainties

The problem of uncertainty pervades all attempts to use empirical measurement to implement economic measures which, in theory, appear to be unexceptionable. Environmental economics are no exception to this, and the world of environmental economic policy assessment is strewn with attempts to measure the marginal willingness to pay or the marginal damage costs utilising a conventional or modified econometric and other economic/statistical tests, or, alternatively, even more ingenious attempts to put reliable values on parameters which are needed to make these estimates. By and large, these attempts have not been successful, the reasons for this including:

– the data is so strongly correlated that the parameter estimates are unreliable;
– there is insufficient data to undertake a sufficiently rigorous statistical analysis;
– the statistical models used may be inappropriate for the purposes to which they are being applied in this instance.

The question of uncertainty is associated with the question of measurement, which is discussed below.

5.8.3 Measurement

The measurement of the levels of pollution being emitted from a variety of sources, the ambient level of pollutant in the various environmental media, and the effect of the pollutants on human health, building structure, and the density and nature of flora and fauna, for example, are extremely difficult to measure. In addition, there are a number of influences which will be specific to a particular circumstance because of synergistic effects. The use of imprecise measures as a basis for economic instruments which will have ubiquitous effects can be one reason for being reluctant to use such measures in the first place.

5.8.4 Political acceptability

The issue of political acceptability relates to most factor demand curves in industry being relatively inelastic in the short run. The implication is that for a direct economic instrument to have an effect it is necessary that a relatively large increase in input prices must be brought about (a large increase in marginal costs) to receive a relatively small quantitative response. Any such policy is likely to be met by intensive lobbying from the particular sector concerned, and particularly those firms (usually the larger enterprises) who are more efficient at pollution control and therefore will bear a large proportion of the total costs. Whilst this may be more true of direct instruments such as pollution taxes and less true of other instruments such as exchangeable pollution permits, the lobbying undertaken by industry and trade associations against such measures is, perhaps, evidence of their concern about their introduction.

All of these reservations notwithstanding, the use of economic instruments in environmental policy has gradually increased over the past two decades, and appears still to be increasing. The continued use of discharge fees in France, despite early difficulties, and their adoption in Germany, both bear witness to the fact that they are seen as an effective measure for water pollution control. The proposed use of a carbon tax to reduce emissions of gaseous oxides of carbon by the European Community is further evidence of a widespread use of a particular economic instrument to achieve a particular environmental policy target.

Further examples, such as the use of recycling credits under the Environmental Protection Act 1990 in the United Kingdom to encourage the recycling of recyclable materials from household waste is further evidence of the increasingly broad perception of the value of economic instruments in this context, although its manner of implementation, to some extent, is also evidence of the problems in application. There can be no doubt that the use of economic instruments as a tool of environmental policy is established, and will increase over the coming years, particularly as experience of their use is gained across a wide range of countries.

6. ADMINISTRATIVE CONTROLS

6.1 The use of administrative powers

6.1.1 The administrative departments of any government are necessarily involved in the process of pollution control. Policy statements may be written into legislation, or committees of ministers or particular ministers may be given a duty to formulate policy. Even without a statutory duty, a minister is expected to formulate policy and supervise its execution. Without that, there would be a gap between the sovereign power and the executive agencies. The use of all administrative powers must then conform to the policies thus formulated.

Three examples of the latter may be taken from Denmark, the United Kingdom and the Netherlands.

In Denmark there is a council of cabinet ministers chaired by the Prime Minister. It is the highest authority on environmental matters, and determines general policy on national physical planning and environmental management, and all regional development plans are subject to its approval.

In the United Kingdom, the Water Act 1973 Section 1, now repealed, provided that

> It shall be the duty of the Secretary of State and the Minister of Agriculture, Fisheries and Food .... to promote jointly a national policy for water .... and .... to secure the effective execution of that policy by the bodies responsible .... .

The Water Act 1991, which repealed that provision has more complex provisions, but provides at Section 83 that

.... the Secretary of State may .... establish water quality objectives for any waters which are (controlled waters) ..... .

In the Netherlands, there are various ministries which make decisions on matters which can affect the environment. Co-ordination is therefore necessary. The Ministry of Housing, Physical Planning and Environmental Management is the co-ordinating body for environmental hygiene and physical planning, and the Minister chairs meetings of the Council for Regional Planning and Environmental Hygiene.[20]

6.1.2 Administrative actions then taken may include: the approval and sanctioning of developments proposed by regional or local authorities; the grant of loans or loan sanction; the approval of standards for discharges or products; and the taking or sanctioning of emergency action. The administrative authorities also normally have more generalised supervisory powers to ensure the proper implementation of policy. The use of such powers is discussed at 6.3 below.

6.1.3 Some 30 countries now have in their constitutions statements of rights or duties concerning the environment.[21] The inclusion of such rights and duties in the constitution will be discussed in Chapter VI.

6.2 Administrative and judicial powers

6.2.1. There is here, however, a difficult distinction to be drawn between the use of administrative powers and the discharge of judicial functions. Where there is a dispute between two or more persons, whether on facts, law or procedures, the dispute is often settled by persons who can act as independent arbiters. Where their decision is to be based only on the issues between the parties, they are considered to be acting judicially. It is then normally considered to be a principle of vital constitutional importance that those persons, in making the decision, should be free from influence by the Government and its agencies.

Difficulties can arise in cases in which there are both judicial and administrative elements – commonly referred to as 'quasi-judicial'. It is usually possible in such cases to separate the two elements. The judicial function can be performed by an independent arbiter, by whatever title he is given, and his findings sent to the appropriate minister. The minister then applies government policy, and issues the final decision. It is important in those cases, however, that the arbiter's findings are published, not only because this facilitates the preparation of any appeal, but also because the public is then able to see the results of the independent judicial enquiry, and how the policy has been applied to its findings.

6.2.2 Often, however, quasi-judicial decisions are made entirely by the minister, normally with the help of advice from experts, who may be from his own department.

---

[20]The Netherlands ministerial and co-ordinating structure is complex. For a more detailed account see Emvironmental Resources Ltd., *The Law and Practice Relating to Pollution Control in the Netherlands*, pp.6-7, and Environmental Resources Ltd., *The Law and Practice Relating to Pollution Control in Member States of the European Communities - Recent Developments* (Graham & Trotman, London, 1982 and 1986 respectively).

[21]T.T. Smith and P. Kromarek *Understanding U.S. and European Environmental Law*, 'The Future of Environmental Law in Europe' contribution by A. Kiss at p.151. (Graham & Trotman, London, 1989).

Many such decisions are made in the process of hearing appeals from the decisions of control authorities, particularly under consent systems for discharges to water. They are directed to the minister for two reasons. The first is so that he can ensure that the control decisions are decided in accordance with government policy. That may apply not only to general government policy, but also to *ad hoc* policies: e.g. to give support to some industry of vital national importance, or to allow development in areas of natural beauty, or to restrain it as the case may be. The second is to ensure some consistency throughout regional or local jurisdictions, where consistency is wanted, and to ensure consistency over a period of time.

6.3   Supervisory powers and powers to secure implementation

6.3.1   Under a consent system, a minister may be empowered to 'call in' applications for his own decision. This is done for the policy reasons referred to above. The power is usually used for decisions on major developments, where there are issues of national importance and policy implications loom large, e.g. a large estuary barrage scheme in an area of great natural beauty.

6.3.2   Ministers may also be granted a power to give directions to a control authority. Care is often taken, however, not to give them power to instruct authorities to prosecute, or not to prosecute, in any particular case. It is considered that if justice is to be impartial, political influence must be kept out of such decisions. To take an example from another field, the United Kingdom Health and Safety at Work etc Act 1974, dealing with the health and safety in the place of work, at Section 10 establishes a Health and Safety Commission, and a subordinate Executive. Section 11 then provides that

> (3) It shall be the duty of the Commission .... to give effect to any directions given to it by the Secretary of State.
> (4) .... it shall be the duty of the Executive .... to give effect to any directions given to it by the Commission, ... but, except for the purpose of giving effect to directions given to the Commission by the Secretary of State, the Commission shall not give to the Executive any directions as to the enforcement of of any of the relevant statutory provisions in a particular case.

That provision is open to criticism in that it does appear to give the minister a power to intervene indirectly in decisions concerning prosecutions in particular cases. Such a power, when granted in the United Kingdom is more usually in the form in which it appeared in the Water Act 1973, at Section 5, now repealed.

> (2) The Secretary of State may give water authorities directions of a general character as to the exercise by such authorities of [their functions].

6.3.3   Guidelines may also be issued to regional and local pollution control authorities. They may be issued under the title 'guidelines' or 'circulars', and are normally in terms of how the authorities should use their powers. For example: in the United Kingdom Circular 10/73 was issued to all local planning authorities giving guidance on noise standards they should seek to achieve in the use of their planning powers; also various circulars have been sent to pollution control authorities on how they should use their powers in order to comply with EEC directives.

Guidelines have likewise been used to supplement treaty requirements. Under the Kuwait Convention, a Protocol on the Protection of the Marine Environment against Pollution from Offshore Operations, the Regional Organisation is empowered to issue guidelines on environmental impact assessments, and on the use of chemicals in those operations.

There are guidelines issued in Germany which, although not issued by public authorities, have comparable effects. The Association of German Engineers has issued over 200 VDI guidelines on air and noise emissions, the German Institute for Standards has issued DIN standards, and the Committee for Nuclear Energy guidelines on technical requirements for use in licensing procedures under nuclear laws.

Guidelines and codes of practice are not in themselves enforceable. They can, however carry considerable persuasive weight, and a failure to follow them can often have legal consequences. In some legislation the control authority is required 'to have regard' to them.[22] In the case of a minister's guidelines, the minister may refuse to authorise a scheme, in other cases the failure may be weighty evidence in subsequent legal proceedings.

6.3.4   A minister may be granted other powers which can be used effectively to control pollution. Capital investment schemes by public authorities may need his approval, either in accordance with specific legislation, or under a five year development plan. He may withhold that approval until certain conditions for protection of the environment have been met.

Similarly, loans for capital investment may need his approval, and that approval may be withheld for like reasons. In the United Kingdom, controls over discharges to sea were in the past exercised in this way, to fill gaps in the existing environmental laws. Local authorities wishing to build pipelines to the sea to be used as sewage outfalls would have to raise large loans, and such loans needed ministerial approval. The minister would not give that approval until he was satisfied by hydrological tests that the discharges would not be carried back to pollute beaches. The tests themselves were often inadequate in not taking into account industrial discharges which might in the future be permitted into the sewers, but in the absence of proper pollution control laws, they did serve some useful purpose. Approvals for the construction of sewage treatment works, also, can provide a means of control in ensuring that the size of the works and the type of plant installed would be adequate.

The use of both such powers can, in the longer term, influence the development of pollution control management throughout the jurisdiction.

6.4   Economic planning

6.4.1   Many states, even with different forms of government, plan the development of their economies, and use their governmental powers to ensure that development takes place in accordance with the plan. Frequently, this takes the form of successive five year plans.

Decisions made in preparing the economic plan can have considerable effect on the environment. This is true whether further development is planned for industry,

[22]See UK Control of Pollution Act 1974 ss.60(4) and 61(5).

agriculture, forestry or tourism. It is proper then, that environmental impact be taken into account. That does not mean that the economic planning agency will engage directly in environmental management. It does mean that it must be aware of probable environmental impacts, and take those impacts into account.

6.4.2 Clearly there will have to be close co-ordination with the work of the land use planners. Consultation is needed at early stages, and in some jurisdictions the land use plan for the territory is made subordinate to the economic plan.

In many cases, there will also be a need to consult pollution control authorities. That will be particularly important if the proposed developments include any hazardous industries.[23]

7. LEGAL CONTROLS – CIVIL

7.1 The term 'civil law' is here used to denote that body of law which protects individuals by giving them rights to compensation, or court orders such as injunctions which compel other persons to refrain from certain actions, or compel them to take certain actions.

Civil liability will be discussed more fully in Chapter V.

7.2 Civil actions and their effects

7.2.1 Civil actions are taken by persons, including corporations, to protect their own interests. Any compensation or court orders in most cases relate only to those interests. Any effects of the court's decision on the environment generally, or other persons' interests in the environment, are purely incidental.

Such incidental effects do occur, however. In many instances, the environment is protected, as when a civil action restrains a person from discharging toxic fumes into the atmosphere, or a toxic effluent into a river. That can also bring benefits to a wide range of other people. The right to bring actions which have such effects is discussed in Chapter V at 6.5.

7.2.2 The effects of actions taken by individuals on their own behalf, however, are haphazard and patchy. The principal reason for that is that the bringing of any civil action depends on there being a person

- whose interests are or will be damaged, and
- who has funds available to run an action which may prove costly in view of the need for expert evidence, and
- who is willing to take such action in the face of the risks and uncertainties of litigation.

The availability of legal aid can help, but while that helps the poor it is often less help to persons in the middle range of incomes, who may have to make a substantial contribution to costs, and to do so may have to put their investments and property at stake. Such a person often decides that it is less risky to tolerate the

---

[23]In Hong Kong, e.g., in 1982 a special study was commissioned on the concentration of hazardous developments on Tsing Ye Island, and controls over hazardous installations elsewhere.

interference, or to move to another area. The use of contingency fees can help, but in many countries they are not permitted.[24]

For that and other reasons, people with middle range or higher incomes tend to move out of polluted areas, and the value of properties there falls. The poor are left to tolerate the pollution. Moreover, that arises not only from a lack of money. In such areas there are then few people with the knowledge, the skill, and the connections, to see that preventive action is taken when a new source of pollution arises. This may be illustrated by two contrasting examples.

The first is from Liverpool, where a small research project was carried out. After heavy rain, some of the roadside drains become blocked, and a small area of the road and possibly the pavement is flooded. The project was to discover how soon the blockages were cleared by the municipal authorities in various areas. It was clearly established that the floods remained longer in the poorer areas.

The second occurred in Bowden, a middle class area in Cheshire, England. A large company sought permission to build a factory in the area. Although it would have been a clean process, an action committee comprising business and professional people was quickly organised, funds were raised, and the application was soon withdrawn.

Thus the worst effects of pollution tend to be felt in the poorer areas. Any government wishing to achieve the same or similar standards of environmental quality in residential areas, must take that tendency into account.

It is notable also, and not unconnected with the above, that where there is already considerable pollution there are often fewer interests to protect. In the United Kingdom, wherever rivers are clean, angling clubs take action against any pollution; but where the river is already so polluted so that there are no fish, and no recreational use of the waters, there is no-one with sufficient interest to protect who will take action. Also where 'water parks' are created, and the waters put to recreational use, the control authority has a stronger case in demanding that industry cleans its waste waters before discharge.

7.2.3 Another reason why reliance cannot be placed on civil actions is that individual rights can be surrendered as part of an agreement, or an individual's interests in the land may simply be bought out.

There is a similar form of protective action which has often been used in the United Kingdom. In one instance, a petrochemical works, adjacent to land on which farmers grew potatoes, discharged ethylene which damaged the potato crops. Annually, the damage to each farmer's crop was assessed, and compensation paid. Eventually, the petrochemical company bought the farmed land and leased it back to the farmers. The lease was at a specially reduced rent, but stated that no compensation could be claimed by the tenant for industrial pollution from the works. That satisfied the farmers, but did nothing to restrain pollution by ethylene. In fact, the company, at least in the short term, would no longer save costs by reducing the output of ethylene.

In other instances brick companies whose works discharge fluorine, which can do damage to cattle, have bought adjoining farm land and leased it back to the farmers, the terms of the lease being that no cattle should be kept on the land. The agreement would be beneficial to the farmers in terms of rent. On the other hand, it did nothing to restrain pollution, and restricted the use which could be made of the land.

[24]On contingency fees, see Chapter V at 6.3.1.

The same techniques may be used in purchasing fishing rights downstream of a discharge. That has much the same effect, although legally the result is different. In the cases outlined above, of the many persons having rights of action, a few, albeit the principal complainants, surrendered their rights to sue. Where fishing rights are purchased, in common law terms a piece of incorporial property has been purchased. The person selling that property thereafter has no property that the law will protect.

7.2.4 That is a problem on which legislation may be needed.

7.3 The broader aspects of civil liability, including the relationship of individual civil rights against control authorities, will be discussed in Chapter V.

8. LEGAL CONTROLS – CRIMINAL

8.1 Classification of controls

8.1.1 It will be useful for the purposes of this study to place the controls in a sequence which will show in a more logical way the range of possibilities available, and permit a more orderly study.

The sequence follows the stages of a person planning an enterprise, acquiring a site, works plant and machinery as necessary, setting in motion his process, treating and discharging his wastes, and subsequently the use of the products which may itself cause pollution, and the final disposal of the products.

8.1.2 There is an advantage in following such a sequence. One of the most important considerations in deciding which form of control to use is the extent to which it can successfully be enforced. As noted in Chapter II at 5.1, successful enforcement involves detecting infringements, which may itself involve continuous or regular monitoring, and also gathering evidence sufficient for a prosecution. For those purposes, the place in the sequence may be significant. Controls imposed at the earlier stages are, in general but not invariably, easier to enforce. If land use planning is refused, or granted subject to conditions, it is easy to see whether or not a building has been erected, and in most cases whether or not the conditions have been met. At a later stage, once an enterprise has been established, it can become difficult for authorities to exercise rigorous control. They are often told by management that the controls will impose unsustainable costs, and result in many employees being dismissed, or even the closure of the works. It is clear too, that controls imposed at an early stage, for example over a few manufacturers of pesticides, are easier to apply than controls over the thousands of farmers who may use their products.

There are notable exceptions. Controls over the users of a product comes at a late stage, but when the users form a small body of people acting under a disciplinary code, as in the case of airline pilots, monitoring and enforcement at that stage can be easy.Again, automatic monitoring of the character and volume of discharges to water, even though done at a later stage in the sequence, can be easily done and is highly effective. As no reliable general rule can be laid down, the ease and effectiveness of enforcement will be examined separately for each form of control.

The sequence is set out in Figure III.

Figure III Range of Control Measures Enforceable by Criminal Penalties

Operation	Control Measure
Licensing of operations	e.g. nuclear installtions, classified installations
Choice of site	land use planning controls
Choice of process	e.g. adoption of clean techniques of production
Equipment to be used	type approvals approval of furnaces
Fuel to be burned	product standards for fuels
Precautions against accidents	e.g. use of blow-out preventers on oil platforms
Product control	product standards
Pre-discharge treatment	e.g. use of best available technology
Place and manner of discharge	consents for discharge
Chemical or physical characteristics of discharge Quantity or rate of discharge	dischargelimits
Use of products in terms of time and places	e.g. motor cycles, aircraft
Recycling of waste or discarded products	
Final disposal of product	treatment before disposal place and manner of disposal

8.2 Land use planning controls

8.2.1 An early and crucial decision in most enterprises is to find a site where the work can be done. In most countries there are controls over the erection of buildings and placing of installations on land, and the use to which the land and buildings can be put.

These normally include some form of zoning, in which zones for industrial, residential and other uses are delineated, coupled with some discretionary powers of regional or local authorities to decide outstanding matters, such as the design of a building, and even a discretion to depart from the zoning restrictions. The extent of these discretionary powers varies from a very wide discretion in the United Kingdom, to more narrowly defined powers in the United States and New Zealand. Yet where the discretion is more limited, there is still usually a power to grant permission subject to conditions.

Even at the stage of drafting their plans for zoning, the planning authorities are exercising some form of pollutions control, and some countries expressly provide that they shall do so. In Denmark each county authority, when preparing its plan, must conduct a survey of pollution sources,[25] and in the United Kingdom, local planning authorities must include in their unitary development plans 'measures for the improvement of the physical environment'.[26]

Thus land use planning authorities and pollution control authorities are both concerned to protect the environment. The former, however, have wider interests: they protect visual amenity, national parks and areas of great natural beauty; and unless there is a separate department of antiquities, they also protect places and things of historic and archaeological interest.

It is thus clear that there is a considerable overlap of powers between the two kinds of authorities. Even where the powers themselves do not overlap, a decision of a planning authority can have a significant effect on the work of pollution control. There is therefore a need in many cases for close consultation between them, and in some cases for a close co-ordination in the exercise of their powers.

At policy level, this may be achieved by giving overall policy control in those matters to a council of ministers, as in Belgium and Greece, or by placing the responsibilities for planning and pollution control within the same ministry, as in the United Kingdom and Denmark. Below that level, there can be frequent consultation between officers. In Cyprus, to ensure that the view of one authority can always be put to the other, a member of the Planning Board is given a place on the Environment Committee, and a representative of that committee attends the meetings of the Planning Board as an observer. In the United Kingdom, as noted below, the planning authorities are required to send notice of certain classes of planning applications to the water pollution control authority. In any case, since good administration calls for frequent consultation, even without statutory requirements or ministerial directives, there is usually frequent informal consultation.

---

[25]National and Regional Planning Act 1973. See also Urban and Rural Zones Act 1969 and Municipal Planning Act 1975.
[26]Town and Country Planning Act 1990 s.12.

8.2.2   On receipt of an application, the planning authority has first to decide whether or not permission shall be granted. The relevant pollution control authorities may inform it that a grant of permission may create difficult or wholly intractable problems of control for them. It may then be reasonably expected that the application will be refused. To facilitate that kind of co-operation, in the United Kingdom local planning authorities are required to consult the water pollution control authority of certain classes of applications it has received which may affect waters.[27]

A request from a control authority may, however, raise a conflict within the planning authority. If the latter is a department of the local authority, it may be under strong pressure to grant the permission, because the proposed development could bring prosperity to the area. In such circumstances, there is a need for some procedure for reference to a minister or other higher authority for a balanced, impartial decision.

8.2.3   Another way in which planning authorities can provide safeguards against pollution is to refuse permission for a noise sensitive development in or near a noisy or potentially noisy area. In the United Kingdom at least, it is recognised that one function of planning authorities is to maintain an appropriate separation between noisy and noise-sensitive developments. Several with major airports within their areas have therefore formulated 'planning policies', which include provisions such as a presumption against permitting the building of houses within the 60 decibel noise contour around the airport.

8.2.4   Whatever and wherever the proposed development, if permission is to be granted, the planning authority may have to consider whether conditions are to be attached to the grant, and what they are to be. Then it could be acting as a pollution control authority in its own right. In Ireland, for example, planning conditions are used extensively for pollution control.[28] It would be a mistake, however, for it to impose conditions on such matters as quantity and character of discharges where the control authorities are empowered to do the same. The latter will have the greater expertise in those matters, will have the personnel, procedures and equipment for monitoring, and will often have more appropriate powers of enforcement. In contrast, the planning authority would probably lack the trained personnel and equipment to enforce such conditions.

8.2.5   Where there is consultation in the early stages of any proposed development, however, a planning authority may be of considerable help by imposing conditions. If it is proposed that a group of houses be built, the authority may grant planning permission with a condition that a private sewage treatment plant be installed, maintained and operated. Where it is proposed to build a group of large storage tanks for oil or chemicals, the authority may grant permission, but as a condition, require that a bund wall be built around the group, of sufficient height to retain all the oil or chemicals which could escape.

In the case of waste disposal sites, the planning authorities have an interest in the purpose for which the site can be used, and is used, after disposal operations have finished. That will to a large extent be determined by the type of wastes deposited

[27]Town and Country Planning (General Development) Order 1988 s.i.813 at Art.18(1)(o) to (n).
[28]See Y. Scannell, *The Law and Practice of Pollution Control in Ireland*, (Graham & Trotman, London, 1982), particularly at p.26.

there and the management of the site. They also have an interest in retaining or restoring the amenity of the site. The waste disposal authorities will be more likely to have an interest in harmless disposal, avoidance of pollution such as the contamination of groundwaters and other possible effects of leachates, and the avoidance of nuisances such as by vermin or windblown litter. Much will depend on the respective responsibilities imposed on the authorities by law. Whatever the division of responsibilities, the planning authorities are likely to have some part to play, and therefore some degree of co-operation will be needed.

8.2.6 Particularly in the field of noise pollution control planning conditions can be of considerable help. That is because, noise being a transient thing, and emissions so often being infrequent or intermittent, some of the controls available to the pollution control authorities may be difficult to enforce. Many would require continuous surveillance for effective enforcement, in contrast to certain controls by the planning authority which are easy to enforce.

For example, where permission was sought for a building which was to house a noisy industrial process, the planning authority could lay down methods of design and construction which would reduce emissions of noise from the building. If the application was for a corrugated asbestos building, the authority could require a cavity wall of brick or concrete, with double glazed windows. In other cases, conditions could restrict the use of the building to quiet processes, or to light engineering generally. In a mixed industrial and residential area, the authority could lay down conditions relating to the times of operation of the process.

Where a whole area is being developed or re-developed, planners acting in conjunction with noise experts can so design the lay-out of the area that noise nuisances are kept to a practicable minimum. Tall buildings such as warehouses, which have uses non-sensitive to noise, can be used to shield sensitive developments from noise intrusion; roads and railways in cuttings are not seen and can hardly be heard, as in Edinburgh; and havens of peace can be provided in sunken gardens, as in the centre of Manchester; while on a less expensive scale, earth mounds and belts of trees can to some extent serve as noise screens. None of those things require regular monitoring, therefore enforcement is simple.

In special cases, such as noise control in national parks, or other areas where ambient noise is kept to a minimum as in 'noise abatement zones', co-operation between planning and pollution control authorities is a necessity if conflict is to be avoided.

In the United Kingdom, the part played by local planning authorities in noise control has been recognised and encouraged by the Department of the Environment. A circular[29] has been issued, giving guidelines and recommended standards on noise from roads, industry and aircraft, and setting out model conditions which may be used. In the former Federal Republic of Germany, the 'Technical Instructions for Noise Control'[30] are used as guidelines for planning.

When it comes to co-ordination of efforts, however, it must be remembered that the two kinds of authorities may work according to different standards. In the United Kingdom, environmental health officers of local authorities, who apply local noise control measures, work mainly in accordance with the common law standard

---

[29]Department of the Environment Circular 10/73.
[30]TA Larm.

of nuisance – the level of interference which would be considered unacceptable by a reasonable person. The planners, on the other hand, may be protecting the amenity of a quiet and attractive area, and therefore apply higher standards.

8.2.7   It is thus clear that in any country, whatever the administrative structure and whatever the laws may be, land use planning is inevitably linked with pollution control, and that planning authorities can usually take a first, and often crucial, step in the control of pollution.

8.3   Licensing of operations

8.3.1   In many cases, planning permission alone is not enough. Some states take the further precaution of requiring a licence to be obtained before certain operations can be commenced. That further precaution relates to the operation itself and the possible consequences, rather than to the economic and structured use of land.

8.3.2   The most rigorous of those licensing controls[31] is exercised over the siting, construction and operation of nuclear installations. Such licensing controls are commonly used in the EEC. (See the EEC official journal at OJ L11 of 20 February 1959.)

There is one feature common to licences for nuclear installations which is elsewhere exceptional. Where a licence is needed for any other kind of installation or operation, it is usual to make known to the operator all conditions of the licence at the outset. He is then able to cost and plan his venture, to be sure that it is economically viable. Nuclear installations are usually constructed by some form of publicly owned company, but regardless of that, safety considerations are so important that it is usual to reserve a right to impose further conditions after the grant of the initial licence.[32] The United Kingdom Nuclear Installations Act 1965, as amended, provides at Section 4 that

> The Health and Safety Executive by instrument in writing shall on granting any nuclear site licence, and may from time to time thereafter, attach to the licence such conditions as may appear to the Health and Safety Executive to be necessary or desirable in the interests of safety . . . ..

In Germany, the installations are licensed by stages, e.g. excavations, construction, specified operations.[33]

8.3.3   Other examples of this kind of licence include those used in many jurisdictions for the disposal of wastes on land[34], and in some countries the sites are chosen by the municipal authorities, e.g. Greece and Italy.[35]

That licensing restriction may be for the protection of amenity in general, for the protection of the soil itself, or as a precaution against the leaching of polluting

---

[31]'Licensing' is here used to include the grants of consent, permits and authorisations.

[32]See, e.g., the French Town Planning Code, Law of 13 December 1936 and the powers of the Head of the Central Safety Service for Nuclear Installations; also the UK Nuclear Installations Act 1965 s.4(1).

[33]Atomic Energy Law, Civil Code BGBI at p.3053 as amended.

[34]See, e.g., Luxemburg Law of 27 July 1978 at Art.4, UK Environmental Protection Act 1990 ss. 35–44.

[35]See Environmental Resources Ltd., *The Law and Practice Relating to Pollution Control in Greece and Law and Practice Relating to Pollution Control in Italy*, (Graham & Trotman, London, 1982).

substances from the deposits into groundwaters. In the United Kingdom those responsibilities are shared, the waste licensing authority being concerned primarily with pollution of the environment and the protection of public health.[36]

8.3.4 The United Kingdom Environmental Protection Act 1990 provides another interesting example. Processes governed under Part I cannot be brought into operation except under an authorisation. Authorisation will not be granted unless the authority considers that the applicant will be able to carry on the process so as to comply with the conditions which would be included in the authorisation.[37] Likewise, a licence to conduct offshore operations for the exploitation of oil resources will not be granted unless the applicant has available both the expertise and the capital resources to comply with all the requirements concerning safety and pollution.

Cyprus is at present considering adopting a similar registration system for certain works for control of emissions to the atmosphere and the control of noise. There is also Australian legislation on similar lines.[38]

8.3.5 Such licensing systems ensure that the operations are placed in a suitable location, and in some cases that they are from the outset constructed and equipped in such a way that they can comply with the relevant pollution control laws.

Many of the requirements of the licence are easily enforced. Only operational conditions applied to a licence require regular inspections.

8.4 Controls over processes, substances, plant and equipment to be used in production.

8.4.1 The common factor in the controls discussed under this heading is that they are all the products of clean technology. Research and development in clean technology can be expensive, and so can be the acquisition of cleaner substances and cleaner techniques. One of the problems facing government is how to encourage that research, and how to persuade industry to adopt its results if they are more expensive that the older methods. Part of the problem lies in the fact that private industry is basically free to choose and adopt whatever method of production it considers to be the most efficient, taking expense into account.

8.4.2 A further problem lies in the internal structure of the majority of industrial enterprises.

In most countries today, industrial enterprises are carried on by corporations. These, more frequently referred to as companies.[39] In law, a corporation is a fictitious person created by law, and all the properties and contractual rights of the business are transferred to it. The corporation owns and runs the business.

---

[36]UK Environmental Protection Act 1990 s.36(2). See also *Land Use Planning and the Control of Water Pollution* Research Paper No.6, (Pollution Research Unit, University of Manchester). pp.243-51, particularly 247.

[37]See s.6(4).

[38]See, e.g. Waste Disposal Act 1970 and Noise Control Act 1975, both of New South Wales; also Environment Protection Act 1971 of Western Australia.

[39]Strictly speaking, the word 'company' may be used of a partnership, in which no separate fictitious person is created and all the property is owned jointly by partners.

Shareholders do not own any of the corporation property, nor are they party to its contracts – they simply have rights such as voting rights, entitlement to a specified share in any dividends declared, and to a share in the proceeds when the company is liquidated.

In commercial terms, a corporation with private investors is an enterprise in which the directors and management provide the skills and expertise, while the shareholders provide the capital. The directors and management owe a duty in law to the corporation, and thence in effect to the shareholders, to maximise the returns on the investments. Any employee exercising discretionary powers, such as a plant manager, has a duty to use those powers to the same end. The powers must be exercised within the terms of the law, and may take the company's long term interests into account.

The directors, managers and employees of corporations which are partly or wholly publicly owned, in so far as the corporation is engaged in work of a commercial nature, owe the same duties. That may be subject, however, to any directions a minister or other public servant may be empowered to give them.

It would be wrong, therefore, for an employee, acting on his own initiative and at the expense of the corporation, to reduce pollution from the works where it was in law unnecessary to do so. It would be a breach of his duty to the corporation, and could lead to his dismissal and replacement by a less conscience ridden employee, or result in the loss of promotion prospects. It would be wrong and unfair to expect that of any employee, whether he be managing director, foreman or labourer.

8.4.3   That does not mean that no company ever takes steps, voluntarily and properly, to abate its pollution. As noted above, it may be proper to do so if in the interest of the corporation. If a corporation which places products on the market in its own name, as with petrol or fertilisers, it may be of benefit to the firm to gain the approval of the public for its clean methods of production or the environmental cleanliness of its products. Indeed, the difference between them and firms which sell only to other corporations for use in their production processes is often apparent.

The former, the 'environmentally conscious' corporations, may then with some justification complain that other, usually smaller, firms in competition with them use cheaper and more polluting processes, thus gaining a commercial advantage. They may even ask for regulations to be passed, compelling the other firms to use clean processes; but they may do so in the knowledge that the smaller firms cannot afford to do so, and thus may be forced out of business, or taken over by larger competitors. A raising of environmental standards can lead to the re-organisation of an industry.

8.4.4   All this raises the problem of how corporations can be persuaded to develop and adopt clean techniques. That includes the use of cleaner substances, and cleaner processes including the equipment required. The adoption of better pre-discharge treatment of wastes, including the installation of arrestment plant, could be considered as part of these changes,[40] but are treated separately in this chapter for two reasons. The first is that they do not necessarily result in a reduction of energy use,

---

[40]See, e.g., the UK Clean Air Act 1956 s.6 on the fitting of new furnaces with plant for the arrestment of grit and dust.

or of waste. The second is that their adoption is a simple matter of tacking on to the end of a production process a new mechanism for treatment or catchment. It does not present the same problems as a radical change in the production process itself.

8.4.5 The problem of persuading industry to adopt cleaner processes resolves itself into two parts, which are in some cases, but not all, separable. The first concerns the research into, and the development of, clean techniques of production. The second is the task of persuading industry to adopt those techniques.

8.4.6 Development of clean technology

Clean technology has been defined to mean

.... the practical application of knowledge, methods and means, so as – within the needs of man – to provide the most rational uses of natural resources and energy, and to protect the environment'.[41]

It must be added that, in any country where industrial enterprises are privately owned, and operate in a 'market economy', any policies proposed for the adoption of clean techniques must take into account the economic factors – a company cannot be persuaded to adopt voluntarily those techniques if that would put the company at a competitive disadvantage against its rivals,[42] and that if companies are forced by law to adopt them, there could be a severe adverse effect on the industry, which could in turn have unfavourable consequences for the economy, at least in the short term. On the other hand, a clean techniques policy based mainly on long term effects could bring considerable long term benefits.

8.4.7 One possible consequence which must be faced is the forcing of a re-structuring of an industry. If the process of adaptation is costly by reason of the need for expensive equipment, acquisition of greater expertise, and the retraining of personnel, the cost may be more than small firms can afford. The larger firms will take over, and the smaller firms, in one way or another, will disappear. The transition itself may be induced as a matter of policy, for the effects could be beneficial to the industry as a whole. Once established, the process may be cheaper, particularly in the reduction of waste and the costs of waste treatment and disposal, even when taking into account only the costs 'internal' to the firm itself. In the wider context, there may be further savings – in the reduction of 'external' costs, i.e. reduction of damage to the environment. It is proper for the government to take both into account. A subsequent effect may be the creation of, or opportunity to participate in, new markets. Many countries today wish to expand their industries, and perhaps to attract new industries, but at the same time preserve the qualities of their natural environment. They will be looking for clean production processes, either established by their own firms or brought in by larger firms from abroad. Some of the industries of the more advanced nations will therefore lose export opportunities if they ignore cleaner technology.

The converse is that smaller states may have to take safeguards against the import of goods, plant and machinery which are unacceptable elsewhere because they impose avoidable damage on the environment.

[41]Economic Commission for Europe *Low Waste and Non-Waste Technology in the Iron and Steel Industry*, (United Nations Publications, 1981).
[42]See 8.4.2 and 8.4.3.

8.4.8   The larger and more far sighted corporations will see and respond to those opportunities. They may have their own resources to engage in research and development work. It is to be expected, however, especially in view of the characteristics of corporations noted in 8.4.2., that the majority of companies may be unable or unwilling to do likewise.

In the main, therefore, sponsorship of the work must come from outside the individual firms. Where there are well established industry associations, they may be expected to undertake at least some of the work. In an industry with many small firms, however, it is unlikely that they would support work which would produce results so expensive that they could not afford to adopt them, and could ultimately result in closure.

8.4.9   Government has a material interest in the development of industry, and is well placed to take the lead in promoting and even sponsoring such development work. The questions then arise – through what agencies, and at who's expense?

Under the UK 'best practicable means' regime, until recent years it was left to the control authority, latterly HMIP, to encourage such work and development, and they did so with certain individual firms, bringing ideas from abroad, and discussing possible solutions. There was, however, no duty to do so, nor any specially formulated strategies, nor resources made available for that purpose. Considering the modern trend to wide-scale developments of new techniques, and the difficulties involved, that attitude is now clearly inadequate.

That regime of best practicable means has now been replaced by one under which HMIP require for some processes the use of the 'best available techniques not entailing excessive cost'. The Chief Inspector has indicated that no allowance will be made for smaller firms that claim that they cannot afford the necessary equipment. They will be expected to raise the money to do so.[43]

As noted above, government has an interest in the development of industry, and for the Government of any developed nation, that must include the development of cleaner techniques. That interest, moreover, is wider than that of individual corporations, which simply have a duty to maximise profits for the corporation and its shareholders. The Government has an interest in the development of industry generally, and in some areas that may include a restructuring of the industry to make it healthier and more competitive, which in some cases can involve the disappearance of small firms. It also has interests in the reduction of wastes and protection of the environment, which can involve costs which are 'external' to the producing firms.

8.4.10   To ensure that the task is done, it is necessary that a government department or agency has a duty to promote research and development. It is preferable, even under a best practicable means or best available techniques not entailing excessive cost regime, that the duty is not imposed on an enforcement authority. Although such an authority may in some cases encourage research and development, it is better left free to concentrate on the adoption, and perhaps adaptation, of techniques.

If there is a department of industry, with a duty to promote the development of industry, that would be an obvious candidate. In any department primarily concerned with the development and welfare of industries, it would also be accept-

---

[43]Personal communication, Chief Inspector of UK HMIP. See also 8.4.17 below.

able. Where, however, the department concerns itself with the welfare of individual firms, to that extent there could be a conflict of interest.

Any department of government with a overriding duty to protect the environment would also be a candidate. The disadvantage it might suffer, however, is not being in close touch with each industry, not being fully informed of their difficulties, and in some cases appearing to be in conflict with the interests of certain industries, especially where the reduction of external costs is a significant consideration.

One solution would appear to lie in co-operation between the two. That could be done by co-ordinated work by a section from each department, or by a separate agency for which the two ministers are jointly responsible. In the United Kingdom, for example, the Department of Trade and Industry and the Department of the Environment have joint responsibility for the Environmental Technology Innovation Scheme. It aims to support collaborative research projects, although single firms are sometimes supported, in cleaner technologies, recycling, waste treatment and disposal, and environmental monitoring. Financial assistance is available.

In some countries there may be other government departments which provide more suitable bases for this work. In the Federal Republic of Germany, the Ministry of Research and Technology, as part of its Clean Technology Programme, has sponsored many projects from basic research to pilot plants, the majority of which would not have been undertaken without support from the Government.[44]

In each case, much will depend on the prevailing political philosophy of the state, and the form and structure of the existing administration. It is a mistake simply to import a form of institution from another state, however well it has worked there. In particular, new relationships with existing departments and agencies have to be worked out, and with a alien form of institution it may not be possible to do that satisfactorily.

8.4.11   Whatever the system of government, in any country which is substantially industrialised, there will be a need for a diffusion of information.[45] The Minnesota University Technical Assistance Programme,[46] and the European Community's Network for Environmental Transfer Technology Transfer,[47] provide examples of that service.

8.4.12   Adoption of clean technology

The second part of the problem[48] lies in persuading industry to adopt the new techniques once they have been developed.

8.4.13   The first difficulty arises out to the existence of tried and proved techniques of pre-discharge treatment, such as chemical or biological treatment plant for discharges to water, and arrestment plant for preventing the release of polluting components of a discharge to air. Where plant is already on the market,

---

[44]J.C. Bongaerts and D. Heinrichs, 'Government Support for Clean Technology Research in West Germany' *R & D Management*, 17, Jan. pp.39-50.

[45]*Environmental Policy and Technical Change*, (OECD 1985).

[46]F.M. Thomson and C.A. McComa, Technical Assistance for Hazardous Waste Reduction, *Environmental Science and Technology*, 21, No.12, pp.1154-7.

[47]See *European Year of the Environment*, EUR 109360, (Commission of the European Communities).

[48]See 8.4.5.

permitting reasonably accurate assessments as to costs, it may present a method more acceptable than new technology, even to a new enterprise. For an existing enterprise, its adoption of the old methods could also cause less disruption. That does not mean, however, that when the external, or social, costs are added, the old techniques are a better proposition for the community as a whole. Taking all proper considerations into account, such as the disposal of wastes collected, conservation of resources and savings in energy, the new technology may be more advantageous to the community without being more attractive to the operating company. It is for the independent authorities established by the state to decide which is to be preferred, on the basis of what would be the best economic/environmental option.

8.4.14   Controls specifying the equipment or processes to be used

The simplest and most direct method of control over processes used is to specify the equipment or process the industrialist must use. Where that is done, the advantage lies in the ease of enforcement. There is no need to wait until unacceptable pollution is detected, and samples taken and analysed. The offence will be in not having the equipment installed, properly maintained and properly used. Such an offence is much easier to detect and prove. It is particulary useful for emissions to the atmosphere, where sampling and analysing can be difficult.

Industrialists, however, do not like to be tied down to using a particular kind of equipment or process. They prefer more flexible controls under which they have freedom to use that which is more appropriate to their particular circumstances, and also so that they are left with freedom of innovation. That freedom of innovation can be a long term advantage to the industry as a whole. There are various ways of giving that flexibility without losing the advantage to the control authority referred to above.

The first is to specify the equipment or method to be used, but to give anyone failing to use it a special defence of proving that he was using an equally efficacious method. That not only allows him to do so, but throws on him the burden of proof that his chosen method was in fact equally efficacious.[49]

A different technique has been used in Greece. Under the former Sanitary Regulations, E1b/221/1965, Section 5 established minimum requirements for sewage and industrial waste. Those wastes had to be treated in such a way that the receiving waters remained suitable for their primary uses. Under Section 14 the prefect for the area granted a licence for a period of up to six months. The licence was conditional on assessment and verification by the local health authority, *inter alia*, that the requirements referred to above would be satisfied.

The control authority could specify the plant to be used for treating industrial effluent before it was discharged to sewers, but its decision was made only after consultation with the discharger and a six month trial period before the choice was confirmed. Likewise, under proposed new legislation in Cyprus, the plant to be used may be specified, but again that will be done only after a trial period.

Another method is to permit the operator to choose the method he prefers, but to make its use subject to the approval of a specified authority. This is done under the Regulations made under the International Convention for the Prevention of

---

[49]See, e.g., the UK Control of Pollution Act 1974 s.68(3).

Pollution from Ships 1973, and its Protocol of 1978. For example, Regulation 6 on oily water separation equipment on ships requires that

> Oily water separating equipment or an oil filtering system shall be of a design approved by the Administration and be such as will ensure that any oily mixture discharged into the sea after passing through the separator or filtering system shall have an oil content of less than 100 parts per million

That will have to be translated into enforceable national legislation, in which it is an offence not to have an approved system, and also an offence to have a system which cannot ensure that the required standard for the discharge is met.

In some cases, success in reducing polluting emissions depends not only on the equipment to be used, but also on the way in which it is installed. The United Kingdom Clean Air Act 1956 Section 3 requires that

> No furnace shall be installed in a building .... unless it is so far as practicable capable of being operated continuously without emitting smoke when burning fuel of a type for which the furnace was designed.
>   Any furnace installed in accordance with plans and specifications .... approved.... by the local authority shall be deemed to comply ....

The provision thus ensures that any approval given may govern the manner of installation as well as design and construction.

Only in cases in which the discharge is of a common character, such as domestic sewage, can the authority confidently lay down what is to be used. In Cyprus, for example, regulations have been prepared to govern the installation and maintenance of sewage treatment plant for hotels. A code of practice on maintenance has also been prepared. That may be supported by a provision that in the event of a failure to follow the code, the onus of proof of proper maintenance lies with the owner of the plant.

8.4.15 Controls over fuels to be used

Within this category there also falls the controls over the fuels used in the production process, or for general heating purposes, or in motor vehicles. They provide a method of control which is relatively easy to enforce.[50]

Where the law specifies the type or composition of fuels, a simple prohibition is sometimes insufficient for adequate enforcement, but needs to be supplemented by associated offences. For example, the UK Clean Air Act 1956 states that if smoke is emitted from a chimney of any building in a smoke control area, the occupier of the building commits an offence. The use of certain fuels is authorised in such areas, and no offence is committed if the smoke was from an authorised fuel. This provision is reinforced by associated offences. Thus it is an offence to acquire any unauthorised fuel for use in a building in a smoke control area, or to sell by retail any unauthorised fuel for delivery to a building in such an area.

8.4.16 Use of discharge limits

The use of discharge limits as a means of controlling pollution is discussed at 8.6

---

[50]They are used by all Member States of the EEC by reason of the following Directives: 75/716/EEC, as amended by 87/219/EEC on the sulphur content of certain liquid fuels; 78/611.EEC and 85/210EEC on the lead content of petrol.

below. It is relevant to comment here on their use, as a means of persuading the discharger to use cleaner techniques of production or pre-discharge treatment.

Where the cleaner techniques give a higher quality discharge than those in current use, even after the latter has been subjected to pre-discharge treatment, and where that is the only advantage offered by the new techniques, regulations requiring that higher standard may suffice.[51] This gives some freedom to the industrialist to decide precisely which techniques he will apply. He may be permitted a reasonable period of use for his existing plant before any changes in standards are imposed on him, thus permitting him to gain a reasonable return on his investment in that plant.[52]

Such a form of control would not be so appropriate, however, when rapid or even steady advances in technology are being made. That would require frequent changes in regulations if the industry were to be required to keep pace with the advances.

On the other hand, researchers have found that there is no proof that regulation leads to stagnation of research and development efforts.[53] Whether or not small firms are adversely affected depends on the severity of the regulations.[54]

8.4.17   Criteria such as 'best available technology'

Normally, it appears that where such steady advances are being made, legislation to require the use of 'best practicable means' or 'best available technology' are more appropriate. Much will depend, however, on how those criteria are applied.

In the United Kingdom, the standard of 'best available techniques not entailing excessive cost' (BATNEEC) has been introduced.[55] Guidance notes have been produced which, *inter alia*, explain the meaning to be given to that phrase.[56]

There is little difficulty with the interpretation of the word 'available', which must be taken to mean 'procurable by the operator of the process in question'.[57]

The difficulty arises with the word 'excessive'. It could mean excessive in relation to the harm to be averted, or excessive for that particular industry, or excessive for some particular operator, e.g. a small firm. Several problems arise from that. If excessive relates to the harm to be averted, taking the community as a whole it would be foolish to spend £2000 to avert harm which could do only £1000 worth of damage. But to take only the costs incurred by the community as a whole is an over simplification.[58] The pre-discharge costs and any other costs of disposal are borne by the operator of the process, whereas the damage costs are borne by many persons, some of whom have no interest in the process or its products. To permit the

---

[51]Compare the use of presumptive limits used in UK by HMIP before the Environmental Protection Act 1990 came into force. The Inspectorate had power to require the use of best practicable means. The Chief Inspector published 'presumptive limits' in the form of emission limits. If a discharger kept within those limits he was presumed to be using the best practicable means.

[52]See, e.g., the UK Water Act 1990 Sched.10 para 7.

[53]See Environmental Policy and Technical Change, (OECD 1985).

[54]On this subject see R. Rothwell and W. Zegfeld, Industrial Innovation and Public Policy, (Frances Pinter, London, 1981).

[55]See Environmental Protection Act 1990 Part I.

[56]Integrated Pollution Control - a Practical Guide, (issued by Department of the Environment 1981).

[57]Ibid, para 5.6.

[58]See Chapter I at 4.1.5(b).

operator to continue with an old production or treatment process because the cost of using a new one would exceed the cost of the damage done to other persons could be very unfair on them, dependent on how much benefit they gain from the process, e.g. in terms of employment or products.

An alternative interpretation would be to consider what would be excessive cost for that particular industry to bear. The regulatory authority is usually required to balance the value of the material wealth created by the industry against damage to the environment. What is often forgotten, however, in formulating legislation to achieve that balance, is to ensure that those who suffer a disproportionate share of the damage have a moral right to compensation. The process achieves justice only if it takes into account the balance of advantage to the individual also, which can be achieved in many cases by awards of compensation. Unfortunately, in at least one case, the operators compliance with regulations meant a denial of compensation for the persons who may have suffered damage therefrom.[59]

Finally, excessive can be considered in relation to the costs a particular firm may be required to bear. In the past such consideration has been given in favour of small firms, so that they would not be driven into liquidation. Relaxation of controls for their benefit, however, can slow or even halt the progress to better environmental protection. Improvements in the technology required can lead to a restructuring of an industry, with benefits to itself and to the nation as a whole.[60]

There is another criterion which is widely used in the application of controls over offshore operations for oil and gas. The operators are required to use 'good oilfield practice'. That is understandable where the research and development into less damaging techniques is going on in, or is promoted by, the industry itself. It means, however, that the standards are being set by the industry, not by the state or any independent body. What are needed in those circumstances are strong national authorities to ensure that all possible progress is being made, or international bodies such as the Paris Commission[61] which itself has considerable expertise, to ensure likewise.

8.4.18   Effluent charges

A further possibility is the use of effluent charges. These are financial charges imposed according to the type and quantity of pollutants discharged. If the charges are calculated by reference to the damage which would have been done by an uncontrolled discharge, this method has the merit of transfering the 'external' costs to the discharger. That can be an effective way of persuading the discharger to use cleaner techniques of production, better pre-discharge treatment, or better arrestment techniques. To that extent it could be an incentive to use cleaner processes or better pre-discharge treatment.

---

[59]See Chaper I at 4.4.5, particularly the claims made on behalf of Fidel Budden and Merlyn Albery-Speyer.

[60]For the response to this problem in the UK, see *Integrated Pollution Control – a Practical Guide*, (issued by the Department of the Environment 1991), para 5.8. to 5.13. Note that a distinction is made between new and existing processes. See also Chapter II at 12.2.5., and this chapter at 8.3.4.and 8.4.9.

[61]The administrative organisation for both the Convention for the Prevention of Marine Pollution by Dumping from Ships and Aircraft, Oslo 1972, and the International Convention for Pollution of the Sea from Land Based Sources, Paris 1974.

In some jurisdictions, however, the introduction of such charges can encounter difficulties. See 5 above where such charges are examined more generally, and 8.8 below where the use of such charges is discussed in more detail.

8.4.19 Fiscal measures

Fiscal means of encouraging the adoption of new techniques may also be considered. That is not merely an alternative – it can operate alongside legal and administrative means.

This method would simply involve offering a tax advantage, over and above any tax allowances offered for capital spending generally, to any firm which incurs capital expense in adopting cleaner techniques. There would have to be a precise statement of the changes which would qualify for the advantage.

Any country which is a member of a regional economic community, such as the European Community, would have to make sure that the tax provision was not a breach of any obligation not to subsidise or offer any other financial advantage to its domestic industries as against those of others in the community. See, for example, Article 92 of the Treaty Establishing the European Community, Rome 1957.

8.4.20   Contractual obligations

Finally, and probably affecting only a narrow range of domestic industries, public authorities could be required to contract for services or goods only from firms using clean techniques in their production methods, and producing environmentally clean goods for sale, such as motor vehicles. That could be done by legislation, although the use of administrative measures would permit greater flexibility within the scheme. In the absence of comparable controls over private companies, however, that could prove a handicap to the public authorities concerned.

8.5   Place and manner of discharge or deposit

8.5.1   Disposal by discharge or deposit refers to the abandonment of control of a substance or article by a person. That does not, however, mean an abandonment of responsibility. Any regime of law which gives adequate protection to the public will provide for legal responsibility, at least at civil law, for damage thus done to any person or his interest after the deposit.[62]

That presents no difficulty if the substance was abandoned in, and remains within, the jurisdiction of one state. Municipal laws on liability can then be enforced. The difficulty arises when the substance abandoned reaches the confines of another state, or enters what are now referred to as the 'global commons', e.g. the high seas, the stratosphere, and any place under no national jurisdiction such as Antarctica. Those difficulties are dealt with in Chapter 8.

8.5.2   For certain intractable wastes, there have been proposals that they be buried underground in a sealed chamber or container, or otherwise sealed so that there can be no seepage. Examples are: the deposit of highly radioactive wastes in natural

---

[62]See the UK Environmental Protection Act 1990 s.61. That extended period of responsibility has been applied also to nuclear installations, see UK Nuclear Installations Act 1965 s.5.

underground caves, disused deep mines or specially constructed chambers;[63] and the deposit of oily sludges in concrete containers or in sealed excavations.[64] For the purposes of pollution control, such burials may be more properly regarded as long term storage. That means that those who put them there must not be considered in law to have abandoned them. It is sensible that they remain responsible for the integrity of such sealed chambers, that the places are shown on maps, and that subsequent use of the land is strictly controlled.[63] In the case of radioactive waste, and any other waste which remains spontaneously active, it would be prudent to require access to the storage space to be maintained, periodic inspections to be carried out, and the possibility of retrieval maintained.[65] It would be prudent also for the law to require that the depositer remained potentially liable, or provided a bond to cover any liability, until the relevant authority had certified that risks could no longer arise from the presence of the deposit.[66]

8.5.3 Prohibitions against discharges and deposits are of two kinds: those which are laid down in absolute terms by law, leaving no discretion to the control authorities; and those effected by a control authority exercising discretionary powers, as by refusing to grant a consent or an exemption, or attaching conditions to a consent.

There are some absolute prohibitions under treaties and regional agreements, e.g. International Convention on the Dumping of Wastes at Sea, 1972, Article IV, Protocol concerning Marine Pollution Resulting from Exploration and Exploitation of the Continental Shelf, 1989, Article X.[67] See also Council Directive 80/68/EEC Article 4, on the protection of groundwater against pollution by certain dangerous substances.

8.5.4 The grant of discretionary powers gives flexibility to the control, permitting variations in severity according to the place, the time or other circumstances. When a control authority receives an application for consent or exemption, the first question to be considered is whether the substance can be recycled for re-use, or for use as a by-product. It is proper for any control authority to consider the possibility of recycling. Likewise, it is proper for it to consider the best environmental option. Whether or not they are duties imposed on the authorities in law, is a matter for the legislature. In some cases that may be advisable. An authority which charges for the facilities it offers, e.g. use of a disposal site, may be tempted to accept an application because to do so will bring extra revenue, even though there may be a better environmental option.[68]

The grant of discretionary powers also creates problems.

---

[63]The UK Nuclear Industy Radioactive Waste Executive (NIREX) has been investigating possibilities of that kind. It now favours keeping the waste underground in places accessible for inspection, i.e. long term storage under controlled conditions.

[64]See *Oil Refineries Waste Survey - Disposal Methods, Quantities and Costs*, Report No.5/89, by (CONCAWE, an oil companies' European organisation for environmental health and protection), p. 18 para 4.4.4.

[65]See above and footnote 63.

[66]See footnote 62. Note also the Swedish strategy for the storage of radioactive waste in chambers deep under the sea-bed, accessible from land by tunnels.

[67]Made under the Kuwait Regional Convention for Co-operation for the Protection of the Marine Environment from Pollution, 1978.

[68]See 9.3.2 below.

8.5.5   If the prohibition relates to a total discharge or deposit, and to a particular place, it will normally be easy to enforce. If it relates only to a possible component of a permitted discharge, it will be as difficult to enforce as any discharge conditions. Those difficulties are discussed in Chapter II at section 5.

There are many other prohibitions which are difficult, if not impossible, to enforce. 'Fly tipping' – the casual but illegal tipping of solid wastes on open land – is notoriously difficult to control. The culprit may go to any place, at any time, where he may not be seen. The same may be said of illegal deposits of the contents of septic tanks. Small contractors, often the owner-drivers of one vehicle, often empty the contents down roadside grids leading to sewers, and individual offences cannot even be detected. One practical answer seems to be to provide conveniently situated facilities for legal deposit.

Another possible answer to this problem has recently been adopted in Mauritius. The first step has been to require all carriers of wastes to be licensed, and to have special plates on their vehicles bearing prominently the word 'waste' followed by the licence number. The second is to empower the police to stop any such licensed vehicle and any other vehicle which appears to be carrying waste. In the case of a licensed vehicle, the policeman can ask the driver where he is taking the waste for disposal, and have a check made on his arrival there. In the case of an unlicensed vehicle carrying waste, an offence will already have been committed. Experience will tell how the system works.

8.6   Character or composition of a discharge or deposit

8.6.1   One common form of control is the imposition of limits on the amounts of various substances which may be discharged or deposited. If there are any quality objectives for the receiving medium, those limits will be calculated to ensure that the objectives are maintained.

8.6.2   There are many examples of these. Under the United Kingdom Clean Air (Emission of Grit and Dust from Furnaces) Regulations 1971[69] there are various limits set in terms of pounds per hour, while the Alkali etc Works Regulation Act 1906 requires that air, smoke or chimney gases from an alkali works shall not carry more than 0.46 grams per cubic metre of hydrochloric acid. Belgium requires that an electricity power station fired by liquid fuel must not emit smoke with more than 5g/Nm3, except that in certain meteorological conditions the limit is 2g/Nm3.[70]

Germany uses a more complex system. Air quality standards are specified in the TA Luft[71] for dust fall, dust concentrations in the air, and eight harmful gases. Values for both short term and long term exposures are given. These are more frequently referred to in Germany as immission standards. Emission limit values are then set for various types of installations. They are based on what is technically

---

[69]1971 s.i.162.

[70]See Belgian reports to the Tenth Congress on International Comparative Law 1978, p.602.

[71]The TA Luft is a general administrative instruction that administative authorities use to enforce the Federal Immission Control Law. Compare the uses of quality objectives and discharge standards explained at section 2 of this chapter.

possible, and are revised regularly to keep pace with technical developments. Compare the use of quality objectives and discharge standards discussed at 2 above.

8.6.3 Controls over the character or composition of the discharge, are used frequently for the control of water pollution, for which quality objectives can be set and easily checked. The objectives are set according to the uses or potential uses of the water, involving decisions which may quite properly include political considerations.

In the United Kingdom the Secretary of State determines the quality objectives for the various stretches or bodies of waters.[72] The control authority, the National Rivers Authority, then seeks to achieve and maintain those objectives[73] through a licensing system. In law, a licence is permission to do something which would otherwise be unlawful. The legislature has therefore made it unlawful to discharge pollutants into the waters.[74] The next step is to permit discharges provided they are in accordance with licences granted by the relevant authority.[75] By empowering the authority to grant licences subject to conditions, at its discretion, great flexibility is achieved.[76]

More recently, the Authority has begun to move from simple conditions which lay down maximum concentrations and maximum quantities for pollutants in discharges which must never be exceeded, to a system of percentiles. Under such a system, the discharge must keep within the limits of his conditions for a certain percentage, such as 95 per cent, of a given period. For the other five per cent of the time, there must be no readings which greatly exceed the consent limits, or exceed a specified upper limit.[77] That upper limit may be specified as an absolute maximum in the consent. The Authority has used the system hitherto for sewage effluent, but in a recent report[78] has stated a proposal to extend this to trade effluents, and also to impose a fixed upper limit.

The advantage of the system is that it makes allowance for minor variations in the performance of plant and equipment, which cannot be attributed to the fault of the discharger. Moreover, the limits to which the percentile rule will apply can be slightly stricter, giving the same overall performance as under the older method. Such percentiles can be used for some constituents, in parallel with absolute limits for others.

It must be noted, however, that a percentile system cannot be operated without continuous or regular monitoring so that performance over the whole period can be checked. It follows that where continuous or regular monitoring is particularly difficult or expensive, the method could be inappropriate.

---

[72]Water Resources Act 1991 s.83.

[73]It is under a duty to use its powers to ensure, so far as practicable, that those quality objectives are achieved at all times, s.83.

[74]Water Resources Act 1991 s.85.

[75]The words 'consent', 'authorisation' and 'permission' may be used. In these circumstances they are all licences.

[76]See Water Resources Act 1991 S.88.

[77]A more detailed examination of the percentile system will appear in a later volume in this series, dealing with water pollution.

[78]*Discharge Consent and Compliance Policy: a Blueprint for the Future*, Water Quality Series No.1, July 1990. (UK National Rivers Authority). For an explanation of the method and its practical difficulties, see pp. 32-3.

A similar system has long been used in the United Kingdom to govern discharges of oil from offshore production platforms. Oil or oily waters cannot be discharged into the sea, save where exemptions are granted by the Secretary of State, who may grant an exemption subject to such conditions as he thinks fit.[79] Exemption conditions normally require analyses at 12 hour intervals, a monthly average concentration of oil of not more that 40mg/kg, and not more than four per cent of the analyses to show more than 100mg/kg.

8.6.4   Licensing can give more accurate control over the discharges, and hence the quality of the receiving waters, than other methods such as controls over fuels, and fiscal methods. In theory, the same is true of the atmosphere, but the practical difficulties in monitoring are sometimes too great. It may be inappropriate also because there are so many other variables which can affect air quality. It is relevant to note, however, that the United Kingdom Environmental Protection Act 1990, at Section 3(5)(b), empowers the Secretary of State to establish for a substance, limits to the total amount of a substance which may be released into the environment, and to allocate quotas to persons carrying on prescribed processes. 'Release' includes any emission into air, entry into water, and deposit on land. It remains to be seen how widely that power will be used.

Even for rivers, however, there has to be adequate monitoring even where the percentile rule is not used. Where there is automatic monitoring for the parameters to be controlled, there is little difficulty. On the other hand, where monitoring still has to be done by control authority sampling and analysis, the frequency may be inadequate to give close control. In areas where there are many discharges, the authorities may be compelled to rely on monitoring of the receiving medium at selected points to give warning of an illegal discharge, followed by more intensive monitoring to identify the offending discharger. Judicious use of automatic monitoring equipment may be made for that purpose, otherwise where the illegal discharge is for short periods only, it may be impossible to gather sufficient evidence against the discharger.

The efficacy of the control measure may also depend on how the characteristic in question is defined. In the United Kingdom, under the Clean Air Act 1956 Section 1, it is an offence to emit dark smoke from certain chimneys. 'Dark' is defined to be as dark as shade 2 on the Ringelmann chart. In Chicago, the same form of control is used, but the measure is one of opacity. That can make it possible to use automatic monitoring – opacity meters may be installed, or required to be installed, in chimneys. That facilitates a check on emissions at night, when visual detection is impossible. The cost, however, may be justified only in the cases of chimneys serving furnaces with large outputs.

8.7   Poor maintenance and alteration of a product

8.7.1   The problems of poor maintenance and misuse follow on from those of product standards. It is possible to ensure that a motor vehicle, when first manufactured, is capable of being used on a road without emitting noise exceeding 85dB(A), but that does not ensure that it will continue to be capable of doing so.

---

[79]See the Prevention of Oil Pollution Act 1971 at s.23.

It may be that the owner failed to maintain it properly, thus allowing it to deteriorate. It may be that a youth with a motor cycle has substituted for an effective silencer one which emits a loud roar, suggesting power and speed.

The problem in each case is how to ensure proper maintenance and prevent unauthorised alteration.

8.7.2 Maintenance

These paragraphs deal with the maintenance and use of plant and machinery which has been designed and constructed in accordance with product standards, the most common being motor vehicles. The offences normally relate to the use of products which have not been properly maintained, as distinct from maintenance itself.

The problem of ensuring the proper maintenance of motor vehicles presents difficulties. It is possible to have annual testing, as is done in the United Kingdom for all cars after three years from first registration. For those tests to cover noise and gaseous emissions in a country with several million cars, however, means establishing many testing stations, expensively equipped, and with trained and reliable staff. For most countries, that would not be feasible.

A different solution has been tried by the United States. For the control of air pollution from motor vehicles, the Administrator of the Environmental Protection Agency is required by regulation to provide, and from time to time revise, '. . . standards applicable to the emission of any air pollutant from any class or classes of new motor vehicles or new motor vehicle engines ... . Such standards shall be applicable to such vehicles and engines for their useful life . . . whether such vehicles and engines are designed as complete systems or incorporate devices to prevent or control such pollution'.[80]

The Administrator is required to prescribe by regulations that the useful life shall, in the case of light duty engines be a period of use for five years or fifty thousand miles or the equivalent, whichever occurs first. The Administrator is given a discretion to provide different standards for other motor vehicle engines, and for motor cycles and motor cycle engines.

A variation on this method is under consideration by Cyprus for the control of noise from industrial equipment. In new legislation initial operating standards will be laid down which must not be exceeded when the equipment is in operation. There will be a second set of noise levels which will apply when the equipment is five or more years old. The second allows for the degree of deterioration which might be expected in that type of equipment, even when subject to the normal maintenance.

France has tackled the problem in a similar way by requiring that when a motor vehicle is in use, noise emissions should not exceed the type approval standard by more than 5dB(A). If a vehicle on the road sounds noisy, the owner can be required to take it to a testing station. That method, however, can leave many offenders unpunished and free to offend again, as noted below.

Many countries have approached the problem by first making it an offence to by-pass or alter the silencer, and to require the owner to maintain it properly. For example, the United Kingdom Road Vehicles (Construction and Use) Regulations 1986, at Regulation 54 (1) provides that

---

[80]US Federal Register Title 42, Subchapter II, Part A s.7521.

Every vehicle propelled by an internal combustion engine shall be fitted with an exhaust system including a silencer, and the exhaust gases from the engine shall not escape into the atmosphere without first passing through the silencer

Paragraph (2) of the same regulation provides further that

Every exhaust system and silencer shall be maintained in good and efficient working order and shall not be altered so as to increase the noise made by the escape of exhaust gases

Paragraph (3) permits compliance with certain EEC directives as an alternative.[81]

Both provisions are, of course, easy to enforce. Excessive noise can be heard, and the absence of a silencer, or presence of a defective silencer, can easily be discovered through roadside inspection by a police officer. They are often supplemented by a further provision making it an offence to emit excessive noise, or noise which is a nuisance or a disturbance. The offences in practice complement each other, evidence of one being evidence of the other also.

On the other hand, there are difficulties in enforcing fixed objective standards when the vehicle is in use. The essence of the problem is that for few car emissions can effective roadside checks be made, and if the owner is required to take it to a testing station for checking, he may have the fault repaired before he does so. The fault is thus corrected, but under that system anyone can safely leave such a fault uncorrected until he is caught. 'Back street dealers' in used cars could become regular offenders with no fear of punishment.

Cyprus will try to overcome this difficulty by proposed new regulations. When a driver is stopped by a constable because of a noisy exhaust, the constable will radio to the testing station to enquire whether the vehicle has been sent in within the previous 12 months, or the owner has been required to take in any vehicle within that period. If so, the vehicle is held until taken in by a man from the testing station. Otherwise, the owner can present it there for testing at any time within the following four days. That method, worked out with the co-operation of the local police, may be suitable for a compact area of jurisdiction, but not necessarily elsewhere.

The government of the Netherlands experimented for some time with a noise meter which could be clamped to the exhaust pipe, so that sounds from other sources would have a proportionately minimal effect. Unfortunately, the experiment did not give results satisfactory enough to encourage adoption of the method.

The same problem arises with gaseous emissions from vehicles, with the exception of smoke from diesel engines. Portable apparatus is available to measure the opacity of that smoke. In the circumstances in many countries, when a vehicle is stopped, a radio call can bring out a man with the apparatus for a roadside check, although in some areas that could be a time-consuming procedure.

8.8 Pollution charges

8.8.1 In section 5 of this Chapter, the use of economic and fiscal measures was considered in general terms. Here, the use of pollution charges is discussed more specifically as a method of control over discharges to water. They are suitable only for the control of such discharges, and their use is therefore so limited.

---

[81]Directives 77/212, 81/334, 84/372, or 84/424; or for a motor cycle other than a moped, 78/1015.

8.8.2 Terms used

'Tax' is used to denote a payment made to a national or local treasury, to be applied for any national or local purpose.

'Levy' means a payment demanded for a particular purpose, not necessarily related to services received.

'Charge' is here used to denote a payment made in return for services received, facilities made available, or any payment made within the meaning of the polluter pays principle.

8.8.3 Discharges of sewage and trade effluents into sewers have long been the subject of 'charges' imposed by the sewerage authorities, eg in the United Kingdom under the Public Health (Drainage of Trade Trade Premises) Act 1937, the Public Health Act 1961, Part v, and the Water Act 1989, Part II, Chapter III. There are two main differences between charges made for discharges to sewers, and those made to natural waters. The first is that sewers belong to private persons or public authorities, and a discharge into them cannot be regarded as polluting the common environment, or any part of the environment in which the public has an interest. The second is that charges imposed by public authorities for discharges into their sewers are calculated solely as contributions to the capital or running costs of providing conveyance and treatment for the effluent.

Nevertheless, those charges provide useful precedents which merit consideration.

8.8.4 To get a balanced picture, it must be noted at the outset that effluent charges are normally used as an instrument of control in conjunction with some other method. In England, the sewerage authority imposing charges also exercises a regulatory form of control by granting or refusing permission to use the sewers. In France, effluent charges are imposed on only a limited range of pollutants discharged to waters, whilst the Prefect issues licences over all such discharges, as noted by the O.E.C.D. in their *Pollution Charges in Practice* (Paris, 1980). (See also the amending Decree No. 82-1167 of 30 December 1982.) In the Netherlands, a licensing system is used to control discharges to waters, but there are also 'levies' and 'contributions' by which dischargers are compelled to contribute to the expense of measures taken to prevent or reduce pollution, (See Surface Waters Pollution Act). Finally, in the Federal Republic of Germany, the Waste Water Charging Law, AAG of 1976, was not intended to replace all regulatory controls.

Again, an unbalanced picture may be given if it is not noted that it is virtually impossible to impose charges on pollution from non-point sources, such as run-off from the use of fertilisers and biocides. Because of that, the imposition of charges only on point sources may be regarded as an imbalance in the use of powers as between the two kinds of sources. As noted below, however, the imposition of a fair charge on one, cannot rightly be criticised on the grounds that fair charges are not imposed on others. Moreover, the control of pollution from run-off presents technical difficulties, and in some jurisdictions considerable political opposition.

It was stated in O.E.C.D. publication *Pollution Charges in Practice* cited above, that

Experience has shown that a basis for charges should satisfy the two essential conditions of simplicity and acceptability.

Simplicity is to be achieved by the selection of a limited number of parameters, while acceptability may be achieved by inviting, when selecting the basis on which charges are to be calculated, the participation of those who may be liable.

The plea for simplicity in those terms underlines the difficulties encountered in monitoring adequately for the purpose of charges, and that for acceptability the difficulty of fixing an adequate but justifiable level of charge. Both present difficulties which the O.E.C.D. appears to accept must limit the use of this method.

8.8.5   Monitoring for the purpose of charging

For this purpose it is necessary to measure both the total volume of the discharge, and the concentration of each pollutant in respect of which a charge is to be made. Some measurement may be done by automatic monitoring, otherwise there must be sampling analyses at a frequency sufficient to prevent surges of pollution from remaining undetected.

In many cases the polluter himself is asked to measure the discharge, with the control authority checking fairly frequently. It is difficult to see, however, how that could prevent a determined polluter from releasing a slug of pollutant that escapes detection. Biological monitoring of the river water at a suitable point downstream from the discharge could detect an unusual or grossly excessive discharge, even if released some time in the past, but it is submitted that that would not always detect an excess quantity of a permitted pollutant, especially if that excess were spread over a long period. Only continuous monitoring of water quality at a well-chosen site downstream would be sufficient to detect that, and if automatic monitoring could be done for that parameter, it could be done at the point of discharge.

8.8.6   Rates of charge

It may reasonably be argued that the rate of charge must be fair, but only between the discharger on the one hand, and on the other hand, the control authority and any others who may be affected by the pollution. The authority may be engaged in cleaning the water before it is used, and will be justified under the polluter pays principle in requiring the discharger to pay a fair proportion of those treatment costs. The user of the water, on the basis of the same principle, may demand fair compensation. It would, of course be impracticable for the authority to collect such money on behalf of users. The user would be left to claim compensation in the courts for damage done.

It is submitted that there would be no justification for claiming unfairness as between polluters. If the system is working properly, the polluter paying a charge would have his liability to users reduced to the extent of the charge. In many cases, however, the polluters not paying charges may also be escaping liability to pay compensation. Yet there would not be any merit in those paying the charges to claim that 'they are getting away with it, so why should not we!'.

Charges can have an added value in persuading dischargers to put in their own treatment plant, and it is often claimed that the charges should be raised until they have that effect. That may be true for particular pollutants, but if the authority can treat the receiving water more cheaply, and before any substantial damage is done, in doing so it would be giving a valuable service by keeping down costs. That has long been the justification for public authority sewage treatment works.

Moreover, it is submitted that the administration costs of control, including costs of monitoring, would be better charged as a separate item, so that they could be collected from all dischargers alike, except that any cost of additional monitoring for the purpose of charging could reasonably be added to the charge. That could also obviate the difficulty which the French river basin authorities ran into when many dischargers responded to the incentive to put in better treatment plant, thus reducing the income from charges to such an extent that the authorities got into financial difficulties.

8.8.7 Pollutants within a charging scheme

The following pollution parameters are commonly used in charging schemes:

— organic matter in terms of biochemical oxygen demand and chemical oxygen demand;
— suspended solids;
— salinity;
— toxicity in terms of such substances as mercury, cadmium and their compounds.

Nitrogen compounds are also considered. Bacterial and viral content might also be added. Properly trained and equipped, inspectors would be competent to take samples, but whether that could be done frequently enough for this purpose, in some States at least may be doubted

Temperature may also be taken into account, and is easily monitored, but difficulties can arise because it is not an independent variable. Its effects may vary with the presence of material pollutants.

8.8.8 Redistribution

The monies raised by pollution charges can be used not only by the public authority for treatment of the receiving waters. They may be used to finance management programmes of regional or municipal authorities, including the provision of sewerage systems. Some may be used to help finance industrial treatment plant, especially where there are shared facilities. That can be justified where the level of charge is calculated to provide for such assistance.

In France, some of the monies collected by a river basin agency are used for loans and subsidies to industries and municipalities in the basin. To that extent, monies are redistributed amongst polluters to help with improvements. In so far as that is done, it constitutes a levy rather than a pollution charge, and express statutory provision may be needed to permit such an imposition.

8.8.9 Combination of pollution charges and regulatory system

Control by charges and control by regulation can be operated separately, as they are in France. Alternatively, both sets of controls may be operated by a single body, as in the Netherlands. In the Federal Republic of Germany, the Waste Water Charging Law of 1976 provided that the Lander will collect the charges, and they also are responsible for the implementation of the regulatory systems of permits and consents.

8.8.10 Combination of regulation and charges

The difficulties of adequate monitoring, the cost of that monitoring, and to some extent the expertise required for the calculation of charges, can put the use of such a system beyond the reach of a less wealthy country. To that must be added that in a developing country, where nascent industries are being weaned and nursed to health, and where indigenous industrial concerns are far from wealthy, the imposition of pollution charges could be inappropriate.

There are countries, however, where some pollution charges might be useful if the public authorities had the resources of expertise and finance to carry out adequate monitoring. It is submitted that those difficulties could be overcome by a direct combination of regulation and pollution charges, even for the same pollutants.

That could be done by charging not for the pollutants actually discharged, but in accordance with the maximum which could be discharged under the regulatory consent granted.

The system would operate as a normal consent system. The consent or licence would be subject to conditions which would relate, inter alia, to the maximum quantities of specified pollutants which could legally he discharged in a stated period. To make monitoring simpler, the condition could permit X gallons of discharge on a daily average, the concentration of the specified pollutant never to exceed Y ppm.

For each pollutant there could be several charge bands. The charge would increase as the amount of pollutant which could be discharged legally under that consent increased. The discharger would thus be charged in accordance with the consent granted. A breach of consent levels could still lead to a criminal penalty.

Under such a system, the monitoring required would be no greater than for the simple regulatory system. This would enable any discharger to move into a lower charge band by installing a more effective treatment plant. The scale of charges could be calculated so as to give him an incentive to do so. Changes would be by stages rather than gradual – but improvements are also normally made in stages, as new treatment plant is installed.

A similar basis of charges is used in the United Kingdom for licences to abstract water from rivers. The charge is based on the maximum abstraction permitted by the licence, irrespective of how much is taken.

8.9 Misuse of products

8.9.1 Pollution problems arise also from the deliberate misuse of products. That may lie in the time, place or manner of use. For convenience, storage of products is also dealt with in this section.

8.9.2 *Time of use*

In a mixed industrial and residential area, the conduct of industrial operations in the evening and at night can cause considerable noise nuisance. This can easily be dealt with by planning conditions,[82] or alternatively through noise control provisions. By reason of the nature of the offence itself, there will be adequate evidence for enforcement.

---

[82]See 8.2.6.

In some places the use of motor cycles in holiday areas, at certain times of day or even at any time[83] can be a nuisance to holiday makers, and thus adversely affect the holiday industry. When restrictions on their use are limited to specified times, the police can enforce them more effectively.

Night flights by aircraft are limited at certain airports because of noise nuisance. The limitations can be imposed as planning conditions, or by powers granted to the airport authority. One difficulty arises. If departure from one airport must be during the day, its arrival at another may be during the night, and vice versa. Some agreement between the two may be necessary. There is no difficulty in enforcement, although clearly allowance has to be made for emergencies, and even perhaps for delayed departures.

8.9.3 Place of use

It may be necessary for the reduction of noise nuisances, to keep specified classes of motor vehicles away from noise sensitive areas such as residential estates, schools and hospitals, and areas of high amenity where quietude is a significant element of that amenity. The noise problems are the same for the two, but the enforcement problems can be very different.

It is not a simple matter to keep specified classes of motor vehicles out of an area. Commercial vehicles may be needed for delivery of goods within the area, and noisy motor cycles may belong to young men who live there. Moreover, potential offenders are numerous, and a close watch by police and other officers may be needed for effective enforcement. It must be remembered that the police have many duties, and will not readily co-operate in the enforcement of new laws unless they are persuaded that enforcement will be expeditious and effective. It is wise, if not necessary, to consult the police before drafting any such new laws, on the length of extra time, particularly on the procedures to be followed, and on the extra time likely to be needed for proper enforcement. In England in 1973, when new regulations were introduced for the control of noise from vehicles when in use of the roads, a meeting of chief constables decided that it would not be worthwhile to require their constables to spend time trying to enforce them – the regulations thereafter remained almost totally ineffective.

Commercial vehicles may be forbidden to travel on certain routes for other reasons – they may be carrying toxic or even explosive materials dangerous to life or health. Such vehicles are in many jurisdictions required to be marked according to the character of their loads.[84] Apart from the safety reasons for that requirement, being so marked they are easily identified by the police.

There is much less difficulty with the adherence to specified flightpaths for aircraft. Commercial pilots form a body of men under close discipline by their employers, and in some jurisdictions by the civil aviation authority.[85] Other pilots are licensed, and are usually members of local aero clubs. In both cases the offending planes can easily be seen, and identified by their markings. The 'grounding' of a commercial pilot, and the loss of licence by any other, would be serious blows to them.

[83]See 8.9.3 below.

[84]See, e.g., the UK Dangerous Substances (Conveyance in Road Tankers and Tank Containers) Regulations 1981 s.i.1059 at Reg.14 and Sched.3.

[85]In the UK, pilots receive instructions by means of 'notams'—notices from the Civil Aviation Authority.

Similar restrictions may apply to the use of potentially polluting substances in certain places. The United Kingdom has recently passed legislation concerning 'nitrate sensitive areas', where the use of nitrates can be restricted.[86]

The use of chemicals in offshore operations may also be controlled. In the United Kingdom there is a voluntary scheme, under which the operating companies agree to comply with limitations specified by the Department of Energy.[87] Under the Kuwait Convention Protocol on Offshore Operations, there is an agreement to impose compulsory controls. Each operator will be required to submit a 'chemical use plan' for approval by the relevant national authority. He must thereafter not depart from that plan without express permission[88].

The storage of chemicals may also be controlled in some areas for the protection of nearby waters.[89] Some of the strictest are found in Germany. Under the Water Supply Law, in most cases generally accepted standards must be met, but in some cases special authorisation is needed. Most Lander also have storage regulations. For example, under the Baden-Württemberg Storage Regulations,[90] storage containers must be double walled, with overflow retention tanks provided. Underground installations must have leakage indicators to indicate automatically, optically and acoustically, any leaks in the container walls.

Other problems of enforcement arise with controls over the use of pesticides. Instructions on application can be printed on the package, including instructions on concentrations to be used and times of spraying, and it can be an offence to disobey those instructions. Concentrations are calculated so that no dangerous residues will be left on fruit. Nevertheless, some fruit farmers may decide to play safe, and spray the pesticide in greater concentrations. Others may use 'cosmetic spraying'. That is used where the specified concentration will ensure that, in the case of apples, for example, no insects penetrate the skin to damage the pulp of the fruit. They may, however, not be killed or driven away soon enough to prevent them from making 'trail marks' on the apples. With such marks, the apples are not so easily sold, therefore the grower is tempted to spray with higher concentrations to prevent such marking. Such practices are well known, yet enforcement is still difficult.

If there are available sufficient resources to provide a wide enough coverage of sampling and analysis of the final product, and where necessary of the plant, enforcement can be concentrated at those points. The department of health can provide enforcement officers, while officers of the department of agriculture are free to act as advisers to the farmers, a system which is being considered in Cyprus. That will be supplemented by controls over the sales of pesticides, permitting only registered persons to sell certain pesticides, and requiring them to keep a record of all sales.

That system will not necessarily work elsewhere. Problems with pesticides vary from country to country according to geography, farming practices, and the extent to which pesticides are imported or produced locally.

---

[86]See Water Resources Act 1991 ss.94–96.

[87]Notification Scheme for Selection of Chemicals for Use Offshore.

[88]Protocol concerning Marine Pollution resulting from Exploration and Exploitation of the Continental Shelf, Art.XI.

[89]See UK Water Resources Act 1991 s.92. on water protection zones.

[90]Regulations of 30 June 1966, GesBl as amended.

8.10 Final disposal of products

8.10.1 The final disposal of products when their useful lives have finished is normally covered by the laws on the disposal of wastes generally. Those are supplemented by the separate collection of some products such as waste paper and glass bottles, preparatory to recycling.

There are, however, some which are so polluting, or create such nuisances, that special provisions govern them.

8.10.2 The disposal of certain specific types of wastes is often governed by special legislation. For the disposal of radioactive waste, it is usual to require a licence or authorisation, which specifies in each case the manner of disposal, as in Italy, Ireland and the United Kingdom.[91] or to provide special rules for their disposal, as in Belgium,[92] or to require the wastes to be delivered to special collection points, as in Germany.[93] For all but wastes of low radioactivity, normally supervision is close and enforcement rigorous.

Most waste oils can be recycled for use as lower grade oils, but that can be carried out economically only in large quantities. Therefore in some countries it is subject to special legislation. The European Community has issued Directive 75/439, amended by 87/101, which covers storage and disposal. Several Member States have arrangements for collection points, where oil is collected for treatment and disposal by a public authority or licensed dealer, as in Luxemburg, the Netherlands, Ireland, Germany and Denmark.[94]

Real difficulties, however, are encountered in the disposal of residual sludges. They are derived from oily water separators, from desalters, from the bottoms of crude oil storage tanks, and from large accidental spills. Various methods may be used, including landfill, land farming, deep well disposal, burning as subsidiary fuels in brick or cement kilns or oil fired electricity generating plant.[95] The difficulties are both economic and technical, the latter involving the removal of toxic constituents. Even when a feasible method is found, careful monitoring for toxic residues or toxic discharges to the air may be necessary, although the points of disposal or discharge will be few. Unfortunately, as long as oil is used widely as a fuel, the problem of dealing with oily sludges will remain inescapable.

In addition to collection points, there may also be collection services. In Cyprus, there is a scheme under which used car batteries are collected, for the joint reasons that if they are carelessly discarded the lead can be very polluting, whereas if they are collected it can be recycled. Consideration is now being given to the collection of batteries from small boats for the same reasons.

[91]Italy—Decree of President of the Republic 185 of 1964, at Art.89. Ireland—Nuclear Energy Act 1971. UK—Nuclear Installations Act 1965 at s. 4(1)(d).

[92]Belgium—Royal Decree of 28 Feb. 1963, serving as a General Regulation for the protection of the population and workers. In France there is a National Agency for the Recycling and Elimination of Waste, which is involved, *inter alia*, in the handling and disposal of wastes.

[93]Atomic Law and Regulations made thereunder,

[94]See J.McLoughlin and M.J. Forster, *Law and Practice Relating to Pollution Control in the Member States of the European Communities: a Comparative Survey* (Graham & Trotman, London, 2nd Edition, 1982), pp. 296,292,286 and 281 respectively.

[95]*Oil Refineries Waste Survey—Disposal Methods, Quantities and Costs*. CONCAWE Report No 5/89.

There are now good grounds for considering the collection of old refrigerators, so that the cfc gases can be drawn off before disposal. Techniques have now been developed which make such schemes feasible.

A further problem, not yet satisfactorily solved in some countries, is the disposal of old motor vehicles. Even in technically advanced countries, where equipment for recycling and disposal is available, cars are often abandoned by the roadside and in open spaces. In the United Kingdom, if the last owner can be traced, he can be charged with the cost of disposal. The ease with which identification marks can be removed, obliterated or rendered indecipherable, however, makes enforcement difficult. In Kingston, Jamaica, such cars are simply collected at the expense of the municipal authority.

A scheme was devised in Ontario, Canada, for imposing a small fee on the registration of a vehicle. The fee would be returned to the owner when the vehicle was disposed of in an environmentally acceptable location. That scheme, however, was never adopted – the authorities decided that the disposal of old cars was not a sufficiently major problem to justify the scheme.

A slightly more sophisticated version of that scheme has since been adopted in Sweden, apparently with some success. An owner of a vehicle may 'de-register' it on production of a 'scrapping certificate'. He is then paid a 'scrapping premium' of Skr300. A scrapping certificate may be issued only by a local authority which has a special reception facility, or by a person who is authorised by the county administration, to dispose of scrap vehicles. (See Appendix C for the Swedish system generally.)

Some of the larger private manufacturers of cars are also tackling the problem. BMW of Germany is now producing a car constructed mainly of recyclable material, and offering to provide recycling facilities. The success of the scheme will depend, of course, on the location of the facilities.

For other wastes that are toxic, dangerous or otherwise difficult to dispose of, there are usually special provisions in more general terms. The common feature is that such wastes must be taken to some place licensed to receive them, and there must be some check on their movement and disposal.[96] Other safeguards are often added, such as supervision by a specially appointed agent,[97] or discretionary powers vested in an authority to determine the place and manner of disposal.[98] Cost of disposal of some of those wastes can be very high, therefore supervision must be close and continuous to ensure proper compliance.

[96]See Directive 78/319/EEC on toxic and dangerous waste.
[97]The German Regulation on Waste Agents, 26 Oct. 1977, BGB1 I. See also Appendix F at 5.4.
[98]See UK Environmental Protection Act 1990, s.62.

Chapter IV

Enforcement

1. FORMS OF ENFORCEMENT

1.1 Civil, and other forms of control not enforced directly by criminal penalties

1.1.1 Enforcement by administrative, economic and fiscal means, vary from state to state, and little can usefully be said of the processes in general terms.

1.1.2 Much can be said of the enforcement of civil remedies, although civil rights generally are dealt with in Chapter V, and the enforcement of individual rights in Chapter VI.

1.2 Criminal

The enforcement of criminal provisions presents problems common to most states, and is dealt with below.

2. POWERS AND DUTIES OF AUTHORITIES ENFORCING CRIMINAL PROVISIONS

2.1 Enforcement process

2.1.1 An enforcement authority is the person or body which, under the law of the country, has a power or duty to enforce the provisions of a specified piece of legislation. In many cases that will be a duty. It is preferable that it should be so for two reasons. The first is that otherwise the authority may fail to enforce properly, through laxity or because of favourable discrimination. The second is that if it is a duty, the authority itself can be forced to take action if it is practicable to do so.[1]

---

[1] In the United Kingdom, by order of mandamus, see Chapter VI at 6.2. In the United States by a citizen suit, see Chapter V at 6.5.3.

This point is of much greater importance if the power to bring prosecutions is denied to others, or if their power to do so is limited.[2]

2.1.2   Enforcement, however, does not necessarily involve prosecution. Often a warning, or even advice, is sufficient. For that reason it is usual to give the authority a discretion whether or not to prosecute in any particular case. The authority may leave the exercise of that discretion to specified senior officers, or to inspectors[3] generally.

2.2   Ancillary functions of the authority and its inspectors

2.2.1   In addition to warnings, inspectors may give advice to the operators of plant on treatment, discharge or deposits of waste. That advice may be of two kinds. It may simply advise the operator that certain methods of disposal would be illegal, or it may go further and advise him on the methods of treatment which would make the substance acceptable for discharge or deposit.

In giving advice on the legality of methods of disposal, the inspector can be expected to know precisely what the requirements are, and in giving such advice he may be regarded as acting properly as a crime prevention officer.

Some inspectors are well qualified and have considerable relevant experience, and in some cases could give advice on methods of treatment. That could be a service of great value to both the operator and the community, but therein lies a danger for him. If he made a mistake in giving such advice, and damage resulted, in some jurisdictions he could be sued by the discharger for making an incorrect statement negligently in circumstances where it was clear that the recipient might act upon it. In the United Kingdom it could be particularly dangerous, for by reason of Section 2 of the Unfair Contract Terms Act 1977,[4] any attempt to opt out of such liability when he gave the advice would be invalid if the damage involved personal injury. In many states, therefore, inspectors are very properly instructed to advise only on which methods of treatment or discharge would satisfy legal requirements.

Where such liability could arise, the state may decide to pass legislation exempting the authority and any inspector from liability for negligent advice given bona fide in the discharge of their functions, or given in connection therewith.[5]

2.3   Persons with enforcement powers

2.3.1   The persons who have rights to bring proceedings for the enforcement of criminal laws varies from state to state. Rights to take steps to ensure that enforcement measures are in fact taken, necessarily vary accordingly. As the latter are significant mainly as the rights of individuals exercised in order to protect their interests, however, they are dealt with in Chapter VI.

---

[2]See 2.4 below.

[3]Inspectors normally have powers of enforcement. Wherever the term is used in this chapter, it is assumed that they have.

[4]Unfair Contract Terms Act 1977, S. 2. The act applies to notices as well as to contracts.

[5]In the past, some states have given general protection to their officers, e.g. Cyprus, Protection of Public Officers Act.

2.3.2 Probably the most widely distributed right to bring criminal prosecutions is found in England. In examining those rights, it is important to distinguish between powers and duties to enforce the law.[6]

The police have a duty to enforce the criminal law. In order to do that they have a power to bring criminal proceedings if they think fit, but alternatively they may simply warn a suspected offender.

Many other public bodies are enforcement authorities for particular pieces of legislation, and under some statutes have a duty to enforce.[7] That means, of course, enforce in the wider sense, which does not necessarily mean criminal proceedings in every case. That raises two points which are of some importance in the administration of justice.

The first is that there is some danger in giving discretionary powers to prosecute to a political body such as an elected local authority. Pollution control, in so far as it concerns environmental standards and the provisions of legislation, inevitably involves political issues.[8] Once the law and standards are fixed, however, political considerations have no proper place in the enforcement of the provisions. The danger is that members of a political body, when making decisions on enforcement, may knowingly or unknowingly permit political considerations to intrude.

It may be argued that in some cases political considerations have a proper part to play. In one case, for example, an industrial plant in a small town was discharging acid fumes to the atmosphere. Work was being done in co-operation with the pollution control authority to reduce the discharge, but the process of finding a satisfactory solution took several years. The control authority, being part of a department of government, was anxious that production at the plant should be maintained, and satisfied that the operator was doing all he could be expected to do under the law administered by that authority. The local authority, on the other hand, had power to bring proceedings both for a public nuisance as a criminal offence, and for an injunction to restrain the operator from emitting such a discharge. The grant of an injunction would have meant the closure of the plant. It brought no such proceedings. The apparent reason was that it was more concerned, in a period of high unemployment, to retain jobs for its work people in the town. The company responsible for the discharge employed forty per cent of the labour force there. The local authority would also have lost local tax revenue if the plant had closed. Those considerations, particularly the former, were valid political considerations. That is not to say that the local authority itself should have been the arbiter. The matter could have gone to court where an impartial judge would have been the arbiter, granting compensation if that was merited, and exercising his discretion whether or not to grant an injunction

The second point is that it is preferable that there is a duty to enforce, and that there is a legal process by means of which individuals can compel the authority to do its duty, so far as that is practicable, as noted at 2.1.1 above and at footnote 1.

[6]See 2.1.1 above.
[7]See United Kingdom Clean Air Act 1956, S. 29, and Water Resources Act 1991 s.84.
[8]See Chapter I at 4.2.3

2.4 Restrictions on the power to prosecute, and the powers of individuals to take action

2.4.1 There lies a danger in giving a single authority, or set of authorities, the exclusive right to prosecute for certain offences, especially where that is a power as distinct from a duty. That leaves the authority free to refrain from prosecuting for certain types of offences, or to refrain from prosecuting certain classes of offenders. That could even amount to the exercise of a power of dispensation,[9] a power which in England has been expressly denied to the Crown by the Bill of Rights, 1689.

2.4.2 In the United States, criminal prosecutions are brought on behalf of the states. An individual acting on his own behalf is able to bring a civil complaint, which could lead to the award not only of compensation, but a fine.

Alternatively, an individual may bring a citizen suit against the Administrator of the Environmental Protection Agency, or against the relevant state authority, or even against a person who, without the necessary permit proposes to build a major works from which there will be emissions to the atmosphere. For a more detailed explanation of citizen suits see Chapter V at 6.5.3.

2.4.3 In Scotland, criminal prosecutions are brought by the Lord Advocate as the public prosecutor. To that there are some exceptions.

It is possible for an individual to bring a private prosecution for a common law offence if, *inter alia,* he can show he has suffered injury. Such actions, however, are rare.

A statute creating an offence may grant a right to individuals to bring private prosecutions. Such prosecutions are fairly common.[10]

2.4.4 In England, Canada and certain other Commonwealth countries, it is open to an individual to bring a private prosecution.[11] In England, however, that right to bring a private prosecution is subject to the power of the Attorney General to issue a nolle prosequi to forestall or bring to an end any such proceedings.

Statutes also can take away that right in particular classes of cases; but in their application to pollution offences, such restrictions in recent years have been considerably narrowed.[12] Those that remain can, often but not always, be justified as preventing ill-informed or politically motivated intervention.[13]

The right to bring private prosecutions does provide a safeguard against failure of the authorities to act. Note however, the comments made in Chapter VI at 5.1.

[9]The term 'dispensation' is used here of knowingly refraining from enforcing a law in particular cases or against particular people. To that extent it amounts to a suspension of that law.

[10]For powers of prosecution in Scotland see Renton and Brown, *Scottish Criminal Procedure*, a loose leaf encyclopedia.

[11]On private prosecutions generally, see Chapter VI at section 5.

[12]See Rivers (Prevention of Pollution) Act 1951, S. 8. That act has been repealed, and that provision not re-enacted in the legislation which replaced it.

[13]See the United Kingdom Nuclear Installations Act 1965. S. 25 (3), which was formerly a restiction relating to all offences under the Act. The provision has since been amended so that it now applies only to offences concerning the production of weapons grade plutonium or uranium, and to the maintenance of insurance cover or other security by a nuclear site licensee. The first of those applications can be justified on the grounds of possible politically motivated prosecutions. The justification for the latter is less clear.

2.4.5 In France, no criminal proceeding may be brought without an examining magistrate, known as a *juge d'instruction,* having first examined the charge and the evidence. He then decides whether or not proceedings shall be commenced. He is, of course, independent of the enforcing agencies.

3. SPECIAL POWERS OF ENFORCEMENT OFFICERS, AND NECESSARY SAFEGUARDS FOR THE OPERATOR OR DISCHARGER

3.1 Special powers of enforcement officers

3.1.1 There are certain powers needed for pollution control authorities which are not necessarily given to the ordinary police. In addition to the usual powers of entry into premises, an enforcement officer may be given powers to do any or all of the following:

– examine and investigate as necessary for the discharge of his functions;
– measure and test any equipment or articles;
– take samples of substances;
– take photographs;
– cause articles to be dismantled or substances to be subjected to any process;
– cause articles or substances to be taken away or destroyed so as to remove danger to the environment or human health;
– take articles or substances and retain them to keep them as evidence;
– require that specified equipment, articles or substances left on the premises are not altered or disturbed;
– require the production of books or papers;
– require persons to give him information;
– require persons to afford him facilities and give him assistance to enable him to exercise his powers;
– take with him on entry to the premises any constable, or an expert needed to assist him in the exercise of his powers.

3.1.2 Inspectors may also be granted a power to prohibit the continued conduct of a process, and remove or even destroy any article or substance, if such action is necessary to remove an imminent danger of serious harm to health or serious environmental pollution.[14]

3.2 Safeguards for the operator or discharger

3.2.1 Enforcement officers thus often wield considerable powers,[15] and those powers may easily be abused. That refers not only to possible corrupt use of the powers, but also to abuse by an over zealous enforcement officer determined to bring to justice a person he is convinced is an offender. It must be emphasised that

---

[14]For examples, see the United Kingdom Health and Safety at Work Act 1974, S. 22, the Environmental Protection Act 1990, S. 18, and the Mauritius Environment Protection Act 1991, S. 59.
[15]See also Chapter II at section 5.

they are not to act as judges, but merely to bring a person to court in order that judgment may be made. Certain legislative safeguards may therefore be necessary.

3.2.2 Such safeguards will normally concern powers to question, take statements, and arrest; interviews and the recording of statements; powers to sieze and retain documents, substances, and other things which may be used as evidence; right of access by the accused to independent legal advice; protection of documents handed to his legal adviser for the preparation of his defence.

Most jurisdictions already have rules of law relating to such matters and applicable to police officers. They range from the use of examining magistrates to conduct all pre-trial interrogation, as in France, and from the freedom of police to interrogate subject to a code of practice, as in England, to the greater freedom left to the police in some other jurisdictions. Much will depend on the legal traditions and practices of the particular state. For enforcement officers, a simple answer is to make them subject to the same legal restraints as the ordinary police of that country. The enforcement officers, however, may have powers beyond those of the police, as noted above. In such cases, special additional safeguards may be needed.

3.2.3 Those safeguards may include any of the following.

(a) Where a sample of a substance is taken, the enforcing officer taking it may be required to give to the occupier, operator or his agent, a portion of the sample to retain for testing or analysis, and for producing the results in evidence. He may also be required to put aside a third portion to be held for such further tests to be made as the court may require. That can be made to apply whether the portion is from a discharge or deposit, or a sample of any other waste product, or any substance used in or produced by the operations.

(b) When any equipment or article is dismantled or subjected to any process for the purpose of checking or testing, it may provide that should be done in the presence of the occupier, operator or his agent.

(c) There may be limitations on the right to see or sieze documents prepared by or for the occupier's or operator's legal adviser, in accordance with the general laws of that country.

(d) There may be appeals against orders to close the process, or to take additional precautions against accidents, or against the destruction or removal of any article.

Chapter V

Civil Liability

1. POLLUTION CONTROL AND CIVIL LIABILITY

1.1 Legislation on control and on civil liability

A large mass of legislation on the protection of the environment has been passed, covering many countries, during the last 30 years. Those laws have mainly imposed controls backed by criminal penalties. Only a small proportion of them have dealt directly with compensation for those who have suffered pollution damage. In the main, civil liability has been left to be dealt with under the general body of civil law, on the same basis as other wrongs.

That practice is understandable. It would have been wrong to have a different set of rules or criteria for pollution damage than for other forms of damage – different standards can be justified only in special cases. In countries with codified systems[1] of law, remedies are usually provided for broad classes of cases, as for nuisances, some of which do not necessarily involve pollution. The standard normally applied is fault liability,[2] but with stricter liability in certain cases.[3] In common law countries, remedies are normally provided under the common law, again on the basis of fault liability[2] but with stricter liability in some cases, notably under the rule in *Rylands* v *Fletcher*.[4] Under both systems there are enacted laws providing for some form of strict liability for pollution damage, often passed in the implementation of international conventions.[5]

The activities which give rise to pollution damage, however, raise problems which suggest that a re-assessment may be needed, at least in some cases. Those problems are examined here, in the context of such activities.

---

[1]Written laws forming a comprehensive code, as distinct from laws developed by the courts through a system of judicial precedent.

[2]See 3.2.

[3]See 3.3.

[4]See 3.3.2.

[5]See, e.g., International Convention on Civil Liability for Oil Pollution Damage, Brussels 1969 at Art. III. See also Chapter VIII at section 5.3 on state responsibility and the standard of 'due diligence'.

2. STANDARDS APPLIED IN CIVIL AND CRIMINAL LIABILITY

2.1   Criminal and civil actions are normally pursued in different courts. In general, the criminal courts award punishments, and the civil courts compensation. Different standards are applied in the two sets of courts. First the standard of conduct which will lead to liability must be determined, then the standard of proof of such conduct sufficient to satisfy the court must be met. The latter, the standard of proof required, is normally higher in the criminal courts. That is understandable – to be condemned for criminal conduct usually carries a greater moral stigma than to have to pay compensation.

In the former, the standard of conduct which will lead to liability, some inconsistency is apparent. That inconsistency is well illustrated by English law. Where river water is polluted by a discharge, before criminal liability can arise under the Water Resources Act 1991 the discharge must carry pollutants in excess of the consent levels,[6] and before it can arise at common law it must cause interference with the enjoyment of public rights to such an extent that the interference would be considered by the ordinary man to be unreasonable.[7] On the other hand, civil liability can arise for any degree of pollution of the river water, however slight.[8] The reverse if found with atmospheric pollution. If dark smoke is emitted from a chimney, or any smoke in a smoke control area, an offence is committed at criminal law.[9] For civil liability to arise, the discharge must be shown to have caused an unreasonable degree of interference to an occupier of property or to the enjoyment of public rights.[10]

2.2   There may be some justification for a difference. As with the standard of proof, it may be said that unless the standard of conduct is significantly bad, there is insufficient justification for condemning that conduct as criminal. But in some legal systems the criminal law is used to support civil redress, for various reasons. Two examples can be given from English law.

The first, and the one of most general application, is the provision for compensation orders. Whenever a person has been convicted by a criminal court for an offence,[11] any person who has suffered from the commission of that offence can apply for such an order. The criminal court is thereby empowered to grant compensation. In practice, however, courts are unwilling to do so unless the amount of the loss in monetary terms is clear. It will not attempt to assess damages for such things as personal injuries, or loss of recreational opportunities. It is therefore little used in connection with pollution offences.

The second is found where an offence is created for the protection of persons of a particular class, such as employees. Any member of that class who has been injured as a result of a commission of that offence may sue in a civil court for compensation. In

---

[6]See Water Resources Act 1991 ss.85 and 88.

[7]Prosecution for public nuisance.

[8]Under the common law on pollution of rivers. See *John Young* v *Bankier Distillery* [1983] AC 691 at 698.

[9]Clean Air Act 1956, S.1 and 11 respectively. In addition to the two examples given, it is relevant to refer to public nuisance. That is a criminal offence, but in some circumstances a civil action will lie.

[10]Civil claims for public and private nuisance.

[11]Excluding an offence causing the death of a person, and a road traffic offence. See Powers of Criminal Courts Act 1973 S.35.

English law he is said to have a 'right of action for breach of statutory duty'. Where, for example, an employer fails to place a guard round a moving part of some machinery, as required by the Factories Act 1961,[12] and a workman's hand is caught by the moving part and is injured, the workman can sue for compensation. He has no need to prove negligence. That right of action seems to be well founded in principle, and certainly it would be reasonable to apply it to many pollution offences. Where a pollution offence has been created for a particular class of persons, and a member of that class suffers as a result of a commission of the offence, it seems logical that he should be awarded compensation. That would give the added advantage of applying the same standard of conduct for the civil action as for the criminal offence.

2.3 If we are to accept that pollution control laws are passed, in part if not wholly, to protect man's interest in the environment, it follows that those whose interests have been damaged as a result of a breach of those laws should be entitled to receive compensation.

That does not mean that every act which causes such damage should be criminal. The damage may arise from simple negligence or other innocent cause. It is submitted, however, that where both civil and criminal liabilities do arise, it would be both logical and fair to base both on the same environmental criteria.

3. FORMS OF CIVIL LIABILITY

3.1 Where an act[13] by one person causes damage to the interests of another, whether by injury to his person, or damage to his property or other interests which the law protects, liability to compensate him can arise.[14] In most systems of law, that person will not usually be found liable unless he was at fault.[15] That is termed 'fault liability'. In exceptional cases, however, he may be found liable without proof of fault. That is termed 'strict liability'.

3.2 Fault liability

3.2.1 Imposing liability on a person only when it can be shown that he was at fault can be justified on the grounds that an ordinary man can be expected to know that the ordinary incidents of life give rise to dangers, and that he can be expected to go about his business aware that accidents can occur, and take such precautions as he can to avoid them.[16] Only when the damage he suffers flows from the fault of some other person, can he be expected to be compensated.

3.2.2 At common law, there is said to be fault liability when the act causing the damage was done intentionally or negligently. Negligence is a failure to take care

---

[12]S.14.

[13]There may be liability for a failure to act, where he has a duty to do so, but that is not relevant in cases of pollution damage.

[14]At common law that act would be referred to as a 'tort', In other systems it would be referred to by another name such as 'delict'.

[15]The meaning of 'fault' is discussed in 3.2.1. below.

[16]On the possible legal consequences of extraordinary dangers, see 3.3.2.

not to injure others by your acts, where injury is a foreseeable consequence of such acts. Liability for omissions can arise only where there was a duty to act.

3.2.3   In countries with codified systems of law, a similar approach has been taken, although the precise rules in those various countries are not necessarily the same.

In Germany, any person whose life, health, freedom or property, or other right, is affected either intentionally or negligently, has a right to compensation.[17] The French Civil Code, at Articles 1382 and 1383, lays down the general rule of fault liability, proof of intention, negligence or imprudence being required. Subsequent articles lay down the stricter form of liability where no fault need be proved. They are dealt with as a form of strict liability under 3.3.

3.3   Strict liability

3.3.1   Liability is said to be strict where the plaintiff can obtain compensation from the person whose act caused the damage, without a need to prove any kind of fault. Because such a form of liability could operate harshly or unjustly in some circumstances, most systems of law permit exceptions in certain cases. Only in one sphere of activity are no such exceptions permitted – that covered by the international treaty on the launching of earth satellites. That therefore may be called 'absolute liability'.

The Convention on Civil Liability for Nuclear Damage (Vienna 1963) states at Article IV that 'liability of the operator for nuclear damage is absolute'. It is submitted that the term is used incorrectly there. That statement is immediately followed by express exceptions to liability, therefore the liability cannot be absolute.

The subject of ultra-hazardous activities and absolute liability is dealt with in Chapter VIII at 6.2.

3.3.2   At common law, the principal area of strict liability is that set out in the case of *Rylands* v *Fletcher*.[18] It was stated there that

> A person who, for his own purposes, brings on to his land and collects and keeps there anything likely to do mischief if it escapes must keep it in at his peril, and, if he does not do so, is prima facie answerable for all the damage which is the natural consequence of its escape.

The scope of the rule, however, is limited to 'non-natural' uses of land. Normal farming practices would be regarded as natural, but many industrial practices, particularly the production or storage of noxious or polluting substances, such as oil in large quantities, would be non-natural. In *Rylands* v *Fletcher* itself, the rule was applied to storage of water in large quantities in a mill lodge.

.   The principle behind the distinction was explained in a later case,[19] in which it was said that there must be

---

[17]B.G.B. (Civil Code) Art.823.
[18](1866) LR 1 Exch. 265, affirmed (1868) LR 3 HL 330.
[19]*Rickards* v *Lothian* [1913] AC 263 at 288.

... some special use, bringing with it increased dangers to others, and not merely the ordinary use of land ...

to which was added

... or such as is proper for the general benefit of the community.

Excluding the additional words, and it must be noted that they were said in 1913, that statement also offers the justification for the rule. Where increased dangers are created, against which the ordinary man cannot reasonably be expected to take his own precautions, liability falls on the one who created the danger.

The exceptions permitted are – act of God,[20] act of a third person, and consent of the plaintiff himself or his contributary negligence.

In the context of environmental pollution, that would appear to offer a sensible rule, but one which is too limited in scope. The limits expressed in terms of 'natural uses' and 'such as is proper for the general benefit of the community' appear inappropriate in today's circumstances. Those limits were formulated in earlier years, before the development of modern industry, modern pesticides and modern practices in farming, and the common law courts have appeared to be reluctant to extend any further the scope of strict liability.[21] In international conventions, however, countries have been more ready to accept strict liability, e.g. for nuclear occurrences, and for spillages of oil at sea.

The French Civil Code applies a form of strict liability in some circumstances. Article 1384 declares that a person is liable for damage caused by the action of things in his care. To avoid liability, the defendant must prove that the damage was attributable to something other than the thing in his care for example *force majeure* or an act of a third party. The liability, when it applies, is referred to as 'objective liability'.

The Italians also have a form of objective liability similar to that of the French. Article 2051 of their Civil Code provides that a person using machinery, industrial plant or other articles in his custody is responsible for its harmful effects from their normal operation or from accidents.[22]

In Germany, compensation can be claimed by a person who had been injured as a result of a violation of a law designed to protect others, under the Civil Code at Section 823, paragraph 2.

4. CRITERIA APPROPRIATE TO LIABILITY FOR POLLUTION DAMAGE

4.1 Disadvantages of fault liability

From the point of view of the plantiff, there can be a serious drawback to fault liability. That is, for various reasons, it may be difficult to prove fault. A pedestrian hit from behind by a motor vehicle may not be able to identify the vehicle or the

---

[20]An act of God in English law occurs in 'circumstances which no human foresight can provide against, and of which human prudence is not bound to recognise the possibility'. *Greenoch Corporation v Caledonian Railway Co.* [1917] AC 556.

[21]See 4.3.2 for a possible extension of the rule to a wider range of pollution cases.

[22]Articles 2050 and 2049 have also been quoted as applying 'objective responsibility', but there appears to be an element of fault in each of those. See M. Guttieres and U. Ruffolo, *Law and Practice of Pollution Control in Italy*, (Graham & Trotman, London, 1982).

driver, and even if he could, would not be able to give evidence on the conduct of the driving. A ship involved in a collision may, at the time of the hearing, be at the bottom of the ocean, displaying there the essential material evidence totally beyond the sight or reach of the court.[23] When a 'blow out' has occurred on a drilling rig, material evidence may have been destroyed in the event, or essential witnesses may have been killed. Apart from these extreme circumstances, many a potential plaintiff is deterred from taking action because of the uncertainty of whether or not he can successfully prove fault, combined with a fear of the cost involved, especially when the defendant is a wealthy company.

Strict liability is often more easy to establish. Therefore, so far as that form of liability is just, justice is more often done.

4.1.1   That difficulty is sometimes removed by presumptions the court is willing to make.

The most common occasion is where the maxim *res ipsa loquitur* – 'the thing speaks for itself', is applied. If damage has been caused, and there is not apparent any way in which it could have been caused except by the negligence of the defendant, the court will presume such negligence. In a leading case on this[24] the following explanation was given.

> There must be reasonable evidence of negligence. But where the thing is shown to be under the management of the defendant or his servants, and the accident is such as in the ordinary course of things does not happen if those who have the management use proper care, it affords reasonable evidence, in the absence of explanation by the defendants, that accident arose from want of care.

That case involved the simple matter of bags of sugar falling from a warehouse on to the plaintiff below. Where the facts are more complex, however, there is often a greater possibility of another cause.

The court has carried this line of reasoning further in the case of *McGhee* v *National Coal Board*.[25] There a workman was given the task of cleaning out brick kilns. He was exposed to clouds of abrasive brick dust, but there were no washing facilities available. He cycled home caked with sweat and grime. After several days he was found to be suffering from dermititis. Although the evidence did not establish a direct causal connection between the brick dust and his dermititis, he succeeded in a claim against his employers. Lord Wilberforce stated at page 1012 that

> .... where a person has, by breach of a duty of care, created a risk, and injury occurs within the area of that risk, the loss should be borne by him unless he shows that it has some other cause.

It is submitted that the reasoning behind that decision could be relevant to many pollution cases. Its application has already been widely recommended for planning and for administrative decisions, under the term 'precautionary principle'.

[23]As in *Joseph Constantine Steamship Line* [1941] 2 All ER 165. Note particularly the judgment of Lord Wright.
[24]*Scott* v *London & St. Catherine's Dock* (1865) H&C 596 per Erle J. at 601.
[25][1972] 3 All ER 1008.

4.2   Reliance on strict liability

The international community of states, in its conventions on liability for pollution damage, has shown a marked preference for strict liability.[26] It is usual, however, to grant exceptions to liability, common ones relating to acts of war or other hostilities, acts or omissions of the plaintiff or third parties with intent to cause damage, and for natural phenomena of exceptional, inevitable and irresistable character.[27] Those exceptions vary in different conventions, and it is the power to permit appropriate exceptions which gives flexibility to that form of liability, and enables the parties to tailor it to particular circumstances.

4.3   'Risk liability'

4.3.1   In providing responsibility for pollution damage, there is much to be said for applying the principle that, in the case of accidental damage, the person who created the risk of the accident is to be liable for the damage done. That may apply in two different sets of circumstances.

The first is found where a person engages in an activity knowing that it can result in a damaging accident, even with no negligence on his part. For many such activities, the risk is quantifiable. Three examples may be given.

> Figures available in 1972 showed that in the circumstances of that time, one accident involving an oil tanker at sea and resulting in serious pollution damage, occurred once every 'thousand tanker years'. With three thousand tankers at sea at any one time in those days, that meant three major pollution accidents per year.
>
> It has been shown that for approximately each 500 exploratory drillings for oil under the seabed, there is one 'blow out'. The exercise of due care, in the present state of scentific knowledge and technical competence, cannot eliminate that risk.
>
> It has likewise been shown that there is likely to be one blow out for every 2,000 well years at production platforms.[28]

In such circumstances there is a strong case for imposing strict liability. Even where that state considers that certain exceptions may be justified, the person who suffers the damage is entitled to at least equal consideration.

The second set of circumstances is where a person who engages in an activity does not know, and could not reasonably be expected to know, the risk he is thereby creating. Again, there is a strong case for strict liability. But for his actions, taken voluntarily and for his own benefit, the damage would not have been done. He may not have been aware of the risk, but there is much to be said for the principle that if one of two innocent persons must suffer the consequences of an occurrence, he who caused it must be the one to bear the loss.

Such a rule would be parallel to that in *Rylands* v *Fletcher*.[29]

---

[26]See, for example, the international conventions listed in 7.3.2. Words such as 'shall be liable' indicate strict liability, subject to any exceptions expressly granted.

[27]See, e.g., the Convention for Civil Liability for Oil Pollution Damage. The last example given in the text is approximately equivalent to the common law Act of God. It may be referred to more succinctly as the Maralyn Munroe clause.

[28]Each drill hole under a platform is called a 'well'. There can be 36 under one platform.

[29]See 3.3.2.

4.3.2 The same principle could be applied where a new product is put on the market. The state of mind of the producer may range from knowing that it could cause some damage, to absolute confidence that no damage could be done. He may be selling a new pesticide, he may be selling a new kind of coat hanger.

A manufacturer of pesticides has stated that even when all tests that the law requires have been carried out on a new product, with satisfactory results, there still remains an area of doubt whether damage may be done by its use.[30] In English law, if an farmer uses that product, and it falls, drifts or is carried outside the area of his land where it does damage, then he is strictly liable under the rule in *Rylands* v *Fletcher*. The producer, however, would be liable only if negligence could be proved. If he had carried out all the tests required by law with satisfactory results, and there was no evidence of further damage, proof of negligence would be impossible. Yet, by selling it for use on farms, he created a risk which did not exist before. To look at it another way, he takes beneficial consequences if no damage is done – justice requires that he should take his share of adverse consequences if damage results.

5. DAMAGE FROM UNATTRIBUTABLE SOURCES

5.1 The problem

Another difficulty arises out of pollution damage. The pollution may have come from any one or more of several sources in the area. Under most systems of law, unless a plaintiff can prove that a particular person or persons are responsible, he can obtain no compensation.[31] For example, oil may float into sea fishing grounds, damaging the fish stocks, but no-one may be able to identify the tanker or tankers from which it came. On the seabed there may lie debris which damages the trawls of fishing boats, and may have come from any one of several production platforms in the area.[32] Until the source is identified, no claim can be made in the courts.

Moves have been made to solve that problem under both voluntary and statutory schemes.

5.2 Voluntary schemes for compensation

A voluntary scheme has been in operation for some years at Milford Haven in Wales. That is an area classified as one of outstanding natural beauty, yet it is a deep water harbour very suitable for unloading large oil tankers. There are three refineries in the vicinity, and several long piers where tankers unload. Oil spills do occur, and it is sometimes difficult to identify the source. Under the scheme, whenever there is an 'unattributable spill', the necessary clearance operation can be organised, for which the port authority and oil companies have agreed to pay in four equal shares.

---

[30]Personal communication, scientist at firm of pesticides manufacturers.

[31]The classic case is that of a paternity suit, where the mother, faced with twins in court, could not be sure which twin had enjoyed that particular responsibility.

[32]There may be a provision requiring indelible identity marks, but otherwise the problem would remains.

There is another scheme, involving the payment of compensation established by the United Kingdom Offshore Operators' Association (UKOOA), in co-operation with fishing organisations, operating in the North Sea. Whenever a fishing boat in the area suffers damage to its fishing gear caused by seabed debris from offshore operations by the oil industry, claims can be made by the owner of the boat against the operator responsible. If the debris cannot be identified as coming from a particular offshore installation, a claim can be made against a fund established by UKOOA. The fund will voluntarily pay

(a) for damage to fishing gear, up to the whole of the loss suffered;
(b) for damage to the vessel, the whole of the uninsurable loss, i.e. that part of the loss the insurer requires the owner to bear himself;
(c) for loss of fishing time
     (i)   for a single boat £3,700,
     (ii) for a pair of boats fishing together £5,500.

5.3   Statutory schemes for compensation

5.3.1   There is a statutory scheme which operates under the United States Outer Continental Shelf Act.[33] The Act first establishes an Offshore Oil Pollution Compensation Fund,[34] raised by a levy on producers of oil from the outer continental shelf. It then provides that there can be claims for economic loss 'arising out of or directly resulting from pollution'. Such claims can be made against the owner or operator of a vessel, other than a public vessel, or of an offshore facility, where there is evidence that that vessel or facility is the source of the damage. The principle of strict liability applies.[35]

The fund itself may be liable, 'without limitation, for all losses for which a claim may be asserted under section 303 ...' to the extent that such losses are not otherwise compensated'.[36] It may thus be liable also when no vessel or facility can be designated as the source of the pollution.[37]

Once the fund has compensated the claimant, it is subrogated to his rights, and can therefore recover such compensation as the law permits against the owner or operator of any vessel or facility which may later be identified.

5.3.2   Japan also has established statutory compensation schemes, but there are differences in the way they operate from that of the United States. For example, the Pollution Related Damage to Health Compensation Law of 1973 established a compensation fund by means of levies on those discharging pollutants to air or water. A person whose health was damaged by such pollutants, who lived in an area designated under the scheme, could claim compensation from the fund.[38] By 1987, however, concentrations of air pollution had decreased as a result of stricter

---

[33]Public Law 95-372.
[34]*Ibid.*, S.302.
[35]*Ibid.*, S.303. Note the exceptions to, and limitations on, liability.
[36]*Ibid.*, 304(2)(f).
[37]*Ibid.*, S.307(b) and S.306(b) and (c).
[38]Pollution Related Damage to Health Compensation Law of 1973.

controls, therefore the application of the scheme to ill-health caused by air pollution was discontinued.[39]

6. ENVIRONMENTAL DAMAGE – WILLING AND COMPETENT PLAINTIFFS

6.1   Civil actions as effective deterrents

6.1.1   Civil actions, or the threat of such actions, can be an effective deterrent to a person contemplating the discharge of a pollutant into the common environment. An individual who has suffered damage, or can show that he is likely to suffer damage, may sue for an injunction to prohibit the discharge. As the penalty for breach of injunction is often imprisonment, that serves as a very effective deterrent. The threat of an action for compensation is much less of a deterrent, but can in some cases be effective.

6.1.2   The effect of civil actions on polluters is, however, uncertain and haphazard. It depends on there being a competent and willing plaintiff. No-one advocates reliance on civil actions as a form of control, but in many jurisdictions the authorities are concerned to ensure that members of the public are able to protect themselves, or are otherwise adequately protected. This section is concerned with how that can be done.

6.2   Want of a competent and willing plaintiff

6.2.1   Environmental damage can be done, causing damage to the interests of many people, with no person able or willing to take legal action to prevent it. The circumstances in which there is that want of an effective plaintiff are various.

6.2.2   There may be a minor nuisance such as a bad odour, or some other slight loss of amenity, either of which affects a wide range of members of the public, but with no one person so badly affected that he considers it worthwhile starting a legal action.

6.2.3   There may be pollution causing physical damage to property, but the person suffering most of the damage may have surrendered his rights to the polluter. This point has already been made and some examples given, in Chapter III at 7.2.3.

It is relevant to add that such surrender of rights by contractual agreement affect only the parties to the contract. Any other persons suffering damage are still free to sue. In practice, however, once the principal complainant has lost his rights, there are often left only persons suffering slight inconvenience or damage, none of whom would be prepared to take action on his own behalf. They may, of course, contribute to support a representative action taken by a few, under the procedure

---

[39]For details of the original proposal, relating to air, water and motor vehicles, see *Development of Environmental Legislation in Japan,* (Ministry of Foreign Affairs, Tokyo, 1973). pp. 95 to 99). For a brief outline of the scheme as enacted, see Schlickman *et al, International Law and Regulation,* (Butterworth, London,1991), p.Jpn-7.

outlined at 6.5.2, but unless there is an organisation representing their interests, that is unlikely to happen. A more likely course would be to persuade the Attorney General or the local authority to take action on their behalf – possibilities examined below at 6.4. As noted there, however, such actions are taken at the discretion of those authorities. The citizen cannot be regarded as having any rights in that respect. Once the principal complainant has thus been emasculated, in most cases the matter lies with the public authorities.

6.2.4   Where wild animals are affected by pollution, it may be impossible to find a person with a legal right to sue. Common law will protect a person's interest in things in his possession. There can be no possession without some degree of control. That control may be minimal – a golf club has been held to be in possession of golf balls lost on its course, even though the club was unaware of the presence of any particular balls, so long as it exercised some control over access to the course.[40]

On the other hand, there could be no possession of dolphins left free to swim when and where they liked, nor peregine falcons in the wild. Even fish in traditional fishing grounds are not reduced into possession until they are within the compass of some net, or otherwise controlled, although there could possibly be an action in negligence for loss or reduction in commercial catches.

It may be said that many states have provided an answer to this problem, by granting the control authority a power to require a polluter to restore the environment to its former condition, including its fauna and flora, as in the United Kingdom Water Resources Act 1991, Section 161. That environment, however, cannot always be fully restored, and there are no provisions for compensation or compensatory measures.

6.2.5   Legislation in Canada is in this respect worth noting. In the province of British Columbia, the Wildlife Act at Section 8 gives the Crown, in the name of the Lieutenant Governor, a right to claim compensation from any person who, without authority, destroys or damages wildlife habitat in an area set apart for the purpose of wildlife management, or public shooting grounds.

6.3   Legal measures to make remedies available

6.3.1   Legal aid for civil actions

There is always the possibility of establishing a legal aid fund, from which persons who have suffered damage to their interests may have all or part of their costs paid, to the extent that they could not afford to pay those costs themselves. It is usual for the poorer litigants to receive full reimbursement of costs, for others to make a contribution to the costs, and for the wealthy to be given no such aid.

There are, however, drawbacks to such a scheme. As noted in Chapter III at 7.2.2 in practice, a poor person can confidently commence an action with nothing to lose. Persons with moderate resources, however, may find that a substantial contribution will be required of them, which will mean a substantial loss if the action fails.

The second drawback is the high total demand made on public funds. In England and Wales, the costs of legal aid in civil cases for the year 1991 to 1992 were

---

[40]*Hibbert* v *McKiernan*, [1948] 2 QB 142, [1948] 1 All ER 860.

£513m gross, reduced to £330m by litigants contributions. In addition the cost of legal advice and assistance, as distinct from aid in litigation, was £99.7m, reduced to £66.1m by applicants contributions. Such costs would be beyond the resources of most less wealthy countries, especially if a large portion of the population was poor.

In the United States, the use of contingency fees overcomes this difficulty in part. A contingency fee is payable to a lawyer only in the event of his winning the case for his client. That offers considerable advantage to a complainant who would not otherwise risk the cost of an action. Such fees, however, can bring a disadvantage to the system of justice as a whole. An advocate often has a duty to the court which overrides his duty to his client. He has a duty not to knowingly mislead the court. If he stands to earn a substantial fee only in the event of winning the case, he may be tempted to ignore that rule. That can be done in various subtle ways. Contingency fees are not permitted in the United Kingdom and other jurisdictions.

6.3.2   Compensation orders

Another possible solution would be to allow any person who had suffered as a result of a pollution offence to ask the criminal court which has convicted the offender to make a compensation order. A brief explanation of such orders is given at 2.2. above. That provision would have the advantage of allowing the person who had suffered the loss or damage to make a simple application to the court, with no need for expensive legal representation, and no risk of having to pay costs. It is noteworthy that any decision to award compensation would be based on the environmental standard used in criminal proceedings for that kind of pollution.

The disadvantage which would probably be encountered is that, as noted at 2.2 above, the criminal courts would be unwilling to embark on the difficult task of assessing compensation in such cases as damage to health, and make awards only where the measure of loss is clear, as in cases of damage to property.

6.3.3   Right of action for breach of statutory duty

A reference has already been made to rights of action for breach of statutory duties, in another context at 2.2 above. It would not depend on some person taking criminal proceedings, but would leave the complainant to run a civil action in the courts. He would have the advantage, however, of not having to prove negligence or any other form of fault, and of being able to succeed on the civil standard of proof, i.e. on the balance of evidence.

Such right of action could be granted to apply to any pollution control statute. Logically, the right would be granted only to those persons for whose protection the offence was created, as explained at 2.2. It would therefore be prudent to give in the legislation some criteria by which it could be decided who would have a right of action.

The disadvantage is that in some cases, particularly where expert evidence is needed, the costs can be high.

6.4   Actions by public authorities on behalf of members of the public

6.4.1   Some countries make provision for an officer of government or a public authority to take action on behalf of the public.

6.4.2 For example, in the United Kingdom the Attorney General, acting on behalf of the Crown which is regarded as the *parens patrae*, may bring an action to restrain the commission or continuance of a public nuisance. The purpose of his taking such action was explained in the Court of Appeal in *A-G v P.Y.A. Quarries*,[41]

> A public nuisance is a nuisance which is so widespread in its range or so indiscriminate in its effects that it would not be reasonable to expect one person to take proceedings on his own responsibility to put a stop to it, but that is should be taken on the responsibility of the community at large.

The Attorney General may in such a case, on his own initiative or on application made by a member of the public commence legal proceedings. In the latter type of case, they are usually referred to as a 'relator actions'. The plaintiff is then 'the Attorney General at the relation of' the complainant. Nevertheless, although the complainant is not the plaintiff, he may ultimately have to bear any costs.

Neither the Attorney General nor the Crown having suffered any damage, however, the action taken can only be for an injunction. Nor can the Attorney General be compelled to take such proceedings – there is no right of appeal against his refusal to do so. He holds the power, however, independently as an officer of the Crown, not as a member of the Government, and is therefore expected to act independently of any party politics.

6.4.3 A similar but wider ranging power is given to English local authorities by Section 222 of the Local Government Act 1972.

> Where a local authority considers it expedient for the promotion or protection of the interests of the inhabitants of their area
>
> (a) they may prosecute or defend or appear in any legal proceedings and, in the case of civil proceedings, may institute them in their own name, and
> (b) they may, in their own name, make representations in the interests of the inhabitants at any public inquiry held by or on behalf of any Minister or public body under any enactment.

Again, the authority cannot be compelled to act.

6.4.4 It will be seen that those provisions give members of the public no rights. The power should not be used, nor its use withheld, for party political reasons, but considerations other than the merits of the case may be taken into account.

Some years ago in the north of England, a factory was emitting polluting gases, which affected the occupants of nearby domestic houses. The Alkali Inspector said that he could do nothing, as the factory was using the best practicable means, yet environmental damage was being done. The factory manager said that 'The housewives were hammering on the factory doors, and if I had been one of them I would have been throwing bricks through the windows'.[42] For ten successive years the annual reports of the chief public health inspector for the authority referred to public nuisances from the factory. The local authority could have started public nuisance proceeding under the provision outlined above, but did not do so. No

---

[41][1957] 2 QB 169 at 191.

[42]Personal communication from the management, under a promise that no publication of the facts will identify the firm.

reason was given for not doing so, but it was known that if the factory had been closed a large proportion of the workforce in the authority's area would have been put out of work at least temporarily. That must be accepted as a valid consideration, but it is submitted that it would have been better for an independent authority to have made the decision after a hearing, or an inspector to have held a public enquiry and published his report before the authority made its decision. (For comments on this case in another context see Chapter IV at 2.3.2.)

6.5   Standing to sue

6.5.1   The general rule in most jurisdictions is that only a person with a legal right which the law will protect can sue for a breach of that right. He is said to have *locus standi* or 'standing to sue'.

6.5.2   *Representative actions and class actions*

In the United Kingdom, representative actions are permitted by

.... a plaintiff suing on behalf of himself and all the members of a class, each member of which, including the plaintiff, is alleged to have a separate cause of cation in tort ...

provided that

.... all members of the class represented shared an interest which was common to them all.[43]

Similarly in the United States a 'class action' may be brought. The words of the provision give a sufficient explanation.

One or more members of a class may sue or be sued as representative parties on behalf of all only if
(1)   the class is so numerous that joinder of all members is impracticable,
(2)   there are questions of law or fact common to the class,
(3)   the claims or defenses of the representative parties are typical of the claims or defenses of the class, and
(4)   the representative parties will fairly and adequately protect the interests of the class.[44]

It is clear that in both those types of action, no person can be represented by another unless he himself has standing to sue on his own behalf. They do not extend the scope of standing to sue – they are merely rules of convenience.

6.5.3   *Citizen suits*

In the United States an extension of the rights of individuals has been granted by provision for citizen suits. The usefulness of the provision must be assessed, however, in the context of a legal system in which private prosecutions are not permitted.

Again, the words of the provision give a sufficient explanation.

---

[43]Rules of Supreme Court 15/12/4.
[44]Federal Code, Rules of Civil Procedure, Rule 23.

Except as provided in subsection (b) of this section, any person may commence a civil action on his own behalf –

(1) against any person (including (i) the United States, and (ii) any other governmental instrumentality or agency to the extent permitted by the Eleventh Amendment to the Constitution) who is alleged to be in violation of (a) an emission standard or limitation under this chapter (Air Pollution Prevention) or (b) an order issued by the Administrator or a State with respect to such a standard or limitation.

(2) against the Administrator where there is alleged a failure of the Administrator to perform any act or duty under this chapter which is not discretionary with the Administrator, or

(3) against any person who proposes to construct or constructs any new or modified major emitting facility without a permit required under part C of subchapter 1 of this chapter (relating to significant deterioration of air quality) or who is alleged to be in violation of any condition of such permit.

Subsection (b) provides that no action shall be taken until 60 days after the plaintiff has given notice of the violation to the Administrator, to the relevant state, or to the violator. Neither shall an action be taken if the Administrator or the relevant state has commenced and is diligently prosecuting a civil action to require compliance with the standard, limitation or order.

6.6 Proposed rights of action by conservation associations

6.6.1 In addition to or alternative to those means, the right to bring civil actions could be extended to cover wealthy conservation associations, which could then bring actions in the interests of the general public to quash decisions of the authorities, or for the grant of injuctions of against private companies restraining them from undertaking damaging developments.

The rule generally applied at present is that the only persons who can sue at civil law are those who have suffered, or can show that they would suffer, an infringement of a right that the law will protect, and in many cases who have also thereby suffered loss or damage. Conservation associations will not normally themselves have such rights, and rarely will they be able to show loss or damage to the association's property or interests.

6.6.2 As noted above, it may not be worthwhile for any individual to commence an action, the Attorney General may refuse to take a relator action, and the local authority for reasons of its own may be unwilling to act.

It is claimed that in those circumstances a conservation association with an interest in such matters could give a useful service to the public by bringing an action in its own name. For that purpose it would have to have the necessary standing to sue.

6.6.3 If the proceedings are for a normal civil action, such as for negligence, trespass or nuisance at common law, or for the protection of a substantive civil right under a civil code, it is submitted that it is unnecessary to give an environmental association standing to sue – the association can support with both money and expertise an action taken by an individual. The proceedings are then properly confined to consideration of the wrong suffered or anticipated.

6.6.4   The action, however, may be to quash or vary a decision to undertake, or to permit, a particular development. The permit may be in the form of a land use planning permission, a licence under environmental impact legislation or laws relating to hazardous installations, or simply a discharge consent. It may be on the grounds of procedural irregularity, excess of jurisdiction or abuse of power. Where the law permits, it may simply be on the merits of the decision.

6.6.5   Where the action is taken on grounds such as procedural irregularity, excess of jurisdiction or abuse of power, standing may be limited to those who have suffered an infringement of a legal right. An example may be taken from German administrative law.

> Furthermore, the constitutional complaint provided for under federal law and serving to protect the citizen against any violation by the state of the basic right laid in the Basic Law is admissible only if the plaintiff asserts that his rights have been infringed..... Actions before the administrative court are designed to protect individual rights, that is, to safeguard the citizen against any infringement of his rights by a public agency'.[45]

That was given as the prevailing view, but the passage continued by casting some doubt on it.

> But traditionally the administrative process both afforded protection to individual rights and served as a means of control of official action. This dual function is still manifest in the procedural principles contained in the VwGO (especially the principle whereby the court must ascertain all relevant facts of the case, Section 86 VwGO), so that it seems doubtful whether the prevailing view is correct.[46]

6.6.6   In a case in the Luneberg Higher Administration Court in 1969,[47] however, it was said that

> The purpose of Section 47 VwGO is to exclude citizen suits, that is, not only to deter frivolous suits but also to acticipate in a single proceeding a variety of possible subsequent actions for annulment. The purpose of all these provisions is to restrict standing to cases where injury to an individual is involved and thus exclude a 'Popularklage', i.e. the possibility of proceedings being introduced by a party not directly affected.

Whether or not a conservation society will have standing to sue in an action on administrative grounds will thus depend on the purpose of the legislature in giving that right of action. In environmental matters, because of the widespread public concern, and the fact that many people may be affected by the administrative decision in question, there may be some justifiction in granting standing to any person who would suffer a disadvantage from the decision, even though no legal right had been infringed. That would, however, create the problem of distinguishing between environmental and non-environmental cases, and no such clear distinction can be made. A simpler answer would be to allow standing to any person who would be significantly affected by the decision.

---

[45]Eckard Rehbinder, *German Law on Standing to Sue,* (IUCN, 1972), p.13.
[46]Ibid., p.9. See also Sellmann, 'Der Weg zur neuzeitlichen Verwaltungsgerichtsbarkeit', in *Staatsburger und Staatsgewalt* Vol.1 (1963), p.37 *et seq.*
[47]NJW 1970, p.773.

6.6.7 Where, on the other hand, the action is based simply on the merits of the decision, it is submitted that it would be inappropriate to permit an action which would transfer the power of decision to a body other than the governmental agency the decision for which it was responsible in the first place.

An examination of the merits of a decision in the field of environmental law most often involves a balancing of interests, e.g. the production of material wealth against the protection of the natural environment. That will entail in the first place an evaluation of those interests, although such an evaluation itself does not necessarily point to a decision. It may show widespread minor benefits to many, but serious detriment to a few. It may be impossible to evaluate the detriment, where it is, for example, the shortening of human life.[48] It may envolve factors to which many different members of the public, with their many different interests, give different weight. Because of the complexity, and the imponderable nature of some of the detriments, the problem cannot be resolved simply by economic calculations. It may be resolved by a policy decision reached through accepted constitutional processes, such as a fact finding hearing followed by a policy decision.

6.6.8 In practice, such decisions are so closely connected with government policy that they are often regarded as a function of government.

> Traditional democratic theory teaches that government is the appropriate authority to made such value judgements as may be necessary of desirable concerning public needs and public good.

To that was added, however, that

> Environmental law suits, on the other hand, are typically initiated against government agencies by environment protection organisations.[49]

Nevertheless, it seems inappropriate to leave the final decision on the merits of the case to a court of law or other tribunal, except one specially constituted for that purpose. An example of the latter can be seen in Mauritius, where an Environment Apppeal Tribunal has been established which, *inter alia*, makes decisions on the grant of environmental assessment licences.[50]

6.6.9 The use of such a tribunal apart, the more usual, and it is submitted, the more acceptable method is to have the decision made by a government agency, but to lay down procedures to ensure that all interests are properly taken into account, that any policy decisions are made in the light of published findings of fact, and that the proceedings of the agency are subject to judicial review.

6.6.10 It is submitted that to be given an environmental association standing to sue in an action on the merits of the decision, where the association has suffered no damage, is both wrong and unnecessary. It is wrong because a third party intervening, as the environmental association would be, would tend to pursue its own aims, which would not necessarily correspond precisely to those of the

---

[48]See, e.g., Chapter I at the second paragraph in 4.1.5(b), and the example given in Chapter II at 7.2 in the penultimate paragraph.

[49]David D. Gregory, *Standing to Sue in Environmental Legislation in the United States of America* (IUCN, 1972), p.13.

[50]Environment Protection Act 1991, S.45 *et seq.*

aggrieved persons. It is unnecessary because its expertise and financial resources could be put to the service of any person with standing, or any party at the hearing.

6.6.11 Different considerations apply to public enquires. Rules governing enquiries under different laws and for different purposes themselves differ on who can appear. The purpose usually, however, is to permit interested members of the public to express their views in defence of their interests. There is no reason why, at such an enquiry, a conservation association should not be permitted to appear in its own name. An outstanding example of the latter is the appearance at the Windscale Inquiry[51] of the Friends of the Earth, who contributed resources of expertise and money, helping considerably towards a full and well informed enquiry.

7. LIMITATIONS ON LIABILITY

7.1 The term 'limitations on liability' is used to mean monetary limits which may be applied to any specified kind of liability arising from a specified cause, for example,

> Where as a result of any occurrence, any oil is discharged or escapes from a ship to which this section applied, then (except as otherwise provided by this Act) the owner of the ship shall be liable
> (a) for any damage caused outside the ship in the area of the United Kingdom by contamination resulting from the discharge or escape; and
> (b) the cost of any measures reasonably taken after the discharge or escape for the purpose of preventing or minimising any damage so caused in the area of the United Kingdom by contamination resulting from the discharge or escape; and
> (c) for any damage so caused in the area of the United Kingdom by any measures so taken.[52]

7.2 Normal liability from civil actions

7.2.1 When a person establishes his right to damages in a civil suit, he is entitled to payment, in full, of compensation to cover the measure of his loss. That measure will include items precisely calculated to cover loss of or damage to property of known commercial value; and will include also estimates by the court of sums to compensate for pain and suffering, loss of faculty such as eyesight, and estimates to cover losses such as the shortening of his life, and the consequent losses to his family which have been suffered, in accordance with the applicable law. The compensation may take the form not only of providing replacement for what has been lost, but of providing alternatives, such as 'talking books' for a man who has been blinded, or alternative pleasures for a man whose injuries prevent him from engaging in his former recreational pursuits. Nevertheless, it goes no further than that – where compensation for the plaintiff stops, punishment of the defendant begins.

---

[51]*The Windscale Inquiry* (HMSO, United Kingdom, 1978).
[52]UK Merchant Shipping (Oil Pollution Act 1988, s.34 and Sched. 4 Pt I para. 1. The limitations are set out in para. 4.

All the defendant's property within the jurisdiction of the court can be made available for payment of the award, subject to such restraints on that process as the law may impose. Some courts have the power to order payment by instalments, and that will entail payments from future earnings. If the defendant is insured against such liability, he can demand payment from his insurer to the extent of his cover, and in some jurisdictions the insurer can be made directly liable to the plaintiff. All moneys from such sources must be applied until the liability has been met in full.

7.2.2   Where the court finds in favour of the plaintiff, it is in effect saying that the defendant must stand the whole of that loss. The effect of any statutory limitation of liability is to impose on the plaintiff himself the burden of any loss he has suffered over and above a certain sum. The limitation does not eliminate the loss, it leaves it as a burden for the plaintiff to suffer. That is an act of arbitrary legislative power which contradicts the accepted principles of justice, and which it is difficult to justify. It is even more difficult to justify where the defendant retains assets of considerable value, e.g. a ship or an oil well, irrespective of the plight of the plaintiff.

7.3   Provisions for the limitation of liability for pollution damage

7.3.1   The earliest limitations imposed in English law, which did not necessarily concern pollution damage, appeared to be for the encouragement of commercial and industrial enterprise by the protection of entrepreneurs and investors.

The first was the Merchant Shipping Act 1854, Part IX DIII to DVI, which absolved the owner of a merchant ship which, without his fault or privity, caused damage to certain classes of goods, and in other cases, again without his fault or privity, limits his liability to the value of his ship and freight due.

As early as 1856, the Joint Stock Companies Act[53] introduced the now well known practice of limiting the liability of investors in 'limited companies' to the nominal value of their investments.[54]

7.3.2   Today, there are statutory provisions in many countries limiting the liability of defendants for pollution damage, which have been passed in the implementation of the terms of international conventions.

The International Convention on Civil Liability for Oil Pollution Damage 1969, as amended by the Protocol of 1976, provides an agreement on civil liability for oil pollution damage in the territory, including the territorial sea, of a contracting state caused by the escape or discharge of oil from a ship. Article V provides that

> The owner of a ship shall be entitled to limit his liability under the Convention in respect of any one incident to the aggregate amount of 133 units of account for each ton of the ship's tonnage. However, the aggregate amount shall not in any event exceed 14 million units of account.

---

[53] 19 & 20 Vict. Ch 47 s.LXI.
[54] Legally, this is not a limitation on the liability of the defendant, for the company is a person separate from the investors. The effect, however, is similar.

The unit of account is the Special Drawing Right defined by the International Monetary Fund.[55]

The limitation does not apply where the incident occurred as a result of the actual fault or privity of the owner.

There is also the International Convention on the Establishment of an International Fund for Compensation for Oil Pollution Damage, Brussels 1971, under which further compensation is paid from the fund if the damage suffered exceeds in value the liability of the shipowner as limited by the former Convention. The fund itself, however, is protected by an arbitrary limitation on the compensation it may be required to pay, to the effect that the total to be paid under the two conventions shall not exceed 60 million Special Drawing Rights.

The Convention on Civil Liability for Nuclear Damage (Vienna 1963). Article 3 provides that

(a) Under the conditions established under this Convention, the Contracting Parties undertake that compensation in respect of the damage referred to in Article 2 shall be provided up to the amount of 120 million units of account[56] per incident.

(b) Such compensation shall be provided:
   (i) up to an amount of at least 5 million units of account, out of funds provided by insurance for other financial security, such amount to be established by the legislation of the Contracting Party in whose territory the nuclear installation of the operator liable is situated;
   (ii) between this amount and 70 million units of account, out of public funds to be made available by the Contracting Party in whose territory the nuclear installation of the operator is situated;
   (iii) between 70 and 120 million units of account, out of public funds to be made available by the Contracting Parties according to the formula for contributions specified in Article 12.

A Convention on Civil Liability for Oil Pollution Damage Resulting from Exploration for and Exploitation of Seabed Mineral Resources, London 1976, was prepared by representatives of nine states surrounding the North Sea area. The United Kingdom was strongly in favour of limited liability for the operators; Norway was strongly opposed. An attempt was made to accommodate both parties by the inclusion of the following provisions.

The operator shall be entitled to limit his liability under this Convention for each installation and each incident to the amount of 30 million Special Drawing Rights until five years have elapsed from the date on which the Convention is opened for signature and to the amount of 40 million Special Drawing Rights thereafter.

That, however, was qualified by the agreement in Article 15 that

This Convention shall not prevent a State from providing for unlimited liability or a higher limit of liability than that currently applicable under Article 6 for pollution damage caused by installations for which it is the Controlling State and suffered in that State or another State Party; provided however that in doing so it shall not discriminate on the basis of nationality. Such provision may be based on the principle of reciprocity.

[55]Special drawing rights are monetary units of the International Monetary Fund. See Chapter I, footnote 26. On 30 Jan. 1992 1 SDR equalled US$1.39921

[56]A unit of account is similar in character to a special drawing right. See also the Joint Protocol relating to the Application of the Vienna Convention and the Paris Convention, (Vienna 1988).

The draft was agreed and published. The United Kingdom and Norway each waited for the other to ratify. All the other prospective parties also waited. Not surprisingly, in the event none ratified, and the treaty never came into operation

7.3.3 It is clear that the offshore oil industry has consistently sought to have the liability of its members limited. In addition to campaigning for limited liability in the conventions, the industry has instituted three schemes of voluntary payments for pollution damage, In two of those schemes, TOVALOP and OPOL, it offers payments which are voluntary but subject to limitation, and which it seeks to establish as a full settlement of the claim. They are fair offers, but offers which any person with a large claim must be wary of accepting.

In the third scheme, CRISTAL, because of the complexity of the agreement, more complex precautions are taken. (See Contract Regarding an Interim Supplement to Tanker Liability for Oil Pollution, Clause IV(D), (7), (8) and (9).

The first of the schemes to be established was TOVALOP (Tanker Owners Voluntary Agreement concerning Liability for Oil Pollution). Under that scheme, there is both a 'Standing Agreement' and 'Tovalop Supplement'.

The standing agreement applies only where the International Convention on Civil Liability for Oil Pollution Damage does not apply. It thus offers a voluntary payment where there would be no liability under that Convention. The payment is subject to a maximum of US$160 per ton of the tanker's tonnage, or an overall US$16.8m, whichever is the less.

The Tovalop Supplement applies when the vessel is carrying oil owned by a party to the CRISTAL agreement (see below). It comes into effect when a legitimate claim for compensation exceeds what is available under the Civil Liability Convention and the International Fund Convention. Payments under the Supplement, however, are limited to the following

Where the tanker is of 0 to 5,000 tons	US$3.5m
Where the tanker is of over 5,000 tons	US$3.5m, plus US$493 for each ton in excess of 5,000 but subject to an overall maximum of US$70m.

Under both the Standing Agreement and the Supplement, however, by reason of Clauses VIII(D) of the former, and 5(A) of the latter, payments are made subject to the following

Unless otherwise agreed in writing, any payment to a Person by or on behalf of a Participating Owner shall be in full settlement of all said Person's claims against the Participating Owner, the tanker involved, its master, officers and crew, its charterer(s), manager or operator and their respective officers, agents, employees and affiliates and underwriters, which arise out of the incident.

The major oil companies back that offer with a further supplementary scheme called CRISTAL (Contract Regarding an Interim Supplement to Tanker Liability for Oil Pollution). Its provisions are complex, but the effect is to give further compensation to the following maxima.

Where a tanker is of 0 to 5,000 tons	US$36m
Where the tanker is of over 5,000 tons	US$36m, plus US$733 for each ton in excess of 5,000 tons, but subject to an overall maximum of US$135m.

It will be noted that in both the TOVALOP and CRISTAL schemes, the limitation of liability is linked to the tonnage of the vessel – not to the ability to pay for the damage done. It is submitted that such a criterion for limitation is both irrelevant and unwarranted.

Finally, there is a scheme of voluntary compensation for oil pollution damage from offshore operations. That is OPOL (Offshore Pollution Liability Agreement). Again, there is a fixed limit to the sums offered, this time amounting to an overall maximum for remedial measures and pollution damage of US$100m. Clause VII of the Agreement provides that

> Any payment hereunder to a Claimant by or on behalf or a Party hereto shall be in full settlement of all the said Claimant's Claims against the said Party and against any other Persons associated with the said Party ...... and shall be conditioned upon a Claimant's executing necessary releases and other documents and taking such other action as is reasonable under the circumstances.

7.3.4 Such voluntary schemes serve useful purposes in providing a means of obtaining compensation which avoid lengthy and costly legal proceedings, and the parties cannot be fairly criticised for limiting their voluntary payments. It is clear, however, that for any future international agreements and national legislation they will continue to press for limitation of liability. The subject of limitation therefore merits some consideration.

7.4   Basis of claims for limitation of liability

7.4.1 The earliest instances of statutory limitation of liability, at least in England, granted in favour of shipowners and investors in registered companies, appeared to be given to remove discouragement to enterprise. The modern examples seem to cover those activities in which very high awards of compensation may be given. The awards may be so high that they cannot be covered by commercial insurance policies.

The reasons for claims limitation, and the circumstances in which they can arise, vary from one kind of enterprise to another. As the remaining contenders for limitation in the field of pollution control are the offshore operators of the oil industry, examination of the justification for limitation will be concentrated on them.

7.4.2 The reasons given to justify an arbitrary monetary limitation of an operator's liability are set out briefly in italics below, followed in each case by comments on those reasons.

(a) *The operator may have insufficient means to cover the full measure of damages which might otherwise be awarded.*

This applies to many individuals who, in their ordinary work or the ordinary incidents of their lives, may incur liability. An engineer in charge of a chemical engineering plant could cause a Bohpal type disaster. A man on a pedal cycle could cause a horrendous road accident. In those cases, the court expects the defendant to pay such compensation as he can, to the limit of his resources. A defendant company may be forced into liquidation, or a person into bankruptcy, as a result – the law gives them no protection. Limitation of liability could have the reverse effect – it could lead to the bankruptcy of the plaintiff.

The precaution normally taken against the contingency of the defendant being unable to pay the compensation awarded is compulsory insurance. Provisions requiring compulsory insurance have been included in all the conventions on civil liability referred to in 7.3.2. Those provisions require compulsory insurance to the extent of the statutory limit to liability.

(b) *The operator may find it impossible to obtain insurance cover for unlimited liability.*

In earlier days of offshore operations, it was not possible to obtain full cover for pollution damage. Operators put a considerable load on the insurance market; the cover for one offshore platform alone could be US$ 500M. Insurers were unwilling to give, in addition to that, unlimited cover for pollution damage, partly because it was doubtful if the market could take the additional load, and partly because there was little experience to refer to in that field, so that the risk could not be adequately quantified.[57]

It is probably possible to obtain such cover now, provided the operator is willing the pay the premium demanded.[58] The major operators now have also a mutual insurance scheme provided by an organisation of theirs called Oil International Ltd, (OIL).

Even if full insurance cover is not available, the ordinary principles of justice require that the operator himself stands the loss. An operating company is usually one formed separately from the oil companies, and is therefore a separate person. Oil companies, however, are often the major shareholders. As such, they are protected by another form of limited liability – the limitation of a shareholder's liability to the nominal value of his shareholding.[59] The oil companies, who share the benefits of the limitation, are very wealthy organisations; and the operating company, except in the most extreme cases, still has very valuable assets in its operating licence and its well.

(c) *Facing the uncertainty of liability without limitation, the operator would be unable to make reliable financial estimates on which to base his decisions and future plans.*

Given the possibilities of insurance cover referred to in (b) above, this problem disappears.

Even where the uncertainty still exists, this is merely one of the many uncertainties which face nearly all business enterprises. Of course, it is good business practice to reduce those uncertainties, and that can be done by passing them on to other persons. Where, however, that other person is an innocent bystander, who takes no part in the enterprise, has nothing to gain from it, but merely stands in fear and trepidation unable to protect himself adequately, it

---

[57]Personal communication leading Lloyd's underwriter in that field.

[58]More recent communication with Lloyd's.

[59]The fact that the shareholder is a different person from the company can in some cases be disregarded. See the English cases *Gilford Motor Company* v *Horne* [1933] Ch 935, *Jones* v *Lipman* [1962] 1 All ER 442. See also the US case *United States* v *Milwaukee Refrigerator Transport Company* 142 Fed 247 (1905) at 255, where the judge said, '... A corporation will be looked upon as a legal entity as a rule ... but where the notion of legal entity is used to defeat public convenience, justify wrong, protect fraud, or defend crime, the law will regard the corporation as an association of persons'.

seems inequitable that the risk of loss should be passed to him. If he does stand to gain marginally, together with most other members of the community as a consumer of oil, at least the loss should be shared proportionately between them.

It has been suggested that those whose persons, property and interests are put at risk should take out insurance. It is doubtful if they could give the insurers the information necessary for an adequate calculation of the degree of risk – essential for any insurer. In any event, that would simply be another way of passing the cost of bearing the risk on to another person.

Limitation of liability does pass the risk from the operator to those who may suffer damage as a result of events to which the limitation applies. This is the converse of the concept of risk liability, discussed at 4.3. Moreover, liability imposed on the operator allows the polluter pays principle to apply. The operator pays the cost of either insurance or direct compensation, then passes that expense back to his customers as part of the costs of the enterprise. The ultimate consumer thus pays, which is in accordance with the associated principle that the persons who take the benefits of an exercise should bear the burdens.

(d) *Operators would be discouraged from embarking on such an enterprise where the liability for pollution damage was not subject to a statutory limitation. To that extent, the exploitation of a country's oil resources would be retarded.*

The extent to which this statement is correct is difficult to assess. Certainly there are countries which have rejected this claim. Norway, a producing country itself, stood out against the limitation of liability when the draft for the London convention 1976 was under discussion, and the failure of the convention to gain ratification was at least in part due to Norway's insistence on retaining a right to impose unlimited liability. Spain has also rejected the idea.[60] Much will, of course, depend on the state of the market in oil, and the degree of risk anticipated in that particular area.

This claim does, however, raise a further consideration. The state may consider that it is more likely to attract development by offering limitation of liability, and that the community will benefit from that development. Applying the principle that he who accepts the benefit must accept the burden, there appears to be in those circumstances an obligation on the community to compensate for any losses suffered by individuals, and not otherwise compensated as a result of the limitation. The community would then pay through to usual organs of state.

There is a precedent for that in the Convention on Civil Liability in the Field of Nuclear Energy, Brussels 1963, At Article 3,[61] it provides that compensation up to five million units of account shall be paid, and that a further amount up to 70 million units of account shall be provided from public funds in so far as loss is suffered but not otherwise compensated.

In principle, there appears in such circumstances to be a moral obligation on the state to cover all the remaining uncompensated loss.

---

[60]In a meeting where this claim in favour of limitation was voiced, a representative of the Spanish Government said that they insisted on unlimited liability without it being a deterrent at least to exploration of their continental shelf. Author's personal recollection.

[61]See 7.3.2.

7.4.3 Any agreements on limitation of liability are likely to be parts of regional agreements. The general pattern of regional agreements is explained in Chapter VIII, but a few observations will be relevant here.

The protection of the marine environment takes many forms, and provides safeguards against many kinds of risks. The sources, the degree of risks and the vulnerability of various parts of the environment vary from region to region, with some homogeneity within a region; and the states of a region usually have a mutual interest in protection. It is therefore usually more easy to reach a regional agreement than one of geographically wider application.[62] The United Nations Environment Programme is aware of that, and has established its Regional Seas Programme under which several regional agreements have already been reached.

7.4.4 It can be said, for the reasons given above, that there is no justification in jurisprudence for a statutory limitation of liability for pollution damage, at least in the circumstances encountered to date. There may, however, be a sound practical reason for accepting it.

One of the problems for states within close proximity to each other arises from trans-frontier pollution. There may be a plaintiff in one state receiving the pollution, and a defendant operator in another state within whose jurisdiction that pollution arose. If the matter goes to litigation, much depends on the national laws of those states, and any international agreements between them. Normally, the plaintiff can sue in the courts of his own country, but can enforce judgment only to the extent that the defendant has property within the jurisdiction of that state. That difficulty is often overcome, however, by conventions on reciprocal enforcement of judgments. Under such a convention, one state agrees to enforce against defendants within its own territory, judgments granted in the courts of another state – on a reciprocal basis with other state parties to the convention. Within any region, such conventions can be of considerable importance to persons suffering trans-frontier pollution, for without them, they may be unable to recover any compensation for their losses.

7.4.5 There is one convention which goes further. That is the Convention on the Protection of the Environment between Denmark, Finland, Norway and Sweden, (Stockholm 1974). Article 3 provides that

> Any person who is affected or may be affected by a nuisance caused by environmentally harmful activities in another Contracting State shall have the right to bring before the appropriate Court or Administrative Authority of that State the question of the permissibility of such activities, including the question of measures to prevent damage, and to appeal against the decision of the Court or Administrative Authority to the same extent and on the same terms as a legal entity of the State in which the activities are being carried out.

> The provisions of the first paragraph of this Article shall be equally applicable in the case of proceedings concerning compensation for damage caused by environmentally harmful activities. The question of compensation shall not be judged by rules which are

[62]The willingness to reach such an agreement is illustrated by the fact that a Protocol concerning Marine Pollution from Exploration and Exploitation of the Continental Shelf, made under the Kuwait Regional Convention 1978, was being prepared, representatives of both Iraq and Iran attended the meetings, even though those states at the time were at war with each other. Author's personal recollection.

less favourable to the injured party than the rules of compensation of the State in which the activities are being carried out.

Such a convention would present some difficulties, however, if the states of the region had different legal traditions, and markedly different rules of law and procedure.

7.4.6   It is quite probable that a state will not enter into any reciprocal agreement if it is to be called upon to enforce full compensation against its own nationals in favour of plaintiffs from other state parties, whereas its own nationals when plaintiffs themselves, can obtain only limited compensation when relying on the agreement. It follows that if any state within a region demands limitation of liability, there will be no mutual enforcement of judgments except on that basis. Some states may therefore accept limited liability simply because half a loaf is better than no bread at all.

Chapter VI

Rights of Individuals

1. NATURE AND SOURCES OF INDIVIDUAL RIGHTS

1.1 Nature of individual rights

1.1.1 The term 'individual rights' is used here to mean substantive rights embodied in the civil law, and enforced by rights of action in the courts. Such actions are brought by individuals to protect their persons, their property and in some cases their economic interests. Any limitations on such rights of action are limitations on the substantive rights themselves – as the Romans of ancient times put it, 'there can be no right without a remedy'.

1.1.2 The normal rule is that only the person who has suffered the damage can bring an action.[1] There are exceptions to that rule, where public authorities are empowered to sue on behalf of the general public, and even where individual citizens can intervene. Those exceptions, and the possible role of conservation associations are discussed in Chapter V at 6.5.

1.2 Sources of individual rights

1.2.1 As noted in Chapter V, many of the rights to sue for pollution damage are provided by the general body of civil law.[2] That was understandable, for it would be wrong to have standards and procedures for pollution damage different from those for other forms of damage. Moreover, it would be too artificial to separate out pollution damage, because many causes of action at common law, and many articles in civil codes, deal with damage which may be classed as polluting concurrently with other kinds of damage, e.g. actions for public or private nuisance.

In a few cases, there are laws giving civil rights which deal specifically with certain sources of pollution damage. The most notable are those passed in accordance with the terms of international treaties, such as those dealing with spillages from tankers, and others concerning releases of radioactive substances. They have

---

[1]Sometimes referred to as *locus standi* or 'standing to sue'.
[2]See Chapter V at 1.1.

been passed to either to protect areas outside national jurisdictions, the 'global commons', or to give special protection from grave dangers against which the individual cannot take adequate precautions. In such cases, rights of individual legal action and compensation are usually granted.

1.2.2 What the legislature can give, however, it can also take away. Any law created by the normal legislative process can be repealed by the same process. To that extent, rights created by such laws cannot be considered as 'guaranteed'. After an election, a legislative assembly of a different political complexion may modify or even take away those rights.

Such modification or loss may even be suffered in the course of normal legislative changes, and may even occur unnoticed. For example, the United Kingdom Parliament passed a Rights of Entry (Gas and Electricity Boards) Act 1954, which specified and restricted the rights of all officers of those public authorities to enter a person's house without his consent. At least one later statute, however, the Gas Act 1986 Schedule 5 at paragraphs 15 to 17, has granted new and more extensive rights of entry, and those earlier restrictions, not being in a written constitution, are thus overridden. Eventually, privatisation extended the rights of entry from public authorities to privately owned registered companies. Those companies could be owned by foreign nationals, who thereby gained rights of entry.

A well drafted statute, supported by sympathetic judicial interpretaton, could reduce the danger of incidental change or erosion of rights, but could not in any sense guarantee the right given

1.2.3 The only way that an adequate safeguard against change can be given is by incorporating the provision into a written constitution which is itself protected in that it can be changed only by a special procedure. In the United States, for example, the constitution can be amended only by the following process.

> The Congress, whenever two thirds of both Houses deem it necessary, shall propose amendments to this Constitution, or, on the application of the legislatures of two thirds of the several States, shall call a convention for proposing amendments, which in either case shall be valid to all intents and purposes as part of this Constitution when ratified by the legislatures of three-fourths of the several States, or by conventions in three-fourths thereof, as the one or the other mode of ratification may be proposed by the Congress; provided that . . . no State, without its consent, shall be deprived of its equal suffrage in the Senate.

By way of contrast, in England, which is notorious for having no written constitution and therefore no constitutional safeguards,[3] such rights can be altered or even abolished by any ordinary Act of Parliament. As noted in Chapter I at 4.4.5., the Civil Aviation Act 1949 Sections 40 and 41 severely limited an individual's right to bring an action in trespass or nuisance from aircraft.

It has been reported that some 30 countries now have provisions in their constitutions concerning the duties of the state or rights of individuals relating to environmental matters.[4]

---

[3]There are some special procedures, e.g. for bills of constitutional importance, and private members bills, but none which give the act when passed any overriding legal force, or make it less easy to repeal than others.

[4]See *Understanding U.S. and European Environmental Law,* (ed. T.T. Smith and P. Kromerak, (Graham & Trotman, London, 1989). The statement is by Alexandre Kiss at p.151.

Provisions in written constitutions can be of two kinds. They can be statements of principles expressed in general terms, such as those of the Greek constitution of 1975, of which Article 24 provides that

> The protection of the natural and cultural environment constitutes a duty of the State. The State is bound to adopt special preventive and repressive measures for the preservation of the environment. Matters pertaining to the protection of forests and forest expanses in general shall be regulated by the law. Alteration of the use of State forests and State forest expanses is prohibited, except where agricultural development or other uses imposed for the public interest prevail for the national economy.

Such provisions are more likely to be found in modern constitutions. Even in older constitutions, however, provisions have been interpreted as giving protection against environmental pollution. Article 40.3.2 of the Irish constitution provides that

> . . . the State shall, in particular, by its laws, protect as best it can from unjust attack and, in the case of injustice done, vidicate the life, person, good name and property rights of every citizen.

In *Ryan* v *Attorney General*[5] it was held that the Article was not exhaustive in its list of human rights, and that by implication the citizen enjoys the right of bodily integrity, and that no process which is or may, as a matter of probability, be dangerous or harmful to the life or health of citizens or of any of them may be imposed on them by an Act of the Oireachtas, the Irish parliament. That imposes a limit on the powers of the legislature, a limit which could apply to environmental matters as well as others.

In *The State (C.)* v *Frawley*[6] that principle was extended to any acts of the executive which 'without justification would expose the health of a person to risk or danger'. That could include acts leading to pollution.

1.2.4 There are advantages to be gained in having the former type of provision. It will have the guaranteed status, noted in 1.2.3. above, which not only protects it from repeal by ordinary statute, but makes it override any provisions in such statutes which are in conflict with it. It will also be a guide to the courts in the interpretation of legislation – quite apart from questions of validity, in cases of doubt the courts will tend to prefer an interpretation which accords with the constitution. It becomes a principle of enhanced importance to which the courts will always have regard.

In addition, the enunciation of the principle in the constitution can set the direction of the mainstream of political thought involving environmental matters.

The danger is that the principle may conflict with other accepted rights, and unduly inhibit, for example, industrial development. The legislature and the courts may lose their powers to balance environmental against other legitimate considerations, and thus lose their powers to reach equitable conclusions.

[5] [1965] I.R. 344. The case was a challenge to the constitutional validity of a statute on the addition of fluorine to supplies of drinking water, which was unsuccessful because the court did not accept that there would be any harmful effect. Had it been persuaded otherwise, there is little doubt that the provision would have been declared unconstitutional.

[6] [1976] I.R. 365.

1.2.5 The latter type, which sets out particular rights of individuals, has the advantage of the rights being guaranteed. Such provisions have the added advantage of being specific about the rights that individuals have.

The danger of creating conflicts with other accepted rights, however, is even greater here. An outstanding example is the grant of rights in the constitution of Cyprus. Article 23 provides that

1. Every person, alone or jointly with others, has a right to acquire, own, possess, enjoy or dispose of any movable or immovable property and has the right of respect for such right.
   The right of the Republic to underground water, minerals and antiquities is reserved.'
2. No deprivation or restriction or limitation of any such right shall be made except as provided in this Article.
3. Restrictions or limitations which are absolutely necessary in the interest of the public safety or the public health or the public morals or the town and country planning or the development and utilization of any property to the promotion of the public benefit or for the protection of the rights of others may be imposed by law on the exercise of such right.
   Just compensation shall be paid for any such restrictions or limitations which materially decrease the economic value of such property: such compensation shall be determined in the case of disagreement by a civil court.

That provision rendered it impracticable, because of the right to compensation, to impose effective land use planning control. The Government has been unwilling to prevent landowners from erecting buildings where they significantly degrade the environment of the area.[7] Although the Town and Country Planning Act was passed in 1972, it has until recently remained impracticable to control much of the proposed development of land.

2. RIGHT TO INFORMATION

2.1 The need for rights to information

2.1.1 The right to information is a necessary prerequisite to the exercise of other rights by which an individual can protect himself against persons who pollute, and against authorities which authorise or permit them to pollute the environment.

2.1.2 Information is needed for the exercise of the following rights.

(a) *Right of objection*
   When a person applies for a licence, consent, permission or authorisation for any kind of activity which may lead to pollution, other persons may wish to object for the purpose of protecting their interests.
      Such a need arises: when land use planning permission is given; when consents are given for discharges or deposits, whether to air, land or water including marine waters; when new developments such as roads and airports

---

[7]In recent years, a large building to hold a department store has been built in one of the few green areas in central Nicosia – despite vociferous public protests.

are planned; when any new industrial project which involves dangerous processes or substances is proposed; and in many other cases.

(b) *Complaints*

People affected by pollution from existing sources may wish to complain to the polluter; to the control authority; to their political representatives; or to the public generally through the press. All are legitimate forms of action to protect their interests. Without a detailed knowledge of the substances discharged or deposited, the manner of discharge or deposit, quantities and times, dispersal and accumulation if known, and corresponding knowledge of discharges of energy such as noise, vibrations, and radioactivity, a person cannot submit a complaint with sufficient degree of particularity. A vague complaint is easily answered or dismissed. Complaints which are particularised can be backed by expert opinion, can more easily be justified, and cannot be so easily answered or dismissed. They are thus more likely to be effective.

It has been argued that it is largely useless, and can be unfairly damaging to the discharger, to give to the general public precise information in scientific terms. The fear is that such information will at best be misunderstood, and at worst will be misinterpreted and raise unjustified fears. In many, if not most countries, that is not true today. Moreover, it deprives of information those who have scientific knowledge and understanding. It also prevents ordinary members of the public from taking the information to experts, to have it interpreted, and to have possible consequences of the discharges or deposits explained. Indeed, they can often consult experts who have a greater knowledge of possible consequences than does the discharger.

(c) *Criminal and administrative proceedings*

Where private prosecutions are permitted, no person can be confident that he can meet the high standards of proof needed in criminal proceedings unless he has a prior source of sound information. Normally, witnesses can be compelled to attend and answer questions, but it is risky to compel the attendance of a potentially hostile witness without knowing beforehand what he is likely to say. In most jurisdictions, a witness need only throw serious doubt on the prosecution case to secure an acquittal.

Likewise, prior information will be needed before a person can confidently embark on proceedings against a control authority, or any administrative proceedings.

(d) *Civil actions*

The need for prior knowledge of the details of discharges or deposits is not so great for the purpose of civil actions, for usually such information can be gained in the proceedings preliminary to the hearing. It would be unwise for anyone, however, to embark on expensive civil proceedings without first being able to test the strength of his case.

2.1.3 *Safeguard against unfair discrimination and corruption*

The publication of details of the grant of licences, consents permits and authorisations is a useful precaution against unfair discrimination or corruption.

In some forms of control, grants of licences etc will be by a central authority. In such cases corruption may be less likely, although by no means impossible: but it is more likely to occur where the powers are vested in local and minor officials.

There is an even greater possibility of improper influence outside the legal definition of corruption. There may be political reasons for a decision, properly applied
by an elected representative. On the other hand, there may be decisions based on
political or personal considerations under pressure from a powerful or wealthy
party supporter.

The forms which corrupt or otherwise unfair practices can take are infinite.

One of the best safeguards against such improper practices is the publication of
all decisions, so that unfair discrimination can be seen.

2.2   Basis of the right to information

2.2.1   In some cases, the lack of available information is the result of statutory
restrictions on the release of information by officers of the control authority. One
example still in force, but now of only limited application is found in the United
Kingdom Rivers (Prevention of Pollution) Act 1961 at Section 12. That section did
not appear in the bill as originally presented to Parliament, but was added at the
request of industrial interests when the bill was in the Second Chamber. It has since
been admitted that the primary purpose of the section was to prevent riparian owners from gaining information that they could use in a civil action against the discharger.

2.2.2   There is, however, a more acceptable reason for such a restriction.

Under many control systems, enforcement officers are given powers: to enter
premises; to examine plant, equipment and substances; to take away samples; and
to require the owner or operator to give information about the operations. With
such legal powers, backed by an express or implied threat of a prosecution, the
officer is able to obtain information he would not be given voluntarily. Those
powers are granted for the purpose of enforcement.

When an officer or agent of government is given a statutory power to obtain
information for a particular purpose, which information would not otherwise be
made available to him, it is in principle wrong, if not legally wrong, to use that
information for other purposes. Therefore the operator of the process is justified in
insisting that the information is not made available to the general public.

Another principle, however, lies in direct conflict with the above. Where a
person discharges into the common environment a substance which could cause
injury or inconvenience to members of the public or damage to their property when
those members are exercising their normal rights, they are morally entitled to know
what the substance is, and any details of the discharge relevant to the injury, inconvenience or damage it may cause. That is an essential prerequisite to the exercise of
his right to take legal or other action to protect his interests.

Normally, the second principle may properly be regarded as overriding, but some
exceptions may reasonably be made. The conflict may be resolved by permitting or
requiring the control authority to publish information relevant to public rights on a
register open to public inspection, and empowering the appropriate minister to allow
exceptions in appropriate cases, e.g. to protect national security or trade secrets.[8]

---

[8]As an example see the provisions on registers in the U.K. Water Resources Act 1991 s.190, and the
Control of Pollution (Registers) Regulations 1989 s.i.1160. The former is set out in Appendix H.

2.2.3 The term 'trade secrets', however, can be given a wide meaning. In *Lancing Linde* v *Kerr*,[9] a case in the English courts concerning a covenent by an employee not to divulge trade secrets or confidential information, Staughton LJ accepted that

> a trade secret is information which, if disclosed to a competitor, would be liable to cause real (or significant) harm to the owner of the secret . . .

He then added

> . . . that it must be information used in a trade or business, and secondly that the owner must limit the dissemination of it or at least not encourage or permit widespread publication.
>
> That is my preferred view of trade secret in this context. It can thus include not only secret formulae for the manufacture of products but also, in an appropriate case, the names of customers and the goods which they buy.

In the same case, Butler-Sloss LJ said,

> 'Trade secrets' has, in my view, to be interpreted in the wider context of highly confidential information of a non-technical or non-scientific nature, which may come within the ambit of information the employer is entitled to have protected.

Although that was a case of a covenant given by an employee, and not necessarily binding in a case concerning effluents, it would be of strong persuasive influence.

It is, of course, a matter of policy whether or not such a wide range of exemptions are to he permitted. An interpretation provision in the Act can ensure that they are not.

2.2.4 Some of the narrower, and more strictly controlled, provisions relating to rights to information are found in the United Kingdom. They often first take the form of restrictions on the release of information by officers of the control authority, except when the release is for the purpose of enforcement of the legislation, as in criminal proceedings, or some associated purpose as when it is given before a commission of enquiry established by the minister. That is then followed by a provision for the keeping of registers open to public inspection. The information to go on the register may be of limited extent, and subject to exemptions. Examples of United Kingdom provisions relating to access to information are given in Appendix H.

The Council of the European Communities has issued a directive 'on the freedom of access to information on the environment'.[10] That requires Member States to ensure that public authorities must make available information relating to the environment 'to any person on request, without his having to prove an interest'. The main provisions of the Directive are given in Appendix H.

The provision of widest scope is the US Freedom of Information Act. That gives to members of the public a general right of access to documents held by public authorities, subject to exceptions for the protection of such matters as national defence, trade secrets, personal privacy, law enforcement and litigation. The main provisions, including those exceptions, are set out in Appendix H.

---

[9][1991] 1 All ER 418. See Staughton LJ. at 425-426, and Butler-Sloss LJ. at 435.
[10]Council Directive 90/313/EEC.

3. RIGHT TO SUBMIT AND HAVE CONSIDERED OBJECTIONS AND REPRESENTATIONS

3.1 Informal representations

When a decision is to be made by a pollution control authority, anyone who has relevant information, and knows who the decision makers are, can submit informal representations.[11] Whether or not those representations are read and taken into account depends on whether that authority considers it politic to do so. They may be ignored, or their receipt may be merely an opportunity to send in reply what arguments they have in support of their intended decision.

3.2 The right to have objections and other representations considered

3.2.1 Where legislation grants powers of decision to authorities, and when others may be affected by that decision, as in the case of a consent, authorisation or licence, it sometimes makes provision for persons to be consulted before the decision is made. They are usually specified persons or bodies, but there may be added a discretion to consult others. Such provisions at the most impose an obligation to consult before a decision is reached. To what extent the authority takes into account what is said depends on the standing of the persons consulted, or the cogency of their representations. An example is given in Appendix H.

3.2.2 More compelling provisions are those which lay down a further procedure to be followed before any decision which conflicts with the representations is made. Usually, that requires the matter to be referred to a minister for decision.

Of particular relevance to the rights of the public is a provision of the United Kingdom Water Resources Act 1991.[12] The National Rivers Authority, before granting a consent to discharge an effluent to inland waters, must first publish the application, then wait for 21 days for representations to be made. If it decides to grant a consent despite representations it has received, anyone who submitted representations is to be informed, and has an opportunity to ask the Secretary of State to call in the application for his own decision. That thus constitutes a form of appeal. The relevant parts of the provision appear in Appendix H.

4. APPEALS

4.1 Purposes of appeal

4.1.1 When a control authority has reached a decision on an application for a grant of a consent, licence or the like, it is usual to grant a right of appeal. The purposes of such appeals, however, vary.

4.1.2 The most obvious purpose is to correct a decision which has been made on faulty or inadequate technical or scientific grounds. Alternatively, the appeal may

---

[11]The term 'representations' is used to include 'objections'.
[12]Schedule 10, paragraph 3.

be made on the ground that in making the decision the authority had failed to take properly into account the interests of all who could be affected thereby. In both cases, the appeal is against the merits of the decision, and the appeal tribunal must be competent to deal with such matters.

4.1.3   Another purpose may be to enable the minister to exercise supervisory jurisdiction over the implementation of policy. Where there is such a need for policy control, he can also be given a power to 'call in' applications in order that he can make the decisions. If a decision has already been reached by a control authority, and a person is dissatisfied on the grounds of the policy applied, that person may be given the right to appeal to the minister.

4.1.4   A third purpose is to have the decision reviewed by an administrative court. Such a court may quash the decision for procedural irregularities or departures from the rules of natural justice. It may also be able to quash it as an abuse of power.[13]

4.1.5   Finally, appeals are good safeguards against corruption and unfair discrimination.[14]

4.2   Types of tribunals

4.2.1   Where an appeal is of the type referred to in 4.1.1, made on the grounds of faulty or inadequate technical or scientific basis, the appeal tribunal must be one which is able to make a judgment on technical or scientific matters. The control authority will have competence in those areas, and it would at first sight seem ludicrous to commit the appeal to a tribunal which does not itself have that competence.

It has commonly been thought that at least some members of such a tribunal should have expertise in the matters on which it is called upon to adjudicate. S.A. de Smith, in his *Constitutional and Administrative Law* stated at page 546 that

A special tribunal may include persons with desired initial qualifications, and others who will acquire them through specialisation and experience.[15]

There are, however, dangers in that kind of appointment.

The first is that although a member of the tribunal may be an engineer, he may not have the knowledge or expertise called for to understand the problems of some specialised branch of engineering which comes before the tribunal. In the United States, dissatisfaction has been voiced at the appearance of a 'nuclear engineer' on a tribunal dealing with a highly specialised branch of that kind of engineering.[16]

There is another danger which causes greater concern. A member of the tribunal who has expertise in the subject matter of the appeal will give to the tribunal the benefit of his expertise by advising the other members. That advice, however, will normally be given behind closed doors when the tribunal has retired to consider its decision. That would be just one expert's view, and in some cases could be open to question by other experts in the same field. Expert witnesses appearing for one of

[13]See 4.3 below, and Chapter II at 7.3(c).
[14]On safeguards against corruption, see Chapter II at section 8.
[15]Penguin Education of Penguin Books Ltd, 2nd Edition, 1973.
[16]Personal communication, official of Westinghouse Corporation.

the parties may have wished to doubt the soundness of that advice, and express a different opinion – if they had had the opportunity of hearing what had been said. Had the same opinion been expressed by a witness in open court, that witness could have been cross-examined, and other expert evidence brought to show that his opinions were ill-founded, mistaken, or did not take into account more recent research. Unfortunately, a party cannot cross-examine a member of the tribunal, and in many cases he will not hear the opinion the member has expressed. Moreover, if the party wishes to contest the decision of the tribunal on a further appeal, he may be handicapped in preparing his appeal in not knowing on what technical or scientific grounds the decision was based.

4.2.2   A more satisfactory system is to empower the tribunal to appoint 'assessors'. They will be experts in the matters under consideration, and their function will be to help members of the tribunal to understand technical and scientific evidence, so that they can make an informed assessment of its relevance and value, and properly apply it to the matters in issue. Their function in the English courts was expressed by Viscount Simon LC in *Richardson* v *Redpath Brown*[17]

> He is an expert available for the judge to consult if the judge requires assistance in understanding the effect and meaning of technical evidence. . . . He may suggest to the judge questions which the judge may put to an expert witness. . . . Where the assessor's advice may affect the judge's conclusion, it may seem desirable to inform the parties what is the advice he has received.

That system preserves the right of the parties to have expert evidence given in open court, and, if Lord Simon's view is accepted by the tribunal, the advice given by the assessor will be made known, also in open court. A party cannot cross-examine the assessor, but he can call expert witnesses to present qualifying or contrary opinions.

4.2.3   Where the appeal concerns matters of policy, clearly it must lie to the minister. In practice, the appeal will often be dealt with by a senior civil servant acting in accordance with known ministerial policy, although on major issues or matters of great public interest reference may be handled by the minister himself. In many cases, where there is no dispute on fact, and no call for expert scientific evidence, there need be no oral hearing. Where there are disputes of fact, the minister may appoint an 'inspector' to conduct a hearing and report to him.[18]

4.2.4   There may also be appeals which raise both questions of policy and technical or scientific issues. In such cases, the technical and scientific issues are best dealt with by persons independent of the minister. The minister may then make his policy decision in the light of the published findings of those persons. Indeed, he may be required to consult independent specialists, although the degree of independence may vary from persons selected by non-governmental institutions, to panels of persons chosen by the minister, to the minister's own scientific or technical advisers. Two examples are given below.

The United Kingdom Food and Environment Protection Act 1985 at Part II deals with licences for the dumping of wastes at sea. The relevant minister grants the

---

[17][1944] AC 62 at 70-71.
[18]The inspector will usually be a civil servant with relevant scientific or technical knowledge. See also Chapter III at 6.2.

licences.[19] An applicant for a licence who has met with a refusal, or who is dissatisfied with the conditions imposed, is entitled to a statement of reasons for the
minister's decision. He may then make representations concerning the decision to
the minister, who must submit them to a committee of persons drawn from a previously constituted panel of experts. The applicant is entitled to an oral hearing
before that committee, either in person or through his representative. The committee produces a report containing findings of fact and recommendations, copies
of which are sent to both the minister and the applicant. The minister must then
reconsider his decision in the light of the report.[20]

Legislation under consideration in Cyprus provides that the Council of Ministers
may be called upon to resolve a dispute between representatives of different ministries on such matters as quality objectives and consent conditions. Before reaching
its decision, the Council of Ministers must appoint a person of suitable qualifications
and experience to hear evidence and submit a report and recommendations.[21]

4.2.5 For any subject on which several government departments have responsibilities, it may be advisable to set up a single board to advise all of them, otherwise different departments may receive different advice. This has been done in the
United Kingdom by the Radiological Protection Act 1970. That sets up a National
Radiological Protection Board, one of its functions being 'to provide information
and advice to persons (including government departments) with responsibilities in
the United Kingdom in relation to the protection from radiation hazards either of
the community as a whole or of particular sections of the community'.

In Mauritius, there is one minister with overall responsibility for the environment,
but other ministries with particular environmental responsibilities. The Mauritian
Environment Protection Act 1991 establishes an Environmental Advisory Council to
advise the Minister of the Environment on the quality of the environment, and make
recommendations to him regarding actions and measures for its improvement.

4.3 Review by administrative courts

Where the purpose of an 'appeal'[22] is to have a review the proceedings for any
procedural irregularity, denial of natural justice or abuse of power, then the matter
will go to a court having powers to deal with breaches of administrative law. Those
courts and their powers are discussed briefly in Chapter II at 7.3.

5. PRIVATE PROSECUTIONS

5.1 Right to bring a private prosecution

In some countries, e.g. England, Canada, an individual may initiate and conduct
criminal proceedings in the ordinary criminal courts against any person, where he

---

[19]That may be the Minister of Agriculture, Fisheries and Food, or the Secretary of State for the
Environment. See S.24 of the Act.

[20]See S.8 and Schedule 3 to the Act.

[21]See the draft Control of Water Pollution Law, Schedule 1 Part II.

[22]The word 'appeal' is used although, strictly speaking, in most cases it is not an appeal against the
merits of the decision, but an application for a review of the proceedings which led to that decision.

has evidence that that person has committed a criminal offence. Such a prosecutor need not have any interest to protect, and need not have been involved in or affected in any way by the alleged offence.

In England, the right is subject to the powers of the Attorney General, acting on behalf of the Crown, to forestall or terminate the proceedings by issuing a *nolle prosequi*. That right is explained in Chapter IV at 2.4.4, but a few further comments are relevant here.

Anyone bringing a private prosecution risks a verdict of 'not guilty', followed by an order that the prosecutor pay the costs of the defence. Consequently, in the past there have been few private prosecutions, and most of those have been for petty offences between quarrelling neighbours. More recently, with the advent of large voluntary organisations to oppose pollution and with substantial funds available, there have been private prosecutions for pollution offences. These have been used as a means not only of directly deterring further pollution, but also to stir control authorities into action, or by taking action where the control authority has thought it not politic to act. Particularly where there are strong voluntary organisations, private prosecutions have proved valuable, even if only as a threat.

There has also recently been a tendency for the public to be more fully informed, and willing to band together in local associations to take action where the authorities fail to do so.

The combined effect of those processes is to make the authorities more responsive to public opinion. If the authorities complain that the campaigning members are ill informed, it is for the authorities to provide them with the necessary information.

In most other jurisdictions, criminal prosecutions are brought by public authorities. A brief explanation of what is done in certain other countries is given in Chapter IV at 2.4.

6. ACTIONS AGAINST THE CONTROL AUTHORITIES

6.1   Where it is legally impossible, or in practice difficult, to bring a private prosecution, the control authorities may be left with a freedom to exercise their discretionary powers to prosecute as they think fit, and in using that discretion they may fail to enforce properly, whether for legitimate or illegitimate reasons. One of the most frequent criticisms of national systems of pollution control is that although the necessary laws have been passed, they are not enforced properly.

There may be many reasons for that. The methods of control may be ill conceived, or laws themselves badly drafted. The International Convention for the Prevention of Pollution of the Sea by Oil, 1954, provided that a tanker shall not be permitted to discharge within a prohibited zone, in effect, water containing more than 100 parts per million of oil. A large part of the Atlantic was a prohibited zone. The United Kingdom passed the necessary implementing legislation. At midnight in mid-atlantic, however, it is difficult to detect discharges from passing ships, even more difficult to identify them as containing more than 100 parts per million of oil. Not surprisingly, between 1954 and the early 1970s, when new legislation came into force, there was only one prosecution for discharge into that area of the high seas. That was only because a patrol aircraft of the Canadian armed forces spotted a ship discharging in daylight into a slick two miles long, and reported his sighting.[23] An effective system of checks and collection of evidence was not in use, nor could such a system have been devised for that offence as set out in the treaty.

Where detection can and has been made possible, a system of monitoring for the collection of evidence may not have been established.

Finally, the enforcement authorities themselves may not always be willing to take firm action. In some cases, that has been because of too much reliance on advice and warnings given to offenders by the inspectors, in others because of political considerations, or because insistence on compliance backed by firm enforcement might throw a heavy burden of cost on a local industry. The last two of those reasons are relevant to the setting of standards, but not in enforcement once standards have been set. Between 1951 and the public's awakening interest in environmental pollution in the 1970s, the English river boards, which enforced water pollution laws in that period, were notoriously unwilling to prosecute. That was doubtless in large measure due to a ministerial circular issued in 1951[24] which advised 'wise and patient administration by river boards, working in close touch with local authorities and industry'. Local authorities and industry were the main polluters! More recently there have been significant changes in enforcement practices, due almost entirely to three causes. The first is the greater availability of information with the introduction of registers, the second the pressure of public opinion, supported by the third which is the power of private prosecution, which was in the earlier days restricted, and in the United States by citizen suits as outlined in Chapter V at 6.5.3.

6.2 Orders of mandamus

6.2.1   In England, and in several other countries with similar legal systems, such as Cyprus, and in the United States, it is possible to apply to the courts for an order requiring a public authority to do its duty, (United States code Annotated Volume 28 section 1361). Wherever a person with a public duty to perform has failed to do so, any person with an interest in the performance of that duty may apply to the High Court for an 'order of mandamus'. After proceedings to enquire into the merits of the application, the court may issue such an order. There are normally rigorous powers of enforcement.

The procedure has been used successfully against the police. In 1966 the Commissioner of Police for the Metropolitan Area of London found enforcement of the gaming laws rendered difficult as a result of certain court decisions. He therefore issued a circular to senior police officers, advising them not to prosecute gaming clubs for breaches of those laws except where there were complaints of cheating, or where the club had become a haunt of criminals. An application was made that he was failing to perform his duty to enforce the gaming laws.[25] The High Court made it clear that it was prepared to issue an order of mandamus, whereupon the Commissioner withdrew the circular.

---

[23]See *Federal Steam Navigation Company Ltd* [1973] 3 All ER 849.
[24]MHLG circular 64/51.
[25]*R* v *Metropolitan Police Commissioner ex parte Blackburn* [1968] 763.

Such an order can succeed where there is shown a clear unwillingness to perform the duty. It is rare, however, that clear evidence of that is available. Pollution control authorities could plead that advice, warnings and threats of prosecution were having effect, and that that was sufficient enforcement. When a second application was made for an order against the Commissioner of the Metropolitan Police, this time to enforce the laws on pornography, he successfully resisted the application on the ground that he did not have enough men for full enforcement.[26] In many cases, pollution control authorities could rely on a similar plea.

6.2.2   A comparable but less direct method is used in Canada. Under the Environmental Protection Act, on a request made by two residents, the minister must investigate an allegation of an offence under the Act. He may then send the results of the investigation to the Attorney General, with whom the decision whether or not to prosecute will than lie.

There is a similar provision in the United Kingdom Alkali Works etc Works Regulation Act 1906 at Section 22.

[26]*R v Metropolitan Police Commissioner ex parte Blackburn* [1973] 1 All ER 324.

Chapter VII

Polluter Pays Principle

1. MEANING AND SCOPE OF THE POLLUTER PAYS PRINCIPLE

1.1. Polluter pays principle as a policy decision

1.1.1   There is no agreed definition of the term 'polluter pays principle', (referred to throughout this chapter simply as the 'principle') nor of any precisely defined scope for its application, nor of any clear agreement on permissible exceptions. That is not surprising, because there is no global treaty on its application, and regional organisations such as the EEC and OECD, and the national authorities, apply it for their own purposes, and subject it to different, often overriding, considerations such as the need for assistance in depressed areas, as with the EEC, or other socio-economic consequences, as with the OECD.

There are also differences in explanations of the purposes and application of the principle, because different authors have in mind its application for different basic purposes. For example, the economist more often has in mind the broad purposes of economic control, taking into account 'social damage' and the 'social cost of further prevention and control'; as distinct from the lawyer, who is more concerned with the protection of particular people, either as groups or as individuals.

1.1.2   It is unlikely in the circumstances of today and the foreseeable future, with economic groups forming, and with developing nations striving for development without degradation of their environments, in a community of self-seeking and often hostile nations, that any generally accepted definition would even be possible. We are therefore left the a world of Alice's Wonderland. 'When I use the word', Humpty Dumpty said in a rather scornful tone, 'it means just what I choose it to mean – neither more not less'. (From Alice through the Looking Glass by Lewis Carroll.)

Nevertheless, the express acceptance of the principle serves a useful purpose. Both separate nations and groups of nations can adopt it as a principle to be applied, for their own purposes and within any overriding terms of their own policies. The adoption of the principle itself, and delimitation of the scope of its application, are matters of policy to be determined by the appropriate government, or by the parties to the treaty, as the case may be.

1.2   Meanings given to the polluter pays principle

1.2.1   An early attempt to give a consistent meaning to the principle was made by the Commission of the European Communities in its communication to the Council.[1]

The Commission defined a polluter as

> someone who directly or indirectly damages the environment, or who creates conditions leading to such damage.

The Commission also stated that

> . . . . costs connected with the protection of the environment against pollution should be allocated according to the same principles throughout the Community.
> To achieve that, the European Communities at Community level, and the Member States in their own national legislation on environmental protection, must apply the principle, under which natural or legal persons must pay the costs of such measures as are necessary to eliminate that pollution or reduce it so as to comply with the standards or equivalent measures which enable quality objectives to be met, or where there are no such objectives, so as to comply with the standards or equivalent measures laid down by the public authorities.
> Consequently, environmental protection should not in principle depend on policies which rely on grants of aid, and place the burden of combating pollution on the Community.

The Single European Act of the Communities has now confirmed the application of the polluter pays principle.[2]

1.2.2   The OECD explained the Principle in similar terms.

> The Polluter Pays Principle . . . implies that in general it is for the polluter to meet the cost of pollution control and prevention measures, irrespective of whether those costs are incurred as a result of the imposition of some charge on pollution emission, or are debited through some other suitable economic mechanism, or are in response to some direct regulation leading to some enforced reduction in pollution.
> The polluter should bear the expenses of preventing and controlling pollution to ensure that the environment is in an acceptable state. The notion of an 'acceptable state' decided by public authorities, implies that through a collective choice and with respect to the limited information available, the advantage of a further reduction in the residual social damage involved is considered as being smaller that the social cost of further prevention and control. In fact the Polluter Pays Principle is no more than an efficiency principle for allocating costs and does not involve bringing pollution down to an optimum level of any type, although it does not exclude the possibility of doing so.[3]

In the language of economists, its effect is to internalise the costs in question.

---

[1]See the Annex to Council Recommendation regarding cost allocation and action by public authorities on environmental matters, 75/436 EURATOM, ECSC, EEC.
[2]Art.130, R.2
[3]See *Note on the Implementation of the Polluter-Pays Principle*, (OECD, Paris, 1974).

1.3   The principle as applied to control measures

1.3.1   Both of those explanations of the principle apply to control measures taken for the elimination or reduction of pollution.[4]

In both it is agreed that the state may decide to accept some level of pollution. The principle is then applied to the costs of prevention of any pollution above that level. That accepts that the appropriate organs of the state may decide that the common environment may be used as a recipient of waste. The question of compensation for damage suffered by any person as a result of such disposal is not addressed. That is a legitimate policy decision which limits the scope of the application of the principle.[5]

As indicated in the quotation from the OECD Report, any imposition of pollution charges, any limits placed on emissions and any process or product standards, all have the effect of applying the principle in that they require the polluter to bear the cost of methods of production or treatment necessary to ensure that acceptable quality objectives for the receiving media are maintained.

1.3.2   Conversely, a failure of the regulatory authorities to enforce the standards set by the state, or any failure to set quality standards which are considered acceptable, would be a breach of the principle.

Likewise, where a Member State of the European Communities fails to observe Community environmental standards, that may constitute a direct or indirect subsidy to the polluter.[6]

1.3.3   The OECD has gone further. It has issued a Recommendation on the Application of the Polluter Pays Principle to Accidental Pollution.[7] The Recommendation is expressed to relate to accidents involving hazardous substances, but it is submitted that it could apply with equal force to all accidents which may lead to damage. It states that

> The Polluter Pays Principle . . . . means that the polluter should bear the expenses of carrying out pollution prevention and control measures introduced by public authorities in member countries, to ensure that the environment is in an acceptable state.

It is stated also that those measures can include.

> measures to improve safety;
> accident preparedness;
> emergency plans and special means of response;
> provision for prompt action following an accident to protect human health and the environment;
> clean up operations.

The measures to which the principle applies may also include

---

[4]See the publication referred to in Footnote 3, and *Council Recommendation on the Application of the Polluter-Pays Principle to Accidental Pollution*, (OECD, 1989). (Both those publications are now out of print.)

[5]See 2 below.

[6]See Kramer, *The EEC Treaty and Environmental Protection*, (Sweet & Maxwell, London, 1990), p.63.

[7]Adopted by the Council on 7 July 1989 at its 712th Session.

> . . . the cost of reasonable pollution control measures decided by the authorities
> following an accident . . . . from which pollution is released.

Such measures may be taken by the operator or by the authorities to avoid or limit
the release of damaging substances, or any spread of environmental damage from
substances already released, e.g. by placing booms in the sea to prevent the spread
of oil. The paper, in paragraph 11 of the Appendix, includes also the cost of
rehabilitating the environment.

They are not to include 'humanitarian measures or other measures which are in
the nature of public services and which cannot be reimbursed to the public authorities under applicable law, nor measures to compensate for the economic consequences of an accident'.[8]

For an accident caused by a natural phenomenon, for which the operator cannot
be made liable under national law, such as an earthquake, which was not foreseeable, or against which no safeguards can be taken, the public authority should
not charge the operator.[9]

2. COMPENSATION FOR POLLUTION DAMAGE

2.1.1 It will be noted that both the EEC and OECD advocate the application of
the principle to the cost of measures needed to maintain acceptable quality
objectives set by the state authorities. In some cases, however, even when quality
objectives are maintained, some damage will be done, if only the degradation of
amenity. The costs of such damage, when quantified in monetary terms, are
considered to be outside the area of application of the principle

That is logical, for if the state cannot require any further reduction, it has no
justification for demanding that the operator should meet further costs.

2.1.2 Both organisations appear to draw a distinction between costs incurred other
than the cost of compensating for damage done, and compensation for damage in
fact done. Both are costs created by the polluter, and in both cases he may
reasonably be required to pay – in the former case by the application of the
principle by the administrative authorities; in the latter by the courts through the
process of civil actions. In the enunciation of the principle, however, no clear line
appears to have been drawn.

2.1.3 In principle, if damage is done, and there is a person who suffers from that
damage in circumstances where a legal right of his has been infringed, the matter is
one for the courts. If damage is done and there is no such person, the application of
the principle does a useful service by filling that gap.

2.1.4 At the time action is demanded, however, no clear line can be drawn
between the two. It is noted at 3.1.7. that the OECD would not consider it a breach
of the principle if the state contributed to acts done to avoid the spread of damage,
to limit further releases of pollutants, or to rehabilitate the environment.

---

[8]See the second publication referred to in Footnote 4.

[9]Note, however, that in the United Kingdom the operators of nuclear installations may be liable for
damage by the escape of radioactivity caused by an earthquake. See Nuclear Installations Act 1965
S.13(4)(b).

In any such case, there may or may not eventually be damage done for which the courts will award compensation. It would seem proper at the outset to require the polluter to pay. By doing so he will either:

(a) be preventing or reducing the damage which may otherwise be done, and thereby reducing his liability to compensate; or
(b) be preventing or reducing damage to the common environment.

The consequences may be a mixture of both.

In the circumstances, it is submitted that it is better for the administrative authorities to require the polluter to pay all those costs. Compensation for any damage to individual interests can then be awarded by the courts.

2.1.5   In practice, the pollution control authorities are well placed and in many cases well qualified to say what preventive measures and damage limitation actions can be taken, and what the costs are likely to be. Where no actual damage is suffered, the authorities can ensure, by various procedures, that the cost is ultimately borne by the operator in accordance with the principle. Where actual damage is done to legally protected interests of people, the question of payment is best left to the courts.

2.1.6   Where discharges are subject to regulatory control, whether in the form of emission limits, prescribed treatment methods, product standards, standards for fuels or the place and method of discharge, no problem of differentiation arises. The only problem will be to decide whether compliance with the regulatory controls absolves the discharger from paying compensation.[10]

Where, on the other hand, the principle is sought to be applied by means of effluent charges, the bases on which those charges are calculated is important. If the division referred to in 2.1.3. is to be maintained, the charge should not in any degree be calculated according to the damage which may be done to the interests of others; otherwise the discharger facing an action for compensation in the courts could claim that he had already paid at least in part. The plaintiff, on the other hand, would never have received payment.[11]

2.1.7   Finally, a public authority may itself claim compensation for an extra burden of costs imposed on it by a breach of pollution control standards. For example, if a source of drinking water has been polluted in breach of control laws, the authority may have to supply water from other sources or by other means. It is submitted that such a claim is one which the authority more properly pursues though the courts. The court as an impartial arbiter can decide on the justification for the complaint, and determine the appropriate measure of compensation.

---

[10]See Chapter I at 4.4.
[11]Any system under which the complainants claimed a share from the charging authority would necessitate a further addition of tribunals or court procedures. It is submitted that such a system would be unweildy, and could never be entirely successful.

3. EXCEPTIONS TO THE POLLUTER PAYS PRINCIPLE

3.1 Agreed exceptions

3.1.1   Both the EEC and OECD have stated that there are permissible exceptions to the application of the principle. Those exceptions are referred to and commented on below.

3.1.2   With the introduction of the principle, some industrial enterprises may face the need for expensive adjustments. In particular, they may find it necessary to change their method of treatment or manner or place of discharge. A reasonable transitional period may be regarded as a justified exception to the principle.

3.1.3   An operator of a hazardous installation may find it necessary to re-locate the installation to reduce the risk of damage to the environment or the health or property of others. If the original location was in conformity with the existing land use plan, it may not be considered a breach of the principle to grant him compensation for doing so.[12]

A similar exception may reasonably be allowed in certain circumstances in which a discharge consent is varied. In at least one jurisdiction, when a discharge consent is granted with conditions relating to quantity or character of the discharge, a time must be stated within which normally there will be no variation. That is for the protection of the operator who may have to install expensive plant in order to comply with the new consent conditions. If the authority nevertheless considers it necessary for the protection of public health or the environment to require a variation of that consent, it may do so; but if the need for the new conditions was foreseeable at the time the original consent was granted, the authority must pay compensation to the discharger.[13]

3.1.4   Where the principle is regarded as covering the cost of treatment necessary to maintain quality objectives, but not treatment needed to achieve higher environmental standards, then any financial assistance to firms seeking to achieve such higher standards will not be regarded as a breach of the principle.

3.1.5   Financial assistance to foster research and development on new techniques for the manufacture of products which cause less pollution, is not regarded by the EEC as a breach of the principle.

3.1.6   The EEC also states that exceptions may be made in the following cases.[14]

(a)   In limited cases where a strict application of the principle would be likely to lead to serious economic disturbances, and where investment affecting environmental protection would benefit from aid intended to solve certain industrial, agricultural or regional structure problems.

(b)   Where, in the context of other policies, e.g. regional, industrial and social, investment affecting environmental protection benefits from aid intended to solve certain industrial, agricultural or regional problems.

[12]See 1.3.1 above.
[13]See Water Resources Act 1991, Sched.10, paras 6 and 7.
[14]Council Recommendation 75/436, Annex.

Neither does the EEC consider any of the following to be contrary to the principle.

(c) Financial contributions which might be granted to local authorities for the construction and operation of public installations for the protection of the environment, the cost of which could not be wholly covered in the short term from the charges paid by polluters using them. In so far as other effluent as well as household waste is treated in those installations, the service thus rendered to undertakings would be charged to them on the basis of the actual cost of treatment concerned.
(d) Financing designed to compensate for the particularly heavy costs which some polluters would be obliged to meet in order to achieve an exceptional degree of environmental cleanliness.
(e) Contributions granted to foster activities concerning research and development with a view to implementing techniques, manufacturing processes and products causing less pollution.

3.1.7 The OECD does not consider that a Member State would be in breach of the principle if it contributed to reasonable control measures decided on by public authorites after a pollution accident had occurred in order to:

– avoid the spread of damage;
– limit further releases e.g. by closure of a plant so as to discontinue emission;
– rehabilitate the environment.

4. APPLICATION OF THE PRINCIPLE IN PRACTICE

4.1 United States

4.1.1 The United States favours interpretation of the principle in 'equity terms',[15] as distinct from the criterion of efficiency. It looks at the allocation of costs between polluters and society at large, and between individual polluters. The impact of future costs imposed on today's polluters is taken into account. The subsidy scheme under the Construction Grant Program, involving a redistribution of costs between an urban population as polluter on the one hand, and society as a whole on the other, is regarded as incompatible with the principle.

4.2 Germany

The German Government accepted the principle on the basis that the polluter must pay for the reduction of polluting effects and also for the restitution after damage has been done. Yet it did not rule out the use of subsidies for the purpose of complying with pollution controls where adequate environmental protection would not otherwise have been given. Normally, those subsidies provide financial aid for investments on environmental protection. The polluter is required to pay the cost after the initial investment has been made.

[15]See *Economic Instruments for Environmental Protection*, (OECD, 1989).

4.3   France

Reliance has been placed on pollution charges as a means of applying the principle. It has been noted, however, that in 1986 those charges would have had to have been increased by a factor of four if they were to have provided proper compliance with the principle. That shortfall, which would otherwise be regarded as a subsidy to the polluters, is not so regarded by OECD,[16] because the subsidies under the scheme are financed by funds raised from the polluters. That means that the polluters as a body pay, but not necessarily each polluter for the costs he himself imposes.

4.4   Netherlands

The approach to the problem in the Netherlands is in principle similar. The Government there considers dischargers in general to be responsible, and levies charges on them to finance its environmental management. It does not consider it necessary to establish that a particular polluter is responsible for particlar management costs to which his levy contributes. Specific charges relating to noise and air pollution have recently been replaced by a charge on fuel consumption. That does not necessarily correspond the noise nuisance or air pollution caused by any particular polluter.

Costs of administration of controls, monitoring and research are met from general public finds. That seems to be, in part at least, a clear departure from the principle.

4.5   Sweden

In Sweden, the costs of administration monitoring and control are charged on the basis of the principle. Penalties for non-compliance are also seen as an application of the principle, but that will depend on what uses are made to the monies collected as fines.

4.6   It has been noted that in most of the countries applying the principle it is not considered to be of overriding concern. In many countries it is said to perform a fund raising function.[17] Nevertheless, so long as those funds are raised from the persons responsible for the pollution, and are used to prevent, reduce or remedy the effects of the pollution, that is the proper purpose of the application of the principle.

5.   SCOPE OF THE POLLUTER PAYS PRINCIPLE

5.1   The polluter pays – in principle

5.1.1   In principle, it appears that there is a just allocation of costs if the polluter pays for all of the following.

---

[16]See footnote 3.
[17]See footnote 3.

(a) Measures taken, by himself or another person on his behalf, to prevent or reduce pollution of the common environment, which would otherwise occur or be likely to occur a result of his actions.
(b) Where the state requires such measures to be taken, any costs incurred by public authorities, or others acting of their behalf, in the administration and enforcement of the controls. That will include: the costs of any routine inspection, sampling and analysis; any exceptional measures reasonably taken, and any costs incurred in enforcement proceedings.
(c) Where any pollutant is discharged and does damage, or it is reasonably expected that it will do damage to the common environment, the cost of removal of the pollutant.
(d) The cost of rehabilitating the environment, including its fauna and flora, after damage has been done and to the extent that rehabilitation is feasible and justified.
(e) Where operations create a known risk of accidental pollution, measures taken:
  (i) to reduce that risk;
  (ii) to reduce the degree of damage which may be done, including the cost of
    – any alarm systems,
    – the formulation of contingency plans, provision of necessary equipment, training and practice in emergency procedures,
    – containment of any pollutant released, e.g. booms to contain oil spills,
    – removal, dispersion or actions taken to render thepollutant less harmful;
  (iii) to inform and safeguard the public, e.g. by broadcast warning, and by evacuation where that is a reasonable precaution;
  (iv) to secure or remove any vehicle or vessel still discharging the pollutant, e.g. towing a ship away from a sensitive area, and the destruction of the vehicle or vessel where that is reasonable;[18]
  (v) by the public services where exceptional action is reasonably taken by reason of the presence of the pollutant.

5.1.2   The principle, it must be added, is concerned only with whether or not the costs are borne equitably between the polluters and the general public. It does not concern itself with the allocation of costs as between polluters. Patent law can ensure that the developer of a new product or process gets the benefit of his research and development, either directly, or indirectly by licensing the production or use of it.

5.1.3   Research can be done outside the industry which, purposefully or fortuitously, leads to cleaner methods of production or treatment. The trend today in some countries is to promote such research.[19] The extent to which operators of polluting installations benefit, and therefore in principle may be required to contribute, can often be calculated only after the event.

There was an interesting example of a method used by the United Kingdom Government some years ago. Household detergents at the time were

---

[18]See International Convention Relating to Intervention on the High Seas in Cases of Oil Pollution Casualties, Brussels 1969 and its Protocol of 1973.
[19]See Chapter III at 8.4 on clean technology.

causing pollution of rivers, particularly the foaming. A form of detergent which was at least 80 per cent biodegradable was sought by the Government. Producers complained that the cost of such a pollutant would be prohibitively high. The government threatened to introduce new legislation if action was not taken. As a consequence the producers embarked on a programme of research and development which led to a detergent which met the government's 80 per cent requirement – and was less expensive to produce than the one it replaced. The polluters as a body had paid. That is also, of course, an example of industry not willing to embark on costly research and development into cleaner products, which would otherwise be available for other purposes or simply for shareholders.

5.1.4   Justice requires also that the polluter pays for any damage suffered by another as a consequence of his pollution. That, however, is normally a matter left to the courts of law, and is therefore not usually referred to as falling within the principle.[20] It is right for two reasons that the courts handle the issues of compensation. The first is that they can then ensure that compensation for pollution damage is awarded on the same basis as for any other form of damage. The second is that the courts are better qualified and experienced to handle such difficult questions as causation, remoteness of damage, and assessment of compensation. Again, it would be wrong, and would create difficult jurisdictional problems, if pollution damage were dealt with separately and on a different basis than other forms of damage.

5.2   'He who takes the benefit . . . .'

5.2.1   It is a recognised principle, accepted in many countries, that the persons who take the benefit of an operation may reasobnably be required to pay all the costs, and bear all the risks of that operation, at least in so far as they are foreseeable consequences. The principle is often a means by which that can be achieved. The operator who uses pollution prevention measures, who pays pollution charges, or pays compensation for damage done, normally passes on that burden of costs to his customers or clients, thus requiring the ones who take the benefits of his operations ultimately to meet the costs.

The disposal of solid wastes illustrates how this principle is applied in practice. Commercial and industrial wastes are from operations which usually benefit only a section of the public – those who buy the products or services of the operator. In most countries, the disposal of those wastes is paid for by direct charges on the operator, who in turn passes on the costs to his customers. They benefit from his operations – and pay the costs of the disposal of the resulting wastes.

For the disposal of domestic wastes, on the other hand, there are usually no direct charges. All members of the public benefit from that service, and all pay through the process of local taxation in whatever form it is imposed.

5.2.2   That principle, however, is easily overlooked, and therefore not always applied. For example, in the United Kingdom, beaches on the southern coasts were often polluted by oil discharged from tankers delivering oil to United Kingdom or European ports. In most cases the tankers responsible could not be identified. Local authorities, many of them at holiday resorts, faced the costly task of cleaning their

---

[20]Note the comment in 2.1.3 and 2.1.4 above.

beaches. The central government for some years paid half the cost of those cleaning operations, but eventually ceased making those contributions. In principle, to the extent that the tankers were bringing oil to the United Kingdom, the government should have paid the whole of those costs. People throughout the country received the benefit of those supplies, and therefore may reasonably have been required, through their taxes or by other appropriate means, to have paid the whole of the cost of making good the damage done.

6. THE POLLUTER PAYS PRINCIPLE – POLICY AND PRACTICE

6.1 Principles are rarely applied in total disregard of all other considerations and anomolous practical consequences. To attempt to do that edges over into fanaticism.

In practice, a government may decide on grounds of policy, for example, to protect an industry which is vital to the national economy, or to assist a nascent industry. In order to do so, it may decide to depart from the principle, and in effect grant a subsidy.

6.2 Some exceptions permitted by the EEC and OECD fall within that class. They include:

(a) assisting with the cost of expensive re-adjustment on the introduction of the principle, (see 3.1.2.);
(b) financial assistance to avoid serious economic disturbances, (see 3.1.6. (a));
(c) meeting the cost of avoiding the spread of damage or preventing further releases, after a pollution accident, (see 3.1.7.);
(d) financial contributions by local authorities to the cost of providing and operating installations for the protection of the environment from polluting discharges by others, (see 3.1.6(c)).

It is submitted that they are policy decisions which deviate from the principle, but which may well be justified in the circumstances.

6.3 The most that can be said for any single nation is that it is right to have regard to the principle, but that in many circumstances a departure from it may be justified. Therein lie grounds for policy decisions which any government, within the terms of its constitution, is free to make.

Where a state is one of a group of nations which have combined for economic, financial or other reasons, or where the state is party to a treaty which covers trading, financial or economic matters, there may be other constraints. As with the EEC, there may be obligations or policies which conflict with the strict application of the principle, such as policies to give aid to certain regions.

The principle is an aid to better management of communal affairs, but is would be wrong to regard it as an overriding principle in all circumstances.

6.4 National legislation

6.4.1 In the case of a single nation, it is useful to declare in legislation the intention that the principle will, as a matter of policy, be applied. That will stand as guidance to administrators, and support them when they make charges in the application of the principle.

6.4.2   It is submitted, however, that that is not sufficient in itself. Doubts will be cleared if powers to impose such charges are included in legislation on specific forms of pollution. Care must be taken, however, to expressly grant such powers on all occasions where the principle is meant to apply. Otherwise it could be argued that the absence of a grant of such power in one particular case, in contradistinction to the cases where the express power was granted, indicates that the principle is not to apply.

Chapter VIII

International Obligations

1. INTRODUCTION

> This we know: the earth does not belong to man: man belongs to the earth . . . All things are connected like the blood which unites one family . . . Whatever befalls the earth, befalls the sons of the earth. Man does not weave the web of life; he is merely a strand in it. Whatever he does to the web, he does to himself.[1]

A wide range of environmental problems are now the subject of international concern – pollution of the oceans and of the atmosphere; transboundary air pollution; pollution of watercourses; and the threat of pollution caused by ultra-hazardous substances. Pollution is of global as well as of regional and national concern because pollution generated in one state may impact seriously upon other states; and because certain environmental problems, global warming for example, are of a magnitude that individual state action is ineffective to resolve them. The line between national and international environmental problems is fast disappearing.[2]

The regulation of pollution at the global and regional levels is a task for public international law, which is the system of law governing relations between states. International law governs nearly every aspect of inter-state relations, including matters such as jurisdiction, claims to territory, use of the oceans, and state responsibility. The international obligations relating to pollution control are found within a specialist area of public international law called international environmental law, though many of the principles referred to are applicable to many other areas of state activity not directly bearing upon the environment. Of particular concern in this chapter is the extent to which international law sets pollution standards, and the enforcement of those standards by or against states and, in certain instances, by or against individuals.

---

[1]Letter from Chief Seattle, patriarch of the Duwamish and Squamish Indians of Puget Sound, to the President of the United States, Franklin Pierce, in 1855.
[2]See Foreword by James Speth to Peter H. Sand *Lessons Learned in Global Environmental Governance* (World Resources Institute, 1990), p.v.

2. THE SOURCES OF INTERNATIONAL LAW

2.1   Where do we find the relevant substantive and procedural rules of international law? The most important sources of international law are treaty law and customary international law, each of which are a rich source of state obligations relevant to pollution control. Treaties are written agreements between states pursuant to which they undertake specific obligations; generally such obligations are binding only upon the states which have indicated their consent to be bound by them. The range of subject matter of such treaties (or conventions as they are also called) is virtually limitless. A treaty may be concluded between two states (a bilateral treaty), or multilaterally, with potentially well over one hundred states bound to those treaty rules. The rules may be confined to states in a particular region – a regional treaty – or globally, in an international treaty expressly designed to regulate the conduct of states globally.

Treaties have been the traditional source of international standards-setting in international law. Two fundamental drawbacks to the embodiment of environmental standards in treaty form may be identified:[3] the unanimity or consensus requirement of their negotiation leads to agreement on a median standard – the lowest common denominator; and the implementation period for treaty obligations can stretch from two years to a decade or more. Treaty negotiation and implementation is a cumbersome process scarcely suited to regulating pollution of a dynamic international environment. This status is to some extent ameliorated through the more imaginative use of treaties with attached protocols, where changing technical standards are embodied in protocols (or annexes) subject to simplified amendment procedures.

2.2   Customary international law is more amorphous than treaty law, constituting state practice combined with *opinio juris sive necessitas*, which embodies the notion that states consider certain action, or inaction, is legally required of them at international law. Both treaty law and customary international law constitute 'hard' law, that is, their rules are firm and binding upon states. Both impose binding legal obligations upon states for the breach of which state responsibility may attach, although in the case of customary international law such obligations may be less specific than treaty obligations.

2.3   However, in the environmental field there is another important category of law known as 'soft' law. This consists primarily of declarations and recommendations made by international conferences and organisations which regulate the conduct of states but for the breach of which the traditional enforcement mechanisms of international law will not apply. Soft law embodies 'rules which have to be considered as law in so far as they fix norms with which states would comply, but which cannot be enforced in the traditional meaning of the term'.[4]

The use of 'soft law' codes of conduct or guidelines as an international law-making or standards-setting device is a relatively recent phenomenon in international law.[5] While a code of conduct or guideline is

---

[3]See Sand, *ibid.*, pp.5-6.

[4]A.C. Kiss, *Survey of Current Developments in International Environmental Law*, IUCN Environmental Policy and Law Paper, No.10 (1976), p.23.

[5]R.E. Lutz and G.D. Aron, 'Codes of Conduct and Other International Instruments' in G. Handl and R.E. Lutz (eds.), *Transferring Hazardous Technologies and Substances: The International Legal Challenge* (Martinus Nijhoff, Dordrecht, 1989), pp.151-7;6. *Ibid.*, p.151.

not an international instrument having the same legal significance under traditional international law as a treaty, . . . it does have legal value in the international legal system. If this approach enables parties, with divergent perspectives and interests, to achieve negotiated agreements about complicated subject-matter, then there is also intrinsic value to this approach.[6]

Such 'concerted unilateralism' allows states to formally preserve national environmental sovereignty whilst facilitating joint technical action.[7] Since codes of conduct may well form the basis of national legislation, or be transformed into binding principles through treaty implementation or into customary international law as a result of state practice (that is to say, 'hardened'), the role of codes of conduct and guidelines as contributors to the international law-making process is potentially a highly significant one. Moreover, unlike treaties and customary international law, soft law may be 'instantly applicable'[8] – if states choose to make it so.

3. TRANSNATIONAL ADMINISTRATIVE LAW

Because of the global dimension to environmental problems, action at the international level has come mainly from two sources: various UN agencies such as the International Maritime Organization (IMO) and the UN Environment Programme (UNEP) and other international organisations such as the Organization for Economic Co-operation and Development (OECD) and the Council of Europe: and non-governmental organisations such as the International Union for the Conservation of Nature and Natural Resources (IUCN). Often concerned with those environmental issues related to their specific areas of concern, these organisations have had a significant impact upon international law-making activity in the environmental sector, particularly at the level of international administrative law.

Indeed, Sand[9] argues that international regulatory measures followed by international organisations and established by treaties comprise a third dimension to classical public international law, operating below the level of hard and soft law, collectively described as 'transnational administrative law'. It is based upon 'mutual recognition of national technical regulation'.[10] He identifies three typical techniques of transnational environmental law-making: standard-setting ('eco-standards'); licensing ('eco-permits') and auditing ('eco-audits'), which are interdependent in practice.

[6]*Ibid.*, p.151.

[7]Sand, 'The Creation of Transnational Rules for Environmental Protection', in M. Bothe (Project Co-ordinator), *Trends in Environmental Policy and Law* (IUCN, 1980), p.317.

[8]It is generally recognised that customary international law may take some time to evolve through state practice, although in some areas this development may be very rapid indeed. For example, see Bin Cheng, 'United Nations Resolutions on Outer Space: "Instant" International Customary Law', *Indian Journal of International Law*, 23/5, 1965.

[9]'The Creation of Transnational Rules for Environmental Protection', note 7, pp.311-20; and *Lessons Learned in Global Environmental Governance*, note 2.

[10]*Ibid.*, p.317.

3.1 Eco-standards

Standards-setting may be facilitated by the 'treaty with attached annexes' approach characteristic of environmental treaties where technical details are left to annexes to which simplified procedures of adoption and amendment apply. This enables technical annexes to be updated to take account of scientific and technological changes without the necessity to invoke cumbersome treaty amendment procedures. The standards may be strictly mandatory, as for example is the case for the radioactive contamination standards under the 1957 EURATOM treaty; or non-mandatory, as under the 1969 FAO/WHO Guidelines for Legislation concerning the registration for sale and marketing of pesticides; or mandatory but with an 'opt-out' clause establishing a notification procedure for states not wishing to be so bound, a technique used with annexes to MARPOL. Moreover, such standards often form a model for standards-setting at the national level, both stimulating the adoption of such standards and ensuring some degree of harmonisation amongst national laws.

3.2 Eco-permits

The issuing of eco-permits – or licenses – is not commonly carried out at the international level but is left, or delegated, to individual states to carry out. For example, 'international oil pollution prevention certificates' are issued by national authorities pursuant to the 1973-78 IMO Convention for the Prevention of Pollution from Ships. Similarly, waste disposal permits are issued under the Oslo and London Dumping Conventions according to black (prohibited) and grey (licence required) lists of substances contained in Annexes to the Conventions. The 1989 Basel Convention on the Control of Transboundary Movement of Hazardous Wastes and Their Disposal provides for waste-export notifications and authorisations, issued by national authorities. Because these licensing regimes are dependent on mutual recognition (or reciprocity) for their effective functioning, they function to ensure national implementation of international standards at the administrative level.

3.3 Eco-audits

Most international standards are set without accompanying back-up – that is, without an institutional machinery to monitor compliance and a regulatory or judicial authority to impose sanctions for the breach of international standards. It is rare for multilateral environmental agreements to provide for compulsory international adjudication of disputes.[11] In general, compliance with standards is achieved through eco-audits – transnational environmental auditing. At the international level this is achieved

---

[11]Moreover, even if the states involved have accepted the compulsory jurisdiction of the International Court of Justice, it has recently become the practice to insert a 'veto clause' in multilateral environmental agreements preventing compulsory third party adjudication. Both the 1985 Vienna Convention for the Protection of the Ozone Layer (and the 1987 Montreal Protocol) and the 1989 Basel Convention on the Control of Transboundary Movements of Hazardous Wastes and their Disposal contain such a clause. It is also always open to states to modify their acceptance of the International Court of Justice's compulsory jurisdiction by making a reservation excepting general or specific environmental matters. Thus, in 1970, the Canadian Government excluded from the compulsory jurisdiction of the Court matters relating to the 1970 Arctic Waters Pollution Prevention Act; acceptance of the compulsory jurisdiction was reinstated in 1985.

through the mechanism of annual reports, the prospect of which is designed to have a deterrent effect upon states contemplating the breach of eco-standards. Such auditing processes occur under one of the protocols to the 1979 Geneva Convention on Long-Range Transboundary Air Pollution which requires annual reports on national programmes, policies and strategies directed towards reduction of sulphur emissions.[12]

It is therefore generally up to national authorities to carry out licensing, monitoring, and enforcement of international standards. Much of the practical implementation and enforcement of international environmental law standards thus occurs at the national administrative level. In so far as international environmental law treaties do impose specific obligations on states, as will be seen below, there is a particular emphasis upon exchange of information, research and monitoring in international environmental law, activities best performed again at the administrative level.

4. THE DEFINITION OF POLLUTION AT INTERNATIONAL LAW

What is the international legal definition of pollution? The following definition, adopted in 1974 by the OECD, has achieved general acceptance by states:

> the introduction by man, directly or indirectly, of substances or energy into the environment resulting in deleterious effects of such a nature as to endanger human health, harm living resources and ecosystems, and impair or interfere with amenities and other legitimate uses of the environment.[13]

With minor amendments this definition has been substantially reproduced in a number of international conventions, including the 1979 Geneva Convention on Long-Range Transboundary Air Pollution and the Montreal Rules of International Law Applicable to Transfrontier Pollution adopted by the International Law Association in 1982. In modified form, it is also found in the 1982 United Nations Convention on the Law of the Sea which addresses not only actual damage, but the risk of damage as well.

The general concept of state responsibility for pollution damage and the definition of pollution employed are interlinked since it is the level fixed for acceptable pollution which also determines the level at which state responsibility will attach for harm caused by 'pollution'.[14] For example, on the definition given above, no pollution would result if, through the introduction by man (in) directly of substances or energy into the environment, the deleterious effects or interferences described did not result. If there is no 'pollution' for the purposes of a convention adopting this definition, then there is equally no question of the application of the liability regime established under a convention in the event of pollution occurring. Other treaty provisions set a harm threshold of 'significant harm' or 'significant adverse effects' which must be crossed before breach of a substantive rule has occurred entailing state responsibility and thus compensation for any resulting harm.

---

[12]See further below, under 5.1.

[13]OECD Council Recommendation on Principles Concerning Transfrontier Pollution, OECD Doc. C(74)224 of 21 Nov. 1974, reprinted in P. Sands (ed.), *Chernobyl: Law and Communication* (1988), p.150. Compare the author's defination, Chapter I at 2.3.3, drafted for his own purposes in 1972.

[14]Stated succinctly as 'to what must the damage be done to be considered pollution and what level of damage is necessary?': Springer, 'Towards a meaningful concept of pollution in international law', (1977) 26 ICLQ 531, p.537; see also *ibid.*, *The International Law of Pollution: Protecting the Global Environment in a World of Sovereign States* (Quorum Books, 1983).

5. GENERAL PRINCIPLES OF INTERNATIONAL ENVIRONMENTAL LAW AND THE PROBLEM OF INTERNATIONAL RESPONSIBILITY

5.1 Customary international law imposes several fundamental duties upon states in terms of their responsibility for environmental harm, duties which have developed through cases involving transboundary air and water pollution in particular. In the 1939 *Trail Smelter* arbitration[15] the US complained of damage caused to trees and crops in the state of Washington by sulphur dioxide pollution emanating from an iron ore smelter in Trail, British Columbia. The arbitral tribunal noted that 'under principles of international law, as well as under the law of the United States, no state has the right to use or permit the use of territory in such a manner as to cause injury by fumes in or to the territory of another or the properties of persons therein, when the case is of serious consequences and the injury established'.[16] The basic duty upon states not to act so as to harm the rights of other states is at the heart of the rules of international law relating to state responsibility. The principle applies equally to shared watercourses. Thus, in the *International Commission on the River Oder* case[17] the Permanent Court of Justice noted that the 'community interest in a navigable river becomes the basis of a common legal right, the essential features of which are the perfect equality of all riparian states in the use of the whole course of the river and the exclusion of any preferential privileges of any riparian state in relation to others'.[18]

5.2

5.2.1 Thus while the sovereignty which a state exercise over its own territory would suggest a certain liberty (or right) to pollute, this is subject to the international legal obligation to refrain from injuring the rights of other states through the use of territory in such a manner so as to cause harm to the territory of another state.[19] This right and the correlative duty was recognised by the arbitrator Max Huber in the *Island of Palmas* case:

> Territorial sovereignty involves the exclusive right to display the activities of a states.
> This right has as corollary a duty: the obligation to protect within the territory the rights
> of other states, in particular their right to integrity and inviolability in peace and in

[15]See 9 *International Law Reports* 315.

[16]*Ibid.*, p.317. This passage was cited with approval by Judge de Castro in his dissent in the *Nuclear Tests* case where Australia sought to halt French atmospheric nuclear testing in the Pacific region on the basis that it was unlawful 'in so far as it involves modification of the physical conditions of and over Australian territory [and] pollution of the atmosphere and of the resources of the sea'. See (1974) *ICJ Reports* 253, p.289. In the event a unilateral declaration by the French Government that atmospheric nuclear testing would be discontinued was held to be binding and the ICJ was not required to proceed to adjudge the merits of the Australian claim as it no longer had any object.

[17]5 *International Law Reports* 83.

[18]*Ibid.*, p.84. See also the *Lac Lanoux* arbitration (12 RIAA 285) involving the diversion of an international river by an upstream state, where the tribunal noted that a state in exercising its own rights must have regard to the rights of other states:

> France is entitled to exercise her rights; she cannot ignore the Spanish interests. Spain is entitled to
> demand that her rights be respected and that her interests be taken into consideration.

[19]This is generally expressed in the maxim *sic utere tuo ut alienum non laedas* (use your own property in such a manner as not to damage that of another).

war, together with the rights which each state may claim for its nationals in foreign territory.[20]

The duty applies even where the harmful effects are caused by trespassers if the territorial sovereignty has knowledge, or the means of knowledge, of the harmful activity. In the *Corfu Channel* case[21] the International Court of Justice emphasised that it was the obligation of every state 'not to allow knowingly its territory to be used for acts contrary to the rights of other states'.[22]

5.2.2   The sovereign right of a state to exploit its own resources in accordance with its own environmental policies, but subject to 'the responsibility to ensure that activities within their jurisdiction or control do not cause damage to the environment of other states or of areas beyond the limits of national jurisdiction' is recognised in Principle 21 of the Stockholm Declaration of 1972. This principle is not legally binding but constitutes 'soft' law; a guideline for the future application of law. But its significance should not be overlooked, particularly as it was laid down at the 1972 United Nations Conference on the Human Environment which forms an important benchmark in the development of international environmental law. Principle 21 has attracted considerable support from states and has been expressly recommended by the United Nations General Assembly as laying down the basic rules governing the international responsibility of states with respect to the environment.[23]

Principle 21 both confirms existing law and adds to it. The confirmation is contained in the recognition that states have an obligation to ensure that activities within their jurisdiction or control do not cause damage to the environment of other states, sometimes more generally expressed as the concept of 'good neighbourliness'. It is innovative in that the principle refers to harm to the environment, not just the territory, of other states. This was one of the first attempts 'to secure recognition of the hitherto vague concept of environment as a concept having legal significance, a development which might eventually affect even the content of states' obligations'.[24] The principle also mentions damage to the environment in areas beyond national jurisdiction, the prevention of which is also recognised in, for example, the 1982 United Nations Convention on the Law of the Sea.

Principle 22 of the Declaration is also worthy of note. It states that

States shall co-operate to develop further the international law regarding liability and compensation for the victims of pollution and other environmental damage caused by activities within the jurisdiction of states or control of such states to areas beyond their jurisdiction.

This is a much weakened text to that originally proposed which would have required states to pay compensation for all environmental damage caused by activ-

[20]2 RIAA 829, p.839.

[21]16 *International Law Reports* 155. The case is not an environmental one; it arose out of an incident involving two British warships which were damaged by mines located in Albanian territorial waters in the Corfu Channel.

[22]*Ibid.*, p.158.

[23]UNGA Resolution 2996 (XXVII) of 15 Dec. 1972, 27 UN GAOR (Supp.No.30) 42. The Resolution received 112 votes in favour, none against and 18 abstentions.

[24]Dupuy, 'International Liability for Transfrontier Pollution' in Bothe, *Trends in Environmental Policy and Law* (IUCN, 1980), p.372.

ities carried on within their territory.[25] Opponents of such a formulation feared that this would incorporate a standard of liability that was strict, or 'no-fault'; as will be seen below, the general standard accepted by states is a lower one of 'due diligence' where states are generally only required to pay compensation for environmental harm caused through a lack of due diligence.

5.2.3   A further general principle[26] of international environmental law relates to the duty to co-operate, reflected in Principle 24 of the Stockholm Declaration which states that 'international matters concerning the protection and improvement of the environment should be handled in a co-operative spirit'. From the *Corfu Channel* case may be deduced the duty to warn other states of known environmental hazards. The duty to inform of environmental hazards is one frequently embodied in international treaties; for example, Article 13 of the 1989 Basel Convention on the Control of Transboundary Movement of Hazardous Waste imposes such an obligation where an accident during the transboundary movement of hazardous waste poses risks to human health and the environment in other states. Other treaties impose an obligation of prior consultation. The International Law Association has concluded that 'a rule of international customary law has emerged that in principle a state is obliged to render information on new or increasing pollution to a potential victim state'.[27]

In the case of shared resources, international law recognises the concept of equitable utilisation of those resources. In the particular context of a shared river or water basin, equitable apportionment of the beneficial uses of the drainage basin, or shared river, between riparian states is a generally recognised principle of international law.[28] This is recognised in state practice with respect to international waterways, the use of which may be regulated by treaty either through the establishment of a regime of joint sovereignty or through provisions regarding the common use of the waterway. Certain rivers, the Danube for example, are subject to a treaty regime to regulate user and administration. Canada and the US, through the 1909 Boundary Waters Treaty, have sought to prevent disputes arising with respect to the waterways shared by these two states. In the event of a dispute regarding the use of boundary waters, the treaty provides for adjudication by an International Joint Commission which in many instances is vested by the treaty with final authority. In addition, injured nationals may pursue their claim in the courts of the state causing the harm.

[25]See generally, Sohn, 'The Stockholm Declaration on the Human Environment' (1973) 14 *Harvard Journal of International Law* 423, pp.493-502.

[26]In addition to treaties and customary international law, a further source of international law is 'general principles of law recognised by civilised nations': see Article 38(1)(c) of the Statute of the International Court of Justice. The principles discussed here could be classified as either customary international law or general principles; either would be characterised as hard, i.e. binding, law.

[27]ILA, *Report of the Sixtieth Conference* 1982, p.173.

[28]See the discussion of the *River Oder* and *Lac Lanoux* cases above. These principles have been elaborated by the International Law Association in the 1966 Helsinki Rules of the Uses of the Waters of International Rivers and by UNEP in Draft Principles relating to Natural Resources Shared by Two or More States.

5.3   The standard of care

In general a breach of a rule of international law by an act or omission, entails state responsibility:

> [I]t is a principle of international law that the breach of an engagement involves an obligation to make reparation in an adequate form . . . .[29]

The standard of care imposed on states will vary according to the nature of the activity causing pollution and the degree of harm caused to other states. There are three possibles types of liability: absolute, strict, or fault liability. Although sometimes used interchangeably to connote no-fault liability, there is a significant distinction between absolute and strict liability.[30] Strict liability still allows for an excuse that the pollution in question was caused by circumstances beyond the control of the polluter, such as the act of a third party (e.g. sabotage) or *force majeure*. Absolute liability would permit no such excuse. It is perhaps not surprising therefore that states have not accepted this onerous standard to regulate their conduct save for the exception of ultra-hazardous activities, described further below.

It has been argued that strict liability should be the standard imposed upon the states in the area of transboundary environmental harm; that states are under an obligation to control or prevent activities within their territory which will cause harm to other states, with absence of fault being no excuse. However, it is doubtful whether this proposition has been accepted as a general one at international law. The case law is inconclusive and treaty practice is variable. Indeed, if a uniform standard were to be identified in the practice of states, it would be one of 'due diligence' rather than strict liability, although the latter is of growing importance. The due diligence standard requires states to exercise diligent control over sources of harm within their territory, a standard which, if met, has the necessary consequence that a state may escape responsibility for harm caused to another state – that some residual transboundary pollution will be regarded as lawful.

Unlike under strict liability then, a standard of due diligence does not render a state automatically responsible for harm caused and introduces some flexibility as to the standard required; 'States will be required to take all necessary steps to prevent substantial pollution and to demonstrate the kind of behaviour expected of "good government"'.[31] This means that

> In accordance with the general principles, States may reasonably be expected to introduce domestic legislation and controls, including sanctions which act as effective deterrents to offenders, based on technical and administrative checks on the use of air and water and arrangements for notifying adjacent countries of serious accidents.[32]

---

[29]*Chorzow Factory* Case (1928) PCIJ Ser. A, No. 17, p.21.

[30]See generally Goldie, 'Development of an International Environmental Law – An Appraisal' in Hargrove (ed), *Law, Institutions and the Global Environment* (Oceana Publications, 1972), pp.104–65.

[31]Shaw, *International Law* (2nd ed. 1991), p.536. 'Good government' means that the standard of conduct expected from it will be that of 'a government mindful of its international obligations': see Dupuy, 'International Liability for Transfrontier Pollution' in *Trends in Environmental Law and Policy*, IUCN Environmental Policy and Law Paper, 1980, p.369.

[32]Kiss, note 4, p.370.

The standard of due diligence is drawn from late nineteenth century international jurisprudence and from common law principles.[33] The elements of remoteness and foreseeability also apply such that the damage must have been caused by the pollution under consideration; the harm caused must be established 'by clear and convincing evidence' said the tribunal in the *Trail Smelter* case.[34] Precautions taken at the outset may not preclude responsibility if 'the risks are foreseeably high ... and damage is in fact caused'.[35] Remoteness and foreseeability pose particular problems in the context of cumulative pollution, a problem inherent in any liability approach to environmental protection whether pursued at international or national level.

The due diligence standard also means that states are not obliged to keep all private individuals and companies within their territory from causing transboundary pollution. However, responsibility would attach to the state for the unlawful acts of its officials which result in injury to nationals of another state. The extent of the state's general responsibility is to ensure that reasonable legislative and executive measures have been taken to regulate conduct under the jurisdiction and control of the state. It is up to the state to ensure that its international obligations are observed within its own territory. Whether a breach has occurred will depend in part upon the nature of the international obligation. Thus, if a convention sets emission standards which are exceeded by the state as a consequence of the actions of an individual, or pollution in violation of international law is caused by unlicensed private actions which by treaty the state is to make subject to prior authorisation, the state will bear international responsibility. State liability for the acts of non-governmental agencies may also be imposed by treaty.[36]

In general terms then, state responsibility arises when the individual act has occurred as a result of a failure of good government; a failure to carry out governmental functions in accordance with the standard of due diligence and in recognition of the state's international obligations. 'Should a state fail, for instance, to provide for the necessary environmental standards and regulations, it would, in case of injuries, be liable for the omission of its legislative organs.'[37]

In each case there are thus a number of questions to ask:

- has damage been caused? If not, is there liability for the risk of damage?
- what threshold of damage must be caused before international responsibility attaches?
- to what types of harm does responsibility attach?

---

[33]*Ibid.*, p.369. The first international use of the expression was in the *Alabama* case arising out of the American Civil War where an arbitral tribunal held that the British Government had failed to exercise due diligence in the performance of its neutrality obligation under the 1871 Treaty of Washington.

[34]Note 15, p.317.

[35]I. Brownlie, 'A Survey of International Customary Rules of Environmental Protection' in L.A. Teclaff and A.E. Utton (eds.), *International Environmental Law* (Praeger, London, 1974) 1, p.4.

[36]See, e.g., Article VI of the Outer Space Treaty 1967 which provides for the international responsibility of states for 'national activities in outer space ... whether such activities are carried out by governmental agencies or by non-governmental agencies'. The Moon Treaty 1979 and the Convention on International Liability for Damage Caused by Space Objects 1972 contain similar provisions.

[37]Brunnee, *Acid Rain and Ozone Layer Depletion: International Law and Regulation* (Transnational Publishers, New York, 1988), p.119.

The answers to these questions will depend upon the nature of the pollution causing or threatening the harm and the degree of harm caused or threatened. It is therefore necessary to examine various types of pollution and the liability regime, if any, applicable.

6. THE TYPES OF POLLUTION

6.1 Air pollution

Air pollution is regulated at every level – international, regional and national.[38] Internationally, the 1979 Geneva Convention on Long–Range Transboundary Air Pollution was negotiated within the UN Economic Commission for Europe (ECE) on the initiative of Scandinavian states concerned about the problem of acid precipitation. It was the first multilateral convention relating to the protection of the environment to include East and West European states as well as the United States and the Soviet Union. It applies to air pollution whose physical origin is situated wholly or in part within the area under the national jurisdiction of one state and which has adverse effects under the jurisdiction of another state. An innovation is that it is not necessary for the affected state to isolate individual emission sources. However, states are only required to 'endeavour to limit and as far as possible, gradually reduce and prevent air pollution, including long range transboundary air pollution', (Article 2) and there is no liability regime established under the Convention, nor a disputes settlement mechanism. The most significant features of the Convention relate to information exchange and consultation, with the types of information to be exchanged set forth in some detail. Three additions have been made to the Convention in the form of protocols relating to long term financing of a monitoring and evaluation scheme

---

[38]See, e.g., the United Nations series 'Air Pollution Studies' which includes annual updates on 'The state of Transboundary Air Pollution'. The series is published under the auspices of the Executive Body for the Convention on Long-range Transboundary Air Pollution. Included is an annual review of national and international strategies and policies for air pollution abatement; forest damage surveys; the effects of mercury and other heavy metals related to the long-range atmospheric transport of pollution; and an analysis of the economic and cost impact of different strategies for abatement of sulphur and nitrogen oxide emissions. This information is compiled on the basis of the information which parties and signatories are obliged to submit annually under the Convention. In addition, under the Protocols:

Parties must also report no later than 1 May of each year on national programmes, policies and strategies for sulphur emission reductions and on progress towards achieving the goal of the Protocol, i.e. the reduction of sulphur emissions or their transboundary fluxes by at least 30 per cent. Furthermore, in accordance with the 1988 ... Protocol ... Parties exchange information on national programmes, policies and strategies that shall serve as a means of controlling and reducing emissions of nitrogen oxides or their transboundary fluxes.

ECE, *The State of Transboundary Air Pollution: 1989 Update* Air Pollution Studies 6, UN Doc. ECE/EB.AIR/25 (1990), p.3.

for Europe, 'EMEP',[39] and to the setting of standards for both sulphur emissions and nitrogen oxides and the transboundary fluxes of each.[40]

It is perhaps the perceived deficiencies of international action which has led to initiatives to combat air pollution at the regional level. In 1977 the OECD noted that the problem was a 'pan-European' one requiring a European solution.[41] The OECD has certainly been active in this area; of particular note is the 1974 Recommendation on Principles Concerning Transfrontier Pollution, which includes the generally accepted definition of pollution cited above, and the supplemental 1977 Recommendation for the Implementation of a Regime of Equal Right of Access and Non-Discrimination in Relation to Transfrontier Pollution. Both Recommendations seek to harmonise environmental policies and to provide for a non-discriminatory right of access by affected individuals to the courts of the polluting state. This latter point is pursued further in the 1977 Recommendation, which in addition to recognising non-discriminatory access by individuals to the administrative and judicial processes of the polluting state extends the same right of standing to environmental protection groups and public authorities in the polluted state. However, the obligations are expressed in weak and permissive language such as 'should consider' and 'should grant', within a Recommendation that reflects 'soft law' at best. Nonetheless, the impact on state practice may be viewed as significant and states are, in any event, encouraged to enter into bilateral or multilateral treaty arrangements in order to implement fully the Recommendations.

In 1982 the Montreal Rules of International Law Applicable to Transfrontier Pollution were adopted by the International Law Association [42] which require states 'to prevent . . . transfrontier air pollution to such an extent that no substantial injury is caused in the territory of another State (Article 3(1)).' This was viewed by the ILA to represent a reformulation of existing customary law.

A wide range of regional organisations have addressed the problem of air pollution, including the Nordic Council[43] and the EC. At this level both standards setting and harmonisation of existing national rules are pursued. For example, the European Community has adopted Council Directive 88/609 designed to reduce the emission of sulphur dioxide and nitrogen oxide from existing large combustion

---

[39]A 'Co-operative programme for the monitoring and evalution of the long-range transmission of air pollutants in Europe', EMEP, has established monitoring stations to detect flows of sulphur dioxide across European borders. Originally funded by UNEP, the Protocol provides for mandatory financing by parties to the Protocol within the geographical scope of EMEP, with voluntary contributions from parties outside EMEP's area.

[40]See the 1985 Protocol on the Reduction of Sulphur Emissions or their Transboundary Fluxes and the 1988 Protocol concerning the Control of Nitrogen Oxide Emissions or their Transboundary Fluxes.

[41]See S. Ercman, 'Activities of the Council of Europe and the European Economic Communities Related to Transboundary Air Pollution' in C. Flinterman, B. Kwiatkowska and J.G. Lammers (eds.), *Transboundary Air Pollution: International Legal Aspects of the Co-operation of States* (Martinus Nijhoff, Dordrecht, 1986), p.131.

[42]The International Law Association (ILA) is a private organisation of lawyers founded in 1873 and dedicated to 'the study, elucidation and advancement of international law, public and private' (Article 2 of the ILA Constitution). The work of the ILA is generally highly respected by international lawyers as authoritative pronouncements of law. The 'teachings of the most highly qualified publicists' form a subsidiary source of law under Article 38 of the Statute of the ICJ.

[43]See the 1974 Nordic Convention for the Protection of the Environment, 1092 UNTS 279; 13 ILM 591 (1974).

plants by 15 per cent by 1993 and by 30 per cent by 1998. EC Directives have also been adopted limiting vehicle exhaust emissions.

6.2 Ultra-hazardous activities

This is one category of activity where it has been argued that international law applies a standard of absolute liability for harm caused by ultra-hazardous activities; that is, it is sufficient to establish that damage has been caused by an activity taking place under the jurisdiction or control of the responsible state. This is an objective form of liability which has been resisted as a general rule applying to all pollution activities. It shifts the burden of proof and of loss from the victim to the state and should operate as an incentive to states to ensure that action is taken with respect to activities carrying the potential of exceptional harm.

What constitutes an ultra-hazardous activity? Consensus has only been reached with respect to nuclear activities as ultra-hazardous, as a general rule. The principle of absolute liability is also found in specific treaty obligations relating to ultra-hazardous but non-nuclear activities. The 1972 Convention on International Liability for Damage caused by Space Objects makes a launching state absolutely liable to pay compensation for any damage caused by its space objects on the earth's surface. Canada sought to rely on this provision in 1978 when the Soviet *Cosmos 954* satellite accidently crashed on Canadian territory. Also relied upon were general principles of law including 'the principle [that] absolute liability applies to fields of activity having in common a high degree of risk'.[44]

As the 1986 incident involving the Chernobyl nuclear reactor demonstrated, the effects of a nuclear pollution incident can be serious and widespread in their effects. The incident also demonstrated that, notwithstanding multilateral treaties banning atmospheric testing of nuclear weapons, placing special obligations on the operators of nuclear ships and on the carriers of nuclear materials at sea, and regarding the protection of nuclear materials, 'there existed no multilateral treaty requiring the provision of prompt and detailed information, either for general air-carried pollution or specifically for radioactive materials".[45] This was very quickly remedied by the International Atomic Energy Authority (IAEA). Established in 1956 to encourage the development of nuclear power, its role is increasingly to ensure the safe use of such power. Arising from the Chernobyl incident were two conventions sponsored by the IAEA, the Convention on Assistance in Cases of Nuclear Emergency and the Convention on Early Notification of a Nuclear Accident. The Notification Convention requires state parties to inform forthwith the IAEA, or the states who are or may be physically affected, of a nuclear accident and to supply both the IAEA and affected states with the detailed information relating to the accident. The provisions of the Notification Convention have been reflected in a variety of bilateral treaty arrangements, some of which strengthen the

---

[44]See the Canadian statement of claim reprinted in 18 ILM 902 (1979), p.907. The claim was settled on 2 Aug. 1981 when the Soviet Union offered to pay CDN$3m in full and final settlement of Canada's claim.

[45]Sands, note 13, p.xix. The earliest treaty providing for assistance in the event of a radiological emergency was the Nordic Mutual Assistance Agreement in 1963.

notification provisions.[46] EC Directive 87/600 of December 1987 provides for the early exchange of information in the event of a radiological emergency.

Under the Assistance Convention, help may be requested of the IAEA and any other state party, but the Convention does not require states to provide assistance. Incentives are provided in the form of reimbursement of costs and of certain privileges and immunities granted assisting personnel and their property. The IAEA has important co-ordinating and information disseminating functions under the Convention; in addition, bilateral and multilateral arrangements are encouraged to facilitate co-operation amongst states in providing prompt assistance. The Convention thus seeks to achieve a balance between the sovereignty of the requesting state, the rights of the assisting state(s), and the interests of the international community in providing a rapid response to nuclear incidents threatening or causing transboundary harm.

6.3   Civil liability

The principle of 'absolute liability' is well-established in the treaties regulating nuclear activities. The first international convention to regulate liability for harm arising from the peaceful use of nuclear energy was the OEEC (now OECD) sponsored 1960 Paris Convention on Third Party Liability in the Field of Nuclear Energy,[47] to which 14 European states are party. The purpose of the Paris Convention is to harmonise national rules with respect to third party liability, insurance against nuclear risks, and to establish a liability and compensation regime for nuclear accidents. It provides that the operator (a private entity or the state itself) of a nuclear installation shall be liable for damage to persons or property, so long as it is proved that the damage was caused by a nuclear incident involving that installation. This causal connection between the incident, the installation, and the harm suffered is sufficient; proof of fault or negligence on the part of the operator is not necessary. Judgments are enforceable in the territory of any contracting party to the Convention. The Paris Convention also requires the operator to maintain insurance or other financial security to meet its maximum liability under the Convention. However, since liability in a nuclear incident might well exceed the stipulated ceiling in the Paris Convention, Euratom sponsored the supplementary Brussels Convention of 1963[48] under which the contracting state in which the installation is situated will be required to provide additional compensation with further compensation available from the contracting states as a whole.[49] Incorporating similar provisions but of intended global application is the IAEA Vienna Convention on Civil Liability for Nuclear Damage 1963, which has attracted eleven parties only two of whom possess nuclear facilities (Yugoslavia and Argentina).

---

[46]For example, in 1988–89 the United Kingdom concluded agreements with Norway, the Netherlands and Denmark which require notification of an accident or activity of 'radiological safety significance' likely to have transboundary effects and of abnormal levels of radiation registered in the notifying State even if not caused by release from facilities or activities in the territory of the notifying State. There are also detailed provisions regarding the exchange of information. See Woodliffe, 'Chernobyl: Four Years On' (1990) 39 *ICLQ* 461, p.464.

[47]956 UNTS 251.

[48]1041 UNTS 358; 2 ILM (1963) 685.

[49]This recognition of the residual responsibility of states to ensure that the operator is able to meet claims up to the liability limits of the Convention, is unique.

Two major weaknesses of the Paris and Vienna Conventions are the small number of states possessing nuclear facilities which are parties to either Convention, and the failure to provide for the costs of environmental clean-up. The first point was addressed in 1988 when the Conventions were linked by a protocol; however, the major nuclear states of the US, Soviet Union and Japan are still not parties to either Convention. The second has not been properly addressed; indeed, as noted above if a state requests assistance from other states under the Assistance Convention, the costs of rendering such assistance may be recouped.[50]

6.4   Other hazardous activities

National legal systems provide a range of civil, administrative and criminal rules and compensation systems for hazardous activities such as the disposal of toxic and hazardous waste and the transport of hazardous and toxic materials by road, rail and sea. The sheer diversity of such rules and the varying quality of the applicable standards, and of their implementation, poses particular problems for the trans-boundary movement of hazardous substances. Such diversity by its very nature discourages the transfer of hazardous yet useful products; and such transfer may occur at the expense of human and environmental health if standards and/or their implementation are set too low. When harm is caused, a diversity of rules impedes the ability to obtain necessary safety information and the development of procedures to deal with pollution incidents involving hazardous substances.[51]

Compounding the difficulty is the fact that multinational corporations are often the vehicle for hazardous transfers and may well be beyond the effective reach of national laws whilst at the same time not traditionally considered subjects of international law. This is not to say that there have not been international attempts to control multinational corporations, primarily through codes of conduct elaborated by international organisations. A code of conduct or guideline, as has already been noted, is a non-binding instrument of principles which generally includes an institutional machinery for their implementation. Typically states, international organisations and multinational corporations participate in the drafting of guidelines. The first attempt to regulate multinational conduct came from the International Chamber of Commerce (ICC) in 1972 with "Guidelines for International Investment', since self-regulation was considered preferable to governmental regulation. Codes of conduct for multinationals have also been adopted by states in organisations such as the UN, the OECD and the EC. Of particular note is the draft UN Code of Conduct on Transnational Corporations and the OECD Guidelines for Multinational Enterprises which form the backdrop for subsequent guidelines directly addressing the issue of transboundary hazardous substances.

Also active has been the World Bank which, following the natural gas explosion in Mexico City and the Bhopal disaster in 1984, established Guidelines for identifying, analysing and controlling major hazard installations in developing countries. It relied heavily on an EEC Directive on the Major Accident Hazards of

---

[50]Indeed, the Convention could apply so that the state in which the nuclear incident occurred provides assistance to an affected state and is able to recover the its assistance costs: see Sands, note 13, p.47.

[51]R.E. Lutz and G.D. Aron, note 5, p.130.

Certain Industrial Activities in drafting these guidelines. In addition, UNEP has established Guidelines on Risk-Management and Accident Prevention in the Chemical Industry, whilst the FAO has adopted a voluntary International Code of Conduct on the Distribution and Use of Pesticides. Following the Mexico City and Bhopal incidents in particular, the General Conference of the International Labour Organization adopted a resolution analagous to a code of conduct which emphasised, *inter alia*,

> that in the design and implication of their industrial development policies, competent public authorities and industry should take fully into account the possible safety and health effects of hazardous substances and processes on workers and the general public, and the basic responsibility of multinational corporations' central management over the organization and control of the management of all their subsidiary units.[52]

A separate yet related problem has been the disposal, or dumping, of hazardous waste in Third World states. In 1988 the Organisation of African Unity adopted a resolution which declared that the dumping of nuclear and industrial wastes in Africa constituted a crime against the African people. One year earlier, UNEP approved the Cairo Guidelines and Principles for the Environmentally Sound Management of Hazardous Wastes. These require the notification and consent of the receiving state prior to the transport of waste, and verification that ultimate disposal facilities are adequate.

In addition, both the OECD and the IAEA have addressed the problem of the transboundary movement of hazardous and radioactive waste. In 1989 the Basel Convention on the Control of Transboundary Movements of Hazardous Wastes and their Disposal was concluded under the auspices of the OECD. This prohibits the export of such wastes to states which are not parties to the convention; which have prohibited their importation and so notified the other parties; or to states which cannot dispose of the waste in an environmentally sound manner. Even if a state party has not prohibited the importation of waste, the exporting state must nonetheless obtain consent in writing to the specific import from the importing state. Written permission must also be sought from transit states. Weaknesses of the Basel Convention include the failure to specify what amounts to 'environmentally sound' disposal, and the absence of a liability regime.

Prior notification and consent is also the basis of the regime established under the IAEA Code of Practice on the International Transboundary Movement of Radioactive Waste. The Code also calls for the establishment of regulatory authorities competent to manage and dispose of radioactive wastes in a manner consistent with international safety standards. This is a further example of the 'transnational administrative law' which Sand argues is developing in the international environmental law field.

6.5   Marine pollution

6.5.1   Principle 7 of the Stockholm Declaration states that

> States shall take all possible steps to prevent pollution of the seas by substances that are liable to create hazards to human health, to harm living resources and marine life, damage amenities or to interfere with other legitimate uses of the sea.

[52]Note 5, p.149.

Accompanying the Declaration is an Action Plan. Of the 109 recommendations comprising the Action Plan, a total of nine are in respect of the marine environment, an indication of the relative importance of the oceans to the global environment.

The sources of marine pollution are diverse, ranging from land-based and air-borne sources to deliberate dumping of waste at sea and pollution from activities on the continental shelf and deep ocean floor. A wide range of treaty activity characterises this area, at bilateral, regional and multilateral levels. Vessel source pollution has been a particular focus of treaty attention where complex liability regimes have been established. These, and the regimes established for other sources of marine pollution, will be canvassed in brief from the viewpoint of the standards set, their enforcement, and the impact at national level of these international law-making activities.

6.5.2   Vessel source marine pollution

Two spectacular oil spills in particular stimulated international and regional leg-islative activity in this field – the *Torrey Canyon* disaster in 1967[53] and the *Amoco Cadiz* in 1978. The *Exxon Valdez* spill in Prince William Sound in 1988 had a similar effect on international law-making. The first Convention for the Prevention of Pollution of the Sea by Oil (OILPOL) pre-dated these disasters, however, for it was concluded in 1954 and prohibited the discharge of oil within 50 miles of land.[54] This was superseded in 1973 by the International Convention for the Prevention of Pollution from Ships (MARPOL) which adopts a framework convention with attached annexes approach characteristic of treaties for environmental protection. Attached to the Convention are five annexes setting forth detail standards with respect to oil, noxious liquid substances carried in bulk, harmful substances carried in packages, sewage and garbage. The procedures for entry into force of the Annexes,[55] and for their alteration in accordance with technological advancement, are simplified. In particular, a tacit acceptance procedure operates with respect to amendments of technical appendices and annexes; an amendment is automatically binding at the expiry of a set period provided no objection has been made to it. In 1978 the Convention was updated and the updated version is referred to as 'MARPOL 73/78'.

There are a number of requirements in respect of the carrying of oil record books and the entering of certain details therein. This record book may be inspected by a contracting state to MARPOL 73/78 on a vessel to which the Convention applies while the vessel is in the port of that state. If the discharges entered are in excess of those established under the Convention then the flag state or, in certain circum-stances, the inspecting port state, may prosecute this breach. MARPOL 73/78 lays down a number of other requirements, including more stringent construction stan-dards for oil tankers.

---

[53]The 1969 International Convention Relating to Intervention on the High Seas in Cases of Oil Pollution Casualties was a direct result of this incident. In 1973 a Protocol was added extending the ambit of the Convention to substances other than oil.

[54]OILPOL was concluded under the auspices of the United Kingdom. Later Conventions have been negotiated under the auspices of a United Nations subsidiary organ, the International Maritime Organization (IMO).

[55]The first two annexes, covering pollution by oil and by chemicals, are mandatory and entered into force in 1983 and 1987 respectively. The remaining annexes are optional, with states able to become parties to MARPOL 73/78 without accepting one or all of them. However, Annex V (garbage) came into force on 31 Dec. 1988; Annex III, covering pollution of the sea by harmful substances carried in packaged form, entered into force on 1 July 1992.

In 1990 an International Convention on Oil Pollution Preparedness, Response and Co-operation was concluded which requires parties to report pollution incidents immediately; to inform states likely to be affected if the spill is serious; and to inform the IMO. Ships are required to carry aboard pollution emergency plans, whilst co-ordinated national and regional emergency planning is encouraged. Although not yet in force, the Convention was used even before its conclusion as the basis for international co-operation in responding to the marine pollution threat posed by the Gulf conflict between Iraq and Kuwait.[56]

6.5.3   Civil liability

Liability for oil pollution is strict under the 1969 Civil Liability Convention where oil from a ship causes damage on the territory or territorial sea of a contracting party. It is the shipowner who is liable, both for the damage caused and for any preventive measures taken. Because liability is strict, there is no necessity to prove fault; however, the shipowner has certain defences available such as civil war, *force majeure*, sabotage, and the negligence of the government authority responsible for maintaining navigational aids.

However, unless the pollution occurred as a result of the actual fault or privity of the shipowner, such liability is limited under the Civil Liability Convention, although the supplementary Fund Convention[57] may apply where the Civil Liability Convention does not. This places financial responsibility on oil cargo interests; oil companies establish and maintain funds in each state party to the Convention to cover claims of this kind. Additional industry schemes, TOVALOP and CRISTAL, operate in this area. TOVALOP covers claims by public authorities against shipowners of charterers for the costs of clean-up on land; liability is fault-based. CRISTAL supplements TOVALOP and extends coverage not only to governmental costs but to costs incurred by private individuals or companies; damage on land and within the territorial sea is also covered.

7.   REGIONAL APPROACHES TO MARINE POLLUTION

7.1   There are number references to the need for regional arrangements in the 1982 Law of the Sea Convention. The first regional organisation designed specifically for marine pollution control was established in 1972. It was a response to the practices of deliberate discharge of polluting substances at sea and commercial dumping. The organisation created was the Oslo Commission established under the Convention for the Prevention of Marine Pollution by Dumping from Ships and Aircraft signed at Oslo in 1972.[58]

---

[56]See IMO Briefing (produced for information purposes only), 24 July 1991 (IMO/B10/91).
[57]The 1971 Convention on the Establishment of an International Fund for Compensation for Oil Pollution Damage.
[58]ST/LEG/SER.B/16, p.457.

7.2 UNEP

No discussion of regional approaches to marine pollution control is complete without reference to the United Nations Environment Programme (UNEP). Established in 1972,[59] UNEP has initiated and carried through a number of marine environment programmes at regional (and global[60]) levels. Its objectives in this sphere are: (i) the promotion of international and regional conventions, guidelines, and action for the control of marine pollution and for the protection and management of aquatic resources; (ii) the assessment of the state of pollution and of living resources; and (iii) the monitoring of marine pollution and aquatic resources.[61] UNEP has sponsored a Regional Seas Programme which encompasses ten regional seas areas and involves 130 governments in: the Mediterranean; the Gulf; West/Central Africa; southeast Pacific; Red Sea; Caribbean; eastern Africa; southwest Pacific; East Asia; South Asia; and the southwest Atlantic. Since 1975 action plans have been adopted for nine regions (South Asia is in preparation), supplemented by 'legislative elements, environmental assessment and management, together with institutional and financial arrangements'.[62] Each Action Plan comprises five basic components:

(a) environmental assessment;
(b) environmental management (with plans for co-ordination and co-operation);
(c) institutional arrangements (secretariat, conferences);
(d) financial arrangements (regional trust funds); and
(e) regional legal instruments.

The blueprint for regional action plans and conventions was developed in the Mediterranean region, with the Mediterranean Action Plan followed by the first regional treaty instruments under the UNEP programme, the Barcelona Convention and Protocols 1976. This is a framework Convention supplemented by appropriate protocols covering, in the instance of the Mediterranean, ocean dumping, emergency co-operation to prevent pollution by oil and other harmful substances, land-based sources of marine pollution, and the designation of specially protected areas.

7.3 Other UN bodies

The Economic and Social Council has establish five regional commissions for Europe (ECE), Asia and the Pacific (ESCAP), Latin America (ECLA), Africa (ECA), and western Asia (ECWA). The activities of the ECE in the context of transboundary air pollution have already been discussed.[63] Each commission has

---

[59]By the United Nations General Assembly on 15 Dec. 1972, G.A. Res. 2997 (XXVII), 26 UN GAOR, Supp. 30, pp.43–5 (1972).

[60]UNEP has adoped global guidelines on Off-Shore Mining and Land-Based Sources of marine pollution, reproduced in P. Sand, *Marine Environment in the United Nations Environment Programme: An Emergent Regime* (Tycooly Publishing, London, 1988), pp.226 and 235 respectively.

[61]See D.M. Johnston and L.M.G. Enomoto, 'Regional Approaches to the Protection and Conservation of the Marine Environment' in D.M. Johnston, *The Environmental Law of the Sea* (Erich Schmidt Verlag) 285, p.325.

[62]M. K. Tolba, Foreword, in P.H. Sand, note 60, at p.vii.

[63]See above, Part 5.1.

also addressed, to varying degrees, the problem of marine pollution; co-operation with UNEP and the relevant Regional Seas Programme being a particular feature of the marine environmental activities of the commissions. This economic dimension to marine pollution control is an essential one given the economic implications of pollution control measures, particularly for developing states, and because financing of, for example, the Regional Seas Programme is ultimately to devolve upon participating states in the relevant region.

7.4   Baltic

In 1974 Baltic maritime states concluded the Helsinki Convention on the Protection of the Marine Environment of the Baltic Sea, which came into force after a seven year delay. Established under the Convention is the Baltic Marine Environmental Protection Commission (BMEPC) which, whilst possessing limited enforcement powers, performs an important role as a permanent centre for information and co-ordination of the parties to the Convention. Monitoring of hazardous substances is left to individual states.

7.5   North Sea

Since the North Sea was the site of two major oil spills in the 1960s and 1970s, it is perhaps unsurprising that the first regional measures to combat marine pollution in the North Sea area focused upon oil pollution. In 1969 an Agreement for Co-operation in Dealing with Pollution with Oil was adopted in Bonn, with amendments in 1972 and 1983. In 1976 the Convention on Civil Liability for Oil Pollution Damage Resulting from Exploration and Exploitation of Seabed Mineral Resources was concluded in London, but has never been brought into operation.

The problem of land-based marine pollution and dumping at sea have been addressed in the broader geographic context of the northeast Atlantic with the Oslo Dumping Convention and the Paris Convention for the Prevention of Marine Pollution from Land-Based Sources. A Protocol in 1987 added pollution of the atmosphere to the ambit of the Paris Convention. In practice the Oslo and Paris Commissions act together through a body called OSPARCOM.

In addition to these specific treaty arrangements, the states surrounding the North Sea have co-operated at ministerial level[64] through the North Sea Conference. The first meeting was held in Bremen in 1984, following by meetings in London (1987) and The Hague (1990). In 1988 the North Sea Task Force was established to co-ordinate the efforts of OSPARCOM and the International Council for Exploration of the Sea (ICES), the latter body being actively engaged in the co-ordination of scientific research in the North Atlantic region.

On 18 February 1991 the North Sea was made a 'special area' under Annex V of MARPOL 73/78. It joins the Baltic, Black, Red and Mediterranean seas under this

---

[64]At the Hague Conference the nine participating states were represented by environment ministers; at the Copenhagen Conference planning for 1993 agriculture ministers will also be invited to attend to discuss, *inter alia*, the use of pesticides as a land-based source of North Sea pollution.

designation where controls on, *inter alia*, the dumping of garbage are much stricter than in other areas.[65]

7.6   Nordic States

In 1974 the Nordic States[66] concluded a Convention on the Protection of the Environment the aim of which 'was to equate, by means of national legislation, the environmental interests of neighbouring countries with those of the country concerned'.[67] Thus, in considering the permissibility of an environmentally harmful activity, the Convention requires Nordic States to consider the effects of that activity in another contracting state which is to be equated with harm caused in the state where the activity is being carried out. Thus the transnational impact of potentially environmentally harmful activities are to be taken into account at the permission stage. In addition, persons harmed have a right to take action in, and to appeal against the decisions of, relevant courts or administrative authorities of other contracting states.

8.   GLOBAL WARMING AND OZONE DEPLETION

The problem of global warming and the anticipated effect of global temperature rise has focused attention on contributors to the process such as deforestation and fossil fuel consumption. Also of concern is depletion of the stratospheric ozone layer which is permitting greater ultraviolet radiation to penetrate the atmosphere to the earth. These are environmental problems of truly global proportions requiring global solutions. Active in proposing those solutions has been UNEP, the global environmental body established by the General Assembly following the Stockholm Conference in 1972.

From the start UNEP was concerned for its involvement to extend beyond general declaratory activities – beyond soft law.[68] The eventual product of UNEP's activities as a global framework convention on the ozone layer – the 1985 Vienna Convention for the Protection of the Ozone Layer, which entered into force in 1988. It is called a framework convention because it provides an institutional structure for the elaboration of individual protocols addressing separate items of concern and establishing specific standards for them. Thus, in 1987 the Montreal Protocol on Substances that Deplete the Ozone Layer was adopted[69] which provides for the phased reduction of CFCs and a freeze on the use of halons. However, the Protocol does not establish procedures for determining non-compliance nor what measures will be taken in the event of such non-compliance. The Protocol has already been modified twice, once in 1989 with the Helsinki

---

[65]For example, the dumping of all garbage is prohibited in a special area, save for food wastes which cannot be dumped within 12 miles of land. Outside of special areas, only the dumping of plastics is subject to a total ban whilst other forms of garbage may be dumped under certain conditions.

[66]Denmark, Finland, Norway and Sweden.

[67]B. Broms, 'The Nordic Convention on the Protection of the Environment' in Flinterman, Kwiatkowska and Lammers (eds.), *Transboundary Air Pollution: International Legal Aspects of Co-operation of States* (Martinus Nijhoff, Dordrecht, 1986), p.141.

[68]See J. Brunnee, note 37, p.227.

[69]Resolutions on the Exchange of Technical Information and on the Reporting of Data were also adopted.

Declaration on the Protection on the Ozone Layer, phasing out CFCs not later than the year 2000, and to phase out halon and other substances harmful to the ozone layer as soon as feasible. Secondly, specific targets were set for CFC and halon consumption in a series of Adjustments and Amendments to the Montreal Protocol in June 1990. This has been supported by parallel developments in the EC, where Regulation 594/91[70] of 4 March 1991 provides that after 30 June 1997 there will be no production of CFCs without first satisfying the Commission that such production is essential.

While leaving matters such as specific standards setting to the protocols, the framework Convention deals with matters of general obligation such as the requirement to co-operate in monitoring, research and information exchange. It requires contracting parties to take appropriate measures to ensure that human health and the environment are protected against the adverse effects[71] of ozone depletion resulting or likely to result from human activities. This includes taking appropriate administrative and legislative action to control, limit, reduce or prevent activities under their jurisdiction and control 'should it be found that these activities have or are likely to have adverse effects resulting from modification or likely modification of the ozone layer'. (Article 2) The Convention also provides for a secretariat and a disputes settlement mechanism.

Despite a UN General Assembly Resolution[72] recognising that climate change is a common concern of mankind and that 'necessary and timely action' should be taken by States to address this issue, progress to combat global warming has been slow. Both the United Nations and UNEP have called for a global conference on environmental and development which is due to take place in 1992 in Brazil. Preparations for a framework Convention on climate change are currently under-way with a view to adopting such a convention at the 1992 conference.

9. ENVIRONMENTAL POLICIES OF THE EC

Mention has already been made of Community legislation under the types of pollution discussed above. Although there is no express mention of the environment in the 1957 EEC Treaty, the Single European Act introduced treaty amendments in 1986 which confirmed the right of EC institutions to legislate on environmental matters.[73] Such activities have been carried out since 1973, when the EC Council approved the First Community Environmental Programme; the Fourth Programme is due to expire at the end of 1992.

These programmes are non-binding indications by the Commission of what it intends to suggest by way of legislation and other initiatives for the period under consideration. Programmes generally cover about four years. Most of these measures are taken in the form of directives, which are not directly applicable in

---

[70]Unlike Directives, Regulations are directly applicable in Member States' legal systems and do not require express implementation by the member State.

[71]'Adverse effects' mean 'changes in the physical environment or biota, including changes in climate, which have significant deleterious effects on human health or on the composition, resilience and productivity of natural and managed ecosystems or on materials useful to mankind'. (Art. 1(2))

[72]UNGA Resolution 45/53 of 6 Dec. 1988.

[73]The Single European Act introduced a new environmental title into the EEC Treaty, Title VII, and three new articles (130R, 130S, and 130T).

member states but 'binding, as to the result to be achieved, upon each member State to which it is addressed, but shall leave to the national authorities the choice of form and methods' (Article 189 EEC). Action is taken at the Community level only when such action can better be attained at that level than at the level of individual Member States (the subsidiary principle). There are now over 200 pieces of Community legislation touching on the environment in eight areas: water pollution; waste; air pollution; chemicals; wildlife; noise; environmental assessment; information and finances; and international conventions. Thus the international environmental obligations of Member States of the EEC may be reinforced, and even strengthened, through the medium of Community law.

10. CONCLUSION

The comparatively recent development of international environmental law is a symptom of humankind's dawning realisation of the importance of the global environment to human survival. It is becoming more difficult to draw a line between nationally and internationally environmentally harmful activities. Increasingly, states will need to provide at the national level for evaluation of the transnational effects of potentially harmful activities.

But international environmental law is concerned with more than simply providing for global environmental impact assessment. Environmental measures aim at both the prevention and reduction of pollution and at the preservation and sustainable use of natural resources. Thus far states have been more able to agree on the reduction of pollution than its prevention and by and large have embodied such obligations in a treaty framework. The task of standards-setting, traditionally carried out via treaty mechanisms, has proved a cumbersome one dominated by the lowest common denominator. Complying with and enforcing these standards is generally left to individual states, to be carried out at the administrative level. Thus coordination and harmonisation of administrative actions is of considerable importance in the environmental field. And, on the international plane, it is often international organisations which are faced with the task of both initiating state action to fill the gaps in international law occasioned by a media or pollutant specific approach to environmental regulation, and setting standards and guidelines for the administrative implementation of the standards agreed by states. In addition there is an increasing role emerging for international organisations in actual standards setting, particularly in framework treaties with technical annexes which leave to an organisation such as UNEP the task of updating the annexes and coordinating their implementation.

Appendix A

United Kingdom

1. TYPE OF CONSTITUTION

1.1 The United Kingdom, which comprises England, Wales, Scotland and Northern Ireland, is a constitutional monarchy. There is no written constitution, and no rights which are protected by special procedures.

There is an hereditary monarch, exercising powers through ministers responsible to Parliament.

1.2 Legislature

In theory Parliament comprises the Monarch and the two Houses of Parliament. In practice the two Houses sit separately, except on ceremonial occasions. The membership of the House of Lords includes hereditary peers and life peers, the House of Commons is formed of 651 members elected for five years on the basis of universal adult suffrage.

To become law, a Bill must be passed by both Houses, except that the House of Lords has no powers over financial measures, and can only delay the passing of a Bill for a period of one year. It nevertheless does valuable work amending Bills, and sometimes persuading the House of Commons to think a second time.

1.3 Executive

1.3.1 Central authority

The central executive is a government of ministers, headed by the Prime Minister. They are responsible to the House of Commons, which may compel them to resign.

Ministers have some legislative powers delegated to them by Parliament. They also exercise supervisory powers over local authorities.

1.3.2 Local authorities

Local authorities are elected bodies, with limited powers to make by-laws, and limited executive powers within their areas.

181

1.4   Judiciary

Lay magistrates form the lowest level of courts. They are assisted by qualified clerks, but do not sit with juries. Sometimes a legally qualified stipendiary magistrate sits.

At an intermediate level, County courts hear civil cases, and Crown court judges, Recorders and Circuit Judges sit to hear criminal cases. All are legally qualified judges. In criminal cases they sit with juries.

At the highest level, there is the High Court, Court of Appeal and the House of Lords. The House of Lords, when exercising its judicial function, is simply a court of judges appointed to sit as the highest court of appeal.

1.5   In civil cases involving scientific matters, including pollution cases, either party may call expert witnesses. Such witnesses may be subject to cross-examination in the usual way. For civil cases, the County Courts and higher courts may also have assessors. (For a explanation of assessors, see Chapter VI at 4.2.2.)

1.6   For certain kinds of dispute, e.g. where the decision is based on expert opinion, statutes have established special tribunals with persons having relevant expertise sitting as members of the tribunal. In the United Kingdom there are no such tribunals for environmental cases. (For a discussion on expert tribunals, see Chapter VI at 4.2.1.).

1.7   The decisions of all lower courts, tribunals and recommendations of all public enquiries are subject to 'judicial review'. That is a review by the High Court to see if they have acted within their jurisdictions, according to law and proper procedure, and have acted fairly.

2. LEGISLATION

2.1   Common Law

This is a body of law, developed through the process of judicial precedents. It is the reasoning which led to the decision which constitutes the precedent.

2.2   Statutes

Statutes are Acts of Parliament. The provisions of statutes override the decisions of common law.

2.3   Subordinate legislation

Parliament delegates some powers of legislation to ministers, local authorities and other public authorities.

2.4   Environmental legislation

There is no framework law. Some statutes, as did the Control of Pollution Act

1974 deal with several forms of pollution. More commonly, however, each statute deals with a particular kind of environmental problem, e.g. Radioactive Substances Act 1960, Prevention of Oil Pollution Act 1971.

3. ADMINISTRATION OF POLLUTION CONTROLS

3.1 Inter-ministerial committees

There is a Cabinet standing committee on the environment. It is chaired by the Lord Privy Seal, and its members include the Secretary of State for the Environment, Chief Secretary of the Treasury, President of the Board of Trade, Minister for National Heritage and the Ministers of Agriculture and Transport.

3.2 Secretary of State for the Environment

The Department of the Secretary of State for the Environment has a wide range of responsibilities, not all concerning environmental control. They cover:
- land use planning;
- rural affairs;
- water supply;
- control of pollution of land, air and water, and pollution by noise and radioactive substances;
- local government;
- housing;
- various other services.
- liaison with other states and international organisations on environmental matters.

The Department also has a Central Directorate of Environmental Protection, which helps to co-ordinate many of the Government's environmental services.

3.3 Other ministries

Other ministries which have duties to promote certain activities, also control any pollution therefrom, e.g.

Ministry of Agriculture, fisheries and Food
promotes agricultural production, and controls pollution from pesticides;
promotes the development of fisheries, and shares with the Department of the Environment the control of pollution of waters.
Department of Energy
promotes the production of energy from nuclear installations, and controls pollution by those installations;
promotes offshore oil production, and controls pollution from those operations.
Department of Transport
promotes transport by road, air and sea, and controls pollution from all three.

3.4   Co-ordination

There is much informal co-ordination through non-statutory committees at the level of senior civil servants.

3.5   Local authorities

Local authorities have pollution control powers over emissions of smoke, grit and dust, over noise emissions, and over local nuisances.

4.   PUBLIC WATCHDOGS

4.1   House of Commons Select Committee on the environment

This committee is established by the House of Commons to keep itself informed of developments and Government actions in the field of environmental protection. It has powers to summon civil servants but not ministers. In all circumstances the civil servant would be subject to ministerial instructions as to how to answer questions. (HC 617 1989–90 para. 8). The selection of chairmen of the committees generally represents the comparative strengths of the parties in the House, although it is accepted that some committees are free to elect their own chairmen. There have been allegations that the political parties themselves recommend members for appointment. It is of the greatest importance, if the committees are to work independently, that party politics does not dominate the selection.
This is just one of a range of select committees.

4.2   Royal commission on environmental pollution

The members of the Royal Commission are appointed by the Government. Its remit is

> to advise on matters, both national and international, concerning the pollution of the environment; on the adequacy of research in this field; and the future possibilities of danger to the environment;
> and to enquire into any such matters referred to us by one of Your Majesty's Secretaries of State or by one of Your Majesty's Ministers, or any other such matters on which we ourselves shall deem it expedient to advise.

It produces major reports, about once a year, which are published generally.

Appendix B

United States of America

1. TYPE OF CONSTITUTION

1.1 True federal constitution, with the residue of powers lying with the individual states. There is a strict separation of powers. There is a Freedom of Information Act in operation.

1.2 Legislature

Congress comprising two houses – House of Representatives, and Senate. They are elected separately.

1.3 Executive

Executive president elected for four years.

Secretaries of State, each appointed by the President, heading Departments of the Federal Administration.

Each state has its own legislature and executive. Residue of powers lies with the States.

There are also local authorities, many of which have passed environmental legislation.

1.4 Judiciary

Supreme Court decides on constitutional issues. Can declare legislation invalid on the grounds that it conflicts with rights granted by the constitution.

There is an hierarchy of state courts. The Supreme Court hears appeals from state courts in accordance with the Constitution.

Criminal proceedings in environmental matters are normally conducted on behalf of the State.

2. LEGISLATION

2.1   The basic law originates from, and closely resembles, English common law. There are relatively minor differences due to different developments in their courts.

2.2   Congress and the state legislatures pass legislation within their own fields of competence, in accordance with the Constitution. Congress has those legislative powers which the Constitution grants to it: the residue of legislative powers remain with the states.

2.3   Environmental legislation

There is a codified system of federal law. Many separate acts have been passed by the federal and by state legislatures, and by local authorities.

3. ADMINISTRATION OF POLLUTION CONTROLS

3.1   The president

3.1.1   In environmental matters, the President discharges all those functions formerly vested in the Cabinet Committee on the Environment. That committee was abolished and its functions transferred to the Domestic Council. The Council was in turn abolished and its functions transferred to the President. He has power to delegate those transferred functions within his Executive Office. Those functions are as follows.

(a)   Take steps to ensure that federal policies and programmes, including those for the development and conservation of natural resources, take adequate account of environmental effects.
(b)   Review the adequacy of existing systems for monitoring and predicting environmental changes.
(c)   Foster co-operation in environmental programmes between federal, state and local governments.
(d)   Seek advancement of scientific knowledge of changes in the environment, and encourage the development of relevant technology.
(e)   Stimulate public and private participation in programmes and activities to protect the environment.
(f)   Encourage timely public disclosure of public and private plans that would affect the quality of the environment.
(g)   Assess new and changing technologies for their potential effects on the environment.
(h)   Facilitate co-ordination of actions taken by departments and agencies of the Federal Government in protection and improvement of the environment.
(i)   Review plans and actions of federal agencies affecting outdoor recreation and natural beauty.

Note
The constitution of the former Cabinet Committee on the Environment may be of some interest.

Chairman   – the President, or in his absence the Vice-President
Members   – the Vice-President
                Secretary of Agriculture
                Secretary of Commerce
                Secretary of Health, Education and Welfare
                Secretary of Housing and Urban Development
                Secretary of the Interior
                Secretary of Transportation
                such other heads of departments and agencies and others as the
                President may from time to time direct.
                Each member of the committee may designate an alternate.

3.1.2   The President transmits to Congress annually an Environmental Quality
Report, which sets out

(a) the status and condition of the main elements of the environment, including
     air, marine estuarine and fresh waters, drylands, wetlands, urban suburban
     and rural environments;
(b) current and foreseeable trends in the quality, management and use of those
     environments;
(c) adequacy of available natural resources;
(d) review of the programmes and activities of the federal, state and local govern-
     ments;
(e) programme for remedying the deficiencies of existing programmes and activ-
     ities.

In producing that report he is advised and assisted by the Council on Environmental
Policy.

3.2   Office of Environmental Quality

3.2.1   The Office of Environmental quality is in the Executive Office of the
President. Its Director is the Chairman of the Council on Environmental Quality.

3.2.2   Its function is to advise and assist the President on policies and programmes
of the Federal Government by:

(a) providing professional and administrative staff and support;
(b) assisting federal departments and agencies in appraising the effectiveness of
     existing and proposed facilities, programmes, policies and activities, and in
     appraising likewise major projects which do not require approval by Congress;
(c) reviewing the adequacy of existing systems for monitoring and predicting
     environmental changes;
(d) promoting the advancement of scientific knowledge of the effects of actions
     and technology on the environment;
(e) assisting in co-ordinating environmental activities in federal departments and
     agencies;
(f) assisting federal departments and agencies in the development of
     environmental quality criteria and standards;

(g) collecting, collating, analysing and interpreting data and information on environmental quality.

The Director is authorised to contract with public and private agencies, institutions and organisations, and with private individuals.

3.3 Council on Environmental Quality

3.3.1 The CEQ has been created in the Executive Office of the President. It has three members appointed by the President to serve at his pleasure, by and with the advice and consent of the Senate. The President designates one of the members to serve as chairman. The Council may appoint experts and such other employees as may be necessary.

3.3.2. The duties of the Council are as follows:

(a) assist and advise the President in the preparation of the Environmental Quality Report.
(b) gather authoratitive information on conditions and trends in environmental quality. Analyse and interpret that information to see if it is interfering or is likely to interfere with the implementation of the general policy on environmental protection as declared by Congress. (See Federal Register, Chapter 55, subchapter 1, Sec.4331.) That is a statement of policy set out in such general terms as '. . . create and maintain conditions under which man and nature can live in productive harmony . . .'
(c) review and appraise the various programmes and activities of the Federal Government in the light of the above policy.
(d) develop and recommend to the President national policies to promote and improve environmental quality. [The part of this work which relates to ecological systems has been transferred to the Administrator of the Environmental Protection Agency.]
(d) conduct investigations, studies, surveys, research and analyses concerning ecological systems and environmental quality.
(e) document and define changes in the natural environment, including plant and animal systems, and to collect data and other information necessary for continuing analyses.
(f) make studies, and to submit reports and recommendations, concerning policy and legislation as the President may request.

3.4 Environmental Protection Agency

3.4.1 The EPA has been established as an independent agency. It is headed by an Administrator and Deputy Administrator, both appointed by the President, by and with the advice of the Senate. They are supported by several assistant administrators.

3.4.2 The functions of the EPA are to:

(a) establish and enforce environmental protection standards, consistant with national environmental goals.

(b) conduct research on the adverse effects of pollution, and on methods and equipment for controlling it.

(c) strengthen environmental protection programmes, and recommend policy changes.

(d) assist others, through grants, technical assistance and other means, to arrest pollution of the environment.

(e) assist the Council on Environmental Policy in developing and recommending new policies to the President.

The mandate on environmental protection legislation is broad. It includes the protection of inland waters and the atmosphere, the suppression of noise nuisances, the control of solid waste management, functions concerning the registration and use of pesticides, and radiation criteria and standards. It is also expected to provide protection in new areas where protection is found to be necessary.

3.4.3   The head of each executive agency is responsible for seeing that all actions necessary for the prevention, control and abatement of pollution which may arise from federal facilities and activities are taken. Each such agency is required to co-operate with the Administrator of the EPA, state, interstate and local agencies in taking such action. The Administrator of the EPA must provide technical advice and assistance to those executive agencies to ensure compliance with applicable pollution control standards.

Each executive agency must submit to the President an annual plan for the control of environmental pollution. The plan must provide for any necessary improvement in the design, construction, management, operation and maintenance of federal facilities and activities, with annual cost estimates. The plan is to provide for compliance with all applicable pollution control standards. The Administrator of the EPA must establish guidelines for developing such plans.

Whenever the Administrator of the EPA or any state, interstate or local agency notifies an Executive agency that it is in violation of an applicable pollution control standard, the latter must consult with the notifying agency, and provide for its approval a further plan to achieve and maintain compliance. The Administrator of the EPA is to make every effort to resolve any conflicts which arise therefrom, and if he cannot do so, must refer the matter to the President.

3.4.4   The EPA – research and development

(a) The Administrator of the EPA, in consultation and co-operation with the heads of other federal agencies, shall take such actions on a continuing basis as may be necessary or appropriate:

to identify research, development and demonstration activities, within and outside the Federal Government, which need more effective co-ordination;

to determine the steps which might be taken under existing law to accomplish or promote such co-ordination, and to provide for or encourage the taking of those steps;

to determine the additional legislative actions needed to ensure such co-ordination.

He is then to co-ordinate that research, development and co-ordination so as to minimise any unnecessary duplication

(b) The Administrator of the EPA was required to submit to Congress in 1977 a comprehensive five year plan for environmental research, development and demonstration. The plan is to be revised annually, each revision to include projections for a 'no growth' budget, a 'moderate growth' budget, and a 'high growth' budget.

(c) The Administrator has been authorised to select a number of full-time permanent staff members of the Office of Research and Development to pursue full-time educational programmes for the purpose of gaining an advanced degree, or taking advanced academic training. The purpose of that is to equip them to carry out the EPA's research projects.

(d) The Administrator has been authorised also to appoint post-doctoral research fellows in addition to its normal full staff complement. He may also engage research associates from outside the Federal Government on the EPA's research, development and demonstration projects.

3.4.5 The Administrator of the EPA has been required to establish a Scientific Advisory Board. The board provides such scientific advice as may be requested by:

The Administrator of the EPA,
The Committee on Environment and Public Works of the Senate,
The committees on Science and Technology, on Energy and Commerce, and on Public Works and Transportation of the House of Representatives.

3.5   The National Oceanic and Atmospheric Administration (NOAA)

3.5.1   NOAA has been established in the Department of Commerce. It is expected to take a lead in developing a national oceanic and atmospheric programme of research and development.

3.5.2   Several existing organisations were merged to form NOAA Its functions therefore relate to a wide range of matters, including:

(a) Weather, marine and river flood forecasting and warning; coast land geodetic survey; observation of the global environment; environmental data service; research on relevant physical and environmental problems.

(b) Strengthening of the fishing industry and the conservation of fish stocks; the marine sport fishing programme.

(c) The development of marine mining and marine resources technology.

(d) Survey of the Great Lakes and their tributary waters; research on their hydrology.

(e) Collection and dissemination of oceanographic data; calibration and testing of oceanographic instruments.

The intention is that this range of interests will enable NOAA to make it possible to develop a balanced federal programme on understanding the resources of the sea, their development and use, whilst maintaining adequate safeguards against over-exploitation or incidental damage.

3.6   National Industrial Pollution Control Council

3.6.1   The Council was established by the President. Its members represent business and industry, and are appointed by the Secretary of Commerce.

3.6.2 Council is to advise the President and the Chairman of the Council on Environmental Quality on programmes of industry which might affect the environment. The advice is to be transmitted through the Secretary of Commerce.

The Council may also:

(a) survey and evaluate the plans and actions of industry in the field of environmental quality;
(b) identify and examine problems on the effects on the environment of industrial practices, and to recommend solutions;
(c) provide liaison between members of the industrial and business community on environmental matters
(d) encourage that community to try to improve the quality of the environment;
(e) advise on plans and actions of federal, state and local agencies which involve environmental quality policies affecting industry, whenever such advice is requested by the Secretary of Commerce, or through him by the Chairman of the Council on Environmental Quality.

4. WORK OF THE ENVIRONMENTAL PROTECTION AGENCY ON STANDARDS AND CONTROLS

4.1.1 The functions of the Federal Environmental Protection Agency are set out at 3.4.2. It will be noted that one function is to establish and enforce environmental protection standards. The purpose of this section is to give a brief outline of how that duty is discharged.

4.1.2 It must be emphasised that this is only a brief outline of one part of the work of the EPA, and even for that part does not purport to be comprehensive. Its purpose is to give some indication of how the system of control works.

4.1.3 For details of the provisions by which this function is discharged, see the United States Code Annotated, 1988, under Title 42 Public Health and Welfare, and subsequent legislation.

4.2 Standards

4.2.1 Environmental standards are set by the Federal EPA For some forms of pollution the maintenance of those standards is secured by enforcement measures taken by the EPA itself, (see 4.2.2 below). In most cases, however, state authorities are left to secure maintenance, subject to the default powers of the EPA

4.2.2 The standards for pesticides and for hazardous wastes are secured by enforcement measures exercised directly by the Federal EPA. No account of what is done is offered here – recourse must be had to the United States Code Annotated, 1988, and subsequent legislation.

4.2.3 The other standards are set by the EPA, but maintained by means of schemes of control proposed by state authorities and approved by the Federal EPA, and by enforcement measures taken within the state.

One example of how that is done is given under 5 below.

5. CONTROL OF POLLUTION OF THE ATMOSPHERE

5.1 National primary and secondary air quality standards

5.1.1 The Administrator of the Federal EPA is required to publish regulations prescribing national primary ambient air quality standards, and national secondary ambient air quality standards for each air pollutant for which air quality criteria have been published under Section 7409 of Title 42. He must first publish proposed standards, and allow a reasonable time of not longer than 90 days for written submissions, before publishing the regulations. The standards may be revised, following that same procedure as for their original publication.

'National primary ambient air quality standard' means a standard, the attainment and maintenance of which is requisite for the protection of public health. It must be based on the issued quality criteria, with a reasonable margin for safety.

'National secondary ambient air quality standard' shall specify a level of air quality, the attainment and maintenance of which is requisite to protect public welfare from any known or anticipated adverse effect associated with the presence of such air pollutant. It must be based on issued air quality criteria.

5.1.2 In particular, the Administrator must promulgate a national ambient air quality standard for concentrations of a period of not more than three hours, unless, based on the criteria issued under Section 7408(c) of Title 42, he finds that there is no significant evidence that such a standard is requisite to protect public health.

5.1.3 The criteria published under Section 7408 shall be reviewed every five years, and the standards varied accordingly.

5.2 State implementation plans

5.2.1 Within nine months of the promulgation of a national primary ambient air quality standard, including any revision thereof, each state, after holding public hearings, shall submit to the Administrator a plan which provides for implementation, maintenance and enforcement of the standard for each air quality control region, or portion thereof.

The state must likewise, as part of or separately from the foregoing, submit a plan for the implementation, maintenance and enforcement of any promulgated national secondary ambient air quality standard.

5.2.2 Within four months, the Administrator shall approve or disapprove of the plan. The plan must:

(a) provide for the attainment of primary standards as expeditiously as practicable, and in no case later than three years after approval, and the attainment of secondary standards within a reasonable time;
(b) include emission limits and timetables for compliance;
(c) include appropriate provision for monitoring, the results being available to the Administrator on request;
(d) include a programme for the enforcement of emission limits;
(e) contain adequate provision for the prohibition of any emission from a

stationary source which will prevent the attainment or maintenance of a primary or secondary standard within another state;

(f) provide necessary assurances for adequate personnel, funding and authority for the purposes of the plan, and requirement for owners or operators to monitor emissions;

(g) provide for inspection and testing of motor vehicles, to the extent necessary and practicable to enforce compliance with emission standards;

(h) provide for procedures for revisions of the plan in order to comply with revisions of primary and secondary standards, or more expiditious methods of achieving such standards;

(i) provide that no major stationary source is to be constructed or modified if the emissions would cause or contribute to concentrations in excess of primary or secondary standards;

(j) meet requirements of Section 7421 relating to – consultation, public notification, prevention of significant deterioration of air quality and visibility;

(k) require the owner or operator to pay to the enforcing authority a fee adequate to cover the cost of dealing with an application and of implementing and enforcing the terms an conditions of any permit.

(See Section 7410(a)(2).)

5.2.3 Once the plan satisfies those requirements, and the requirements of reasonable notice and public hearings, the Administrator must grant his approval.

He must subsequently review the implementation plan to see if it can be revised in relation to stationary fuel burning sources. If he is satisfied that it can, without interfering with the attainment and maintenance of national ambient quality standards, he shall notify the state that a revised plan must be submittcd to him. (See Section 7410(a)(3)(B).)

5.2.4 The state may include in its plan an indirect source review programme. An indirect source is a facility, building, structure, installation, real property, road or highway, which may attract mobile sources of pollution. The programme must be one that can assure or assist in assuring that a new or modified indirect source would not attract mobile sources of pollution which would cause air pollution concentrations to exceed national ambient standards for mobile source related pollutants, or prevent the maintenance of any such standard. (See Section 7410(a)(5)(a).)

5.2.5 There are provisions empowering the Administrator to act where a state fails to submit an implementation plan. (See Section 7410(c).)

There are also provisions empowering the President to deal with national or regional energy emergencies. (See Section 7410(f).)

5.3 Standards of performance for new stationary sources

5.3.1 The Administrator must publish, and from time to time revise, a list of categories of stationary sources which contribute significantly to air pollution and may reasonably be anticipated to endanger public health or welfare. (See Section 7411.)

5.3.2 He must then publish proposed regulations on federal standards of performance for new sources within each category, and give any interested person an opportunity for written comment. Thereafter he must publish the regulations, with such modifications as he deems appropriate. The regulations must be reviewed every four years, and if appropriate revised.

5.3.3 If it is not feasible to prescribe or enforce a standard of performance, he may instead promulate a design, equipment, work practice or operational standard, or a combination thereof, which reflects the best technological system of continuous emission reduction. (cf., UK Environmental Protection Act 1990 at Sections 3, 7(4) and (10).)

If, however, a person owning or operating a new source satisfies the Administrator that an alternative means of emission limitation will achieve a reduction of emissions at least as great as the method prescribed, the Administrator shall permit its use.

Such a person may also apply for a waiver of the Administrator's prescribed requirement so that he can develop and demonstrate an alternative means.

5.4   Emission reduction standards for existing sources

5.4.1 In the case of existing sources the same procedure applies, except that the standard will be one which the state, or in some circumstances the Administrator, considers reflects the degree of emission reduction achievable by the best system of emission reduction, taking into account cost, and any non-air quality health and environmental impact and energy requirements, which the Administrator is satisfied has been adequately demonstrated. (See Section 7411(a)(1)(C) and (c)(1).)

5.4.2 State implementation plans must be produced by a procedure similar to that outlined in 5.2 above. Account may be taken of the remaining useful life of the existing source. (See Section 7411(d).)

Section 7412 deals with hazardous air pollutants separately.

5.5   Federal enforcement

5.5.1 State enforcement plans are normally enforced by the state itself. The Administrator, however, has powers to ensure that enforcement is carried out.

Whenever he finds that a person is failing to conform to an implementation plan, the Administrator may inform both that person and the state. If the failure is not remedied within 30 days, he may order that person to comply with the requirements of the plan, or may bring against him a civil action for a permanent or temporary injunction, or for assessment and recovery of a civil penalty. (See Section 7413. See the section for further enforcement powers of the Administrator.)

5.5.2 Whenever the Administrator finds that violations are so widespread that they appear to result from a failure of the state, he shall notify the state. Should he find that the failure continues for a period of 30 days or more, he shall give public notice of his finding. He may then take action to enforce any requirement of the plan. That will last for a 'period of Federally assumed enforcement' which will end when the state satisfies him that it will enforce its plan. (See Section 7413(a).)

For further powers of enforcement, see Section 7413.

Appendix C

Sweden

1. TYPE OF CONSTITUTION

1.1 Constitutional monarchy.
There is a hereditary monarch. The monarch's executive powers are exercised by ministers responsible to the Swedish Parliament, (see 1.3).

The constitution is based on the Instrument of Government, Act of Succession, and Freedom of Information Act. Each can be amended or repealed only by a special procedure - identically worded resolutions passed in two sessions of the Parliament, with a general election held between; or by a referendum.

1.2 Legislature

The Riksdag is a single chamber parliament of 349 members, elected every three years on the basis of universal suffrage.

1.3 Executive

Central authority	– a government of ministers responsible to Parliament
	– power to issue decrees, granted by the Instrument of Government or by particular statutes.
County administrations	– represent the national government at regional level.
Local authorities	– limited powers in specified fields e.g. social welfare.

1.4 Judiciary

There is a three tier system of courts

– Supreme Court
– Courts of Appeal
– District Courts

Public prosecutors conduct preliminary investigations in criminal cases, and decide whether or not a prosecution is to be brought.

2. LEGISLATION

2.1 Nature Conservancy Act 1964

The Act expressly states that the natural environment is a national asset, to be protected and preserved. It also states that nature conservancy is a function of both national and local authorities. That makes it possible for action to be taken by those authorities for the protection of nature under various pieces of legislation.

2.2 Environment Protection Act and Environment Protection Ordinance

2.2.1   This legislation covers a wide range of controls over 'activities hazardous to the environment', including

(a) discharges of sewage, solid matter or gases from any land, building or plant into any watercourse, lake or any other area of water.
(b) uses of land, buildings or plant in a manner likely to cause pollution of such waters, excluding the construction of such things in those waters.
(c) uses of land, buildings or plant likely to cause disturbance to the surroundings through pollution of the atmosphere, noise, vibration, light etc, except where that is solely the result of an accident.

2.2.2   The main part of the legislation lays down conditions for the conduct of such polluting activities. Pollution damage must be prevented as far as practically possible – unnecessary damage is forbidden. The fifth paragraph of the Act states

> Anyone engaging or intending to engage in polluting activities shall be obliged to take protective measures, suffer any requisite limitation of the enterprise and take every other precaution that might reasonably be required for the prevention or rectification of pollution.

To achieve this, the most efficient technical installations and methods available must be used. A balance is struck between damage effects on the one hand, and the benefits of the activity and cost of environmental protection measures on the other.

Certain factories and plant listed in the Environment Protection Ordinance may not be built without a permit. Permits are needed also for other specified activities, including discharges of sewage.

2.3 Other legislation

There are other pieces of legislation relating to pollution, including legislation on:

(a) water, with particular reference to water supplies and conservation;
(b) roads, designed to avoid conflict with nature conservation;
(c) control of noise and gaseous emissions from motor vehicles;
(d) scrap vehicles;
     This provides an interesting solution to a difficult problem faced in many countries. For an outline of the provision see Chapter III at 8.10.2.
(e) sulphur content of fuel oils;

(f) pollution from vessels in territorial waters and in the Baltic Sea area;

(g) Dumping at sea from ships and other means of transport.

3. ADMINISTRATION OF POLLUTION CONTROLS

3.1 Ministry of Agriculture

This is the ministry which carries political responsibility for most of the measures for environmental protection.

3.2 Environmental Advisory Committee

This committee informs and advises the Government on environmental matters.

3.3 National Swedish Environment Protection Board

3.3.1 The Board is the principal central administrative authority on environmental matters. It comprises a Director General and six members. All are appointed by the Government.

3.3.2 In general, it is responsible for the implementation of any decisions in that field made by the Government and Parliament, the surveillance of developments, and the submission of proposals for any new measures it considers are needed.

It works in accordance with standing instructions laid down by statute.

The standing instructions require the Board:

–   to promote and make proper arrangements for activities within its field of responsibility, in scientific and cultural terms, and including provision for recreational and outdoor facilities;

–   to assist the Franchise Board for Environmental Protection (see 3.5 below) by conducting surveys and field work;

–   to seek safeguards for the conservation of nature in social planning measures;

–   to oppose the use of any unsuitable sites for quarrying, opencast mining etc;

–   to work for the protection of shoreline areas;

–   to direct work on the preparation of an inventory of areas particularly in need of protection;

–   to draft plans for water management, and to co-ordinate measures for water supply and sewage disposal;

–   to direct work on plans for the provision of facilities for outdoor pursuits;

–   to assist county authorities in any work which comes also within responsibilities of the Board.

Other duties of the Board are:

(a) To serve as the enforcement authority for the Environment Protection Act. That Act deals with:

–   discharges of sewage, and solid or gaseous matter from any land, building or plant into any watercourse, lake or any other water area;

–   use of any land, plant or building in a manner likely to cause pollution of a watercourse, lake or other water area, save for construction work in water;

- use of any land, plant or building in a manner likely to cause disturbance through pollution of the air, or through noise, vibration light etc save for accidental disturbance.

    It can also grant exemption from the need for a permit, which would otherwise be required for the building of specified plants and factories. (The permits are granted by the Franchise Board for Environmental Protection)

(b) To serve as the enforcement authority for the Act and the Ordinance made thereunder on products hazardous to health and to the environment. The work is done by its Products Control Board.

(c) To be responsible for the award of state grants towards the costs of municipal sewage treatment plants, and the costs of environmental protection measures in industry.

(d) To plan and award state grants for the provision of outdoor facilities.

(e) To implement hunting legislation, and to submit proposals for open seasons.

3.4   County administrations

The National Government is represented at regional level by county administrations. One of their functions is to manage and supervise environmental controls within their areas. They may grant exemptions from the need for permits, (see 3.5.2).

3.5   Franchise Board for Environmental Protection

3.5.1   The Franchise Board is chaired by a judge. There are three other members are persons with relevant expertise, including one person experienced in industrial matters. It is independent of the Environmental Protection Board.

3.5.2   The function of the Franchise Board is to consider the grant of a permit where, under any statute, a person needs a permit for an activity which may have environmental consequences. The procedure includes oral hearings.

The National Swedish Environment Protection Board, and in some cases the county administrations, may grant exemptions from the need to apply for a permit, on the basis of the merits of each case. The grant of an exemption is preceded by a careful investigation, and the decision of the Board or county administration is final in so far as it may not be appealed or questions. It may, however, be withdrawn at any time.

The Board may also try to negotiate a settlement on the conditions subject to which the permit is granted.

Both the applicant and the Environment Protection Board have a right of appeal to the government against a decision of the Franchise Board. The Board is given the right of appeal in order to act in the public interest.

3.6   Freedom of information

Under the Freedom of Information Act, Swedish citizens and aliens both have a right of access to public documents on the files of government agencies. There are exceptions for the safeguard of certain interests, e.g. national security, personal and financial circumstances of individuals.

3.7 Ombudsmen

3.7.1 There are four Ombudsmen appointed by the Riksdag, each for a term of four years renewable. They are normally judges, and have legally trained staff.

3.7.2 Their chief duty is to see that the courts and civil service enforce the nation's laws, especially those which safeguard the freedom, security and property of citizens. They supervise the actions of legal government authorities, and any persons who exercise public executive powers.

They will also investigate a reported abuse of power by an authority, and may investigate matters on their own authority. They can institute a prosecution in court, but normally make public statements on the acts or decisions of public servants.

3.7.3 Other Ombudsmen have been appointed, otherwise than by the Riksdag, for special fields of work, e.g. Consumer Ombudsman, Ombudsman against Ethnic Discrimination. None have yet been appointed in the field of environmental protection.

4. RESEARCH

4.1 The Research Committee of the National Swedish Environment Protection Board co-ordinates the relevant research. The Nature Conservancy Council, Water Protection Council and Air Protection Council follow developments in their respective fields.

4.2 The bodies contributing to research include:

- universities and colleges, (contract research);
- The Swedish Institute for Water and Air Pollution Research (a research body partly owned by the state);
- The Swedish Meteorological and Hydrological Institute;
- AB Atomenergi;
- The National Defence Research Institute;
- The National Institute for Building Research;
- The Corrosion Institute;
- The National Board of Fisheries;
- The Swedish Natural Science Research Council;
- The National Swedish Board for Technical Development;
- The Swedish Council for Building Research;
- The Swedish Council for Forest and Agricultural Research.

Appendix D

Denmark

1. TYPE OF CONSTITUTION

1.1 Denmark is a parliamentary democracy with a written constitution. There is a system of regional and local authorities, having separate functions. The Central Government retains supervisory powers.

1.2 Legislature

The Danish Parliament – the Folketing, is an elected assembly of 179 members, including two for the Faroes and two for Greenland.
   It has supreme legislative power within the terms of the Constitution
   Some powers of legislation are delegated to ministers and to local authorities.

1.3 Executive

1.3.1 The Central Government is responsible to the Folketing, and subject to laws administered by the ordinary courts.
   The structure of the Government is determined partly by statute and partly by the ministers themselves.
   It has wide powers to entrust administrative functions to local councils, and also to bodies such as 'directorates' and 'boards', which have considerable independence. The Central Government, however, retains wide supervisory powers.

1.3.2 The local authorities are all elected bodies, viz

the metropolitan councils of Copenhagen and Frederiksberg,
fourteen county councils,
local councils, each with a population of at least 6,000.

All have environmental functions, although where possible those functions are given to the local councils.
   Local authorities have powers delegated to them in the fields of building, town planning and environmental protection. They have in recent years been given increasing powers, particularly in the form of authorisations, orders and prohibitions.

The Central Government exercises some degree of supervisory control over them, particularly through general directives, plans, budgetary control and administrative appeals. In some cases, the Government can 'call in' a matter for its own decision.

The courts control the legality of any acts of public administration, whether central or local.

1.4   Judiciary

The judiciary comprise:

a Supreme Court,
two High Courts of Justice,
   all have the usual powers of higher courts, including a power of judicial review
   of administrative acts.
local courts.

2.   LEGISLATION

The Environment Protection Act is the principal piece of legislation on pollution control, covering the atmosphere, inland and coastal waters, disposals of wastes on land and noise nuisances. There is other more particular legislation such as the Sulphur Content of Fuel Act, Chemicals and Chemical Wastes Products Act, Recyling Act and the Marine Environment Act.

3.   ADMINISTRATION OF POLLUTION CONTROLS

3.1   For the purpose of understanding environmental control, it is important to note the following.

(a) 'Ministries' are government departments with political heads as in the United Kingdom. They can deal with complaints about decisions made by subordinate bodies, but the scope of that work has been narrowed in recent years. Such a complaint will now usually be referred to a directorate or board. (See (b) and (c).)

(b) 'Directorates' are central authorities subordinate to the ministries. There may be several directorates under the same ministry. Each directorate is headed by a civil servant, who will have appropriate specialists on his staff. Its work includes making decisions at first instance, and supervising local administrative bodies.

(c) 'Boards' are corporate bodies with specified functions. They may be central or local. Their members may be experts, members of the Folketing or local authorities, or representatives of special interest groups. The ministry or directorate to which the board is responsible has a right to be kept informed of its activities, otherwise it has over it only those powers which are granted by law.

3.2   Ministry of the Environment

The Ministry has six divisions, only one of which deals exclusively with environmental pollution. The others deal with such matters as physical planning and nature conservation. The environmental pollution division has a staff of about 20 persons.

The Minister has been granted wide ranging powers to make regulations under the Environmental Protection Act and various other Acts concerning pollution control. In addition to his own executive powers, he may intervene in decision making by subordinate authorities. The more detailed executive powers are delegated within the Ministry and to other authorities.

3.3   Environment Agency

This is a directorate under the Ministry of the Environment, dealing exclusively with environmental protection. Amongst the staff of 150 are physicians, engineers, biologists, surveyors, lawyers, political scientists and economists. It is entirely subordinate to the Ministry, which may reverse Agency decisions, take over any work not yet completed, and issue directives to it.

The Agency's functions fall into five categories:

(a)   advising the Ministry, e.g. on the drafting of regulations, on particular cases or projects;
(b)   advising authorities other than the Ministry, e.g. local authorities;
(c)   exercising powers delegated to it by the Ministry, e.g. the power to recommend emission standards;
(d)   hearing appeals from decisions taken by local authorities;
(e)   operating most of the public information service.

There is close co-operation between the Agency and the Ministry, e.g. in frequent exchanges of staff, in working jointly on a major project.

3.4   Environmental Appeal Board

Membership of the Environmental Appeal Board is:

President, who must have the qualifications sufficient for a judge of the Court of Appeal.
One or more deputies to the President.
Members appointed by the Minister on the recommendation of
  Federation of Danish Industries,
  Joint Council of Danish Farmers Co-operative Societies,
  Federation of Danish Agricultural Societies,
  Federation of Danish Smallholders Societies,
  (It is assumed that these members will have expert knowledge of production and business economics.)
Members appointed by the Minister from the Environment Agency.
  (These members will have expert knowledge of various branches of environmental science and technology.)

For each case the President or one of his deputies sits with two or four members.

The function of the 'Environmental Appeal Board' is to hear appeals from decisions made in particular cases. Appeal lies only where a statute so provides, and such provision is made only for the more important decisions. These include: decisions concerning specified classes of undertaking which are particularly polluting; orders or prohibitions for the prevention of pollution of groundwaters; permission for sewage discharge into watercourses, lakes or the sea; and orders concerning existing sewage installations of municipal or industrial undertakings.

The Board is considered qualified to deal with legal and technical issues, but not with any based on political responsibility. It cannot, therefore, review municipal decisions on future plans concerning sewage.

The Minister is empowered to issue orders on rules of procedure for the Board. The higher courts can overrule a decision of the Environmental Appeals Board on the basis of administrative law, but such an event would be exceptional.

Appendix E

France

1. TYPE OF CONSTITUTION

1.1 The Constitution of the Fifth Republic, established in 1958, cannot be placed in any of the traditional categories. It combines the characteristics of a parliamentary regime and a presidential regime. Those characteristics are not relevant to our present purpose.

1.2 Legislature

There is a Parliament of two chambers, the National Assembly and the Senate.

All laws are passed by Parliament. The constitution sets out the matters on which laws shall be passed. Of interest in this context, laws pertaining to national planning shall determine the objectives of the economic and social action on the state.

The relationship between Parliament and the Government concerning legislation is complex but, subject to certain conditions set out in the Constitution, the Government may by decree exercise regulatory powers. It may also exercise legislative powers delegated to it by Parliament.

Individual Ministers sometimes have delegated powers to legislate by decrees. Local authorities are also empowered to issue some decrees.

Circulars of a regulatory nature may be issued.

1.3 Executive

1.3.1 President of the Republic
The President is elected directly by universal suffrage for a period of seven years. The Constitution grants him extensive and far reaching powers, in particular the right to dissolve Parliament, right of recourse to a referendum, use of exceptional powers in times of crisis.

He has a free choice in the appointment of Prime Minister, and despite the terms of the Constitution, he can revoke that choice. In practice he determines the policies of the nation.

1.3.2   The Central Government

The Government comprises the Prime Minister, and ministers appointed by the President on the recommendation of the Prime Minister. It carries collective responsibility for its work. In particular, it is responsible to Parliament, which can in practice effect its dismissal. That can lead to a dissolution of Parliament, despite the power of dissolution granted to the President as a personal power.

The powers of state administration are centralised. The central authorities are the President, Prime Minister and Government acting collectively, and individual ministers. There are also subordinate local authorities which in effect carry out state administration, in particular the Prefects, acting within the framework of the Départements.

Local administration is entrusted to decentralised authorities. Of those, the Départements and Communes have a certain autonomy guaranteed by the Constitution. The Law of 25 July 1972 added the Regions, which are involved in some elements of state administration.

2. JURISPRUDENCE

Jurisprudence, in the form of case law on the interpretation of the written law and the opinions of jurists, constitutes an important source of law. It helps the judge to apply the written law to the case before him. He is not bound by precedent, therefore jurisprudence can alter the course of judgments and thus affect the development of the law.

3. ADMINISTRATION OF POLLUTION CONTROLS

3.1   There is no framework law, or law of overall application, dealing with environmental protection, but many separate laws. The law on classified installations, however, is of wide application.

The authorities with responsibilities concerning the protection of the environment can be placed in two categories: those with general responsibilities for environmental protection, and those with special responsibilities which can affect the environment.

3.2   Authorities with general responsibilities for environmental protection.

3.2.1   Ministry of the Environment and the Quality of Life.
This Ministry was created in 1978 with responsibilities which included public works, housing, land use planning and the supervision of architectural development.

The Minister has a duty 'to ensure the protection of sites and the countryside, to improve the environment and to reduce pollution and nuisances of all kinds'. (Decree 7194 of 2 February 1971). More specifically, his powers of supervision or control extend to:

classified installations (See 4.),
hunting and fishing,
national parks and regional natural parks

He is also responsible for interministerial co-ordination in environmental matters for which purpose he presides over such bodies as –

Interministerial Water Mission
Interministerial Committee on National Parks
Interministerial Commission on Regional Natural Parks
National Council for the Protection of Nature

and most importantly, as noted below,

High Committee for the Environment

The delegate for architecture and the environment, appointed in each region, is a subordinate of this Minister.

3.2.2   Interministerial organisations

(a) *High Committee for the Environment*
     Presided over by the Minister for the Environment and the Quality of Life

     35 members   – 15 high ranking officials
                    20 persons selected by the Prime Minister on the basis of their
                    ability and responsibilities.

     A decree of 1975 provided that 'the High Committee is to be aware of the problems of improving the quality of life and in particular the fight against pollution and nuisances of all kinds, of the evolution of the ecological balance, of the protection of nature, of the control of the countryside, the weather and all the other elements which contribute to the quality of life and the environment of man'. It must be aware of current trends in environmental policy, and may submit proposals on that policy to government. To enable it to do that, it must be informed of and consulted on all proposals for further legislation. It presents to government an annual report.

(b) *Interministerial Committee on the Quality of Life*
     This Committee operates under the Prime Minister, and includes a range of ministers. It stimulates, co-ordinates and controls activities concerning the protection of nature and the environment. A fund has been created to finance operations for which the Committee is responsible.

(c) *National Council for the Protection of Nature*
     The Council is presided over by the Minister for the Environment and the Quality of Life. It has 28 members – 14 ex-officio, and 14 elected.
     Its principal function is to advise the Minister on the protection of nature, its fauna and flora, and on the maintenance of appropriate ecological balance in uncultivated areas, particularly natural parks and reserves. For this purpose it elects a permanent committee of its own members, which prepares preliminary reports for submission to the Council. The work can be both legal and scientific.

3.2.3   Regional and local authorities

(a) *Regions*

Because the Government wished to delegate environmental powers to the regional authorities, and in particular to the regional prefects, the Prime Minister in 1970 asked regional prefects to be 'initiators and promoters of an active environmental policy for improvement of the environment and the quality of life' in their regions. In particular, he asked that regulations governing the pollution of water and air, noise nuisances, the deposit of wastes and the abandonment of vehicles should be strictly enforced.

The Minister for the Environment and the Quality of Life has appointed to each region a delegate to participate in environmental work, and to advise local authorities on the protection of the environment, the prevention of pollution and the suppression of nuisances. He puts forward the views of the Minister, and stimulates and co-ordinates activities.

(b) *Départements*

Subject to the supervisory powers of the Minister, départements provide for the control of classified installations (see 4.) hunting and fishing, and for the protection of monuments and sites of historic interest. Within each département is a Bureau for the Protection of Nature and the Environment, which co-ordinates département work in that field, and receives any complaints from the public.

The prefect of the département co-ordinates the environmental work of the communes within his area, and may exercise default powers in that field if a mayor fails in his duties.

(c) *Communes*

The mayor, as head of the commune and in the exercise of his police powers, is responsible *inter alia* for public order, cleanliness and the suppression of nuisances. He therefore deals, amongst many other matters, with excessive noise, odours and the removal of household waste. The communes can also, either alone or in co-operation with other communes, build sewage treatment works and incinerators. By Law 83–8 of 7 January 1983 they were given extensive powers to combat pollution at local level.

3.3   Authorities and agencies with special responsibilities which can affect the environment

3.3.1   Ministries

(a) *Ministry of Agriculture*

Various departments and services within this Ministry have functions concerning the environment, including the Department of Rural Management and Structures and the Forestry Service. The latter participates in the fight against pollution of watercourses.

(b) *Ministry of Industry*

Several specialised departments work in co-operation with the services of the Ministry of the Environment and the Quality of Life.

(c) *Ministry of Education and Ministry of the Universities*

There are specified priority actions for education on the environment and ecology

3.3.2   Interministerial bodies

(a) Interministerial Mission for the Management of Tourism on the Languedoc-Roussillon Coast.
(b) Interministerial Mission for the Management of Corsica.
(c) Interministerial Committee for the Management of the Aquitaine Coast.
(d) Interministerial Mission for the Protection and Management of the Natural Mediterranean Basin.

3.3.3   Other specialised agencies and organisations

(a) Financial port agencies.
(b) Agency for Air Quality, responsible for monitoring air pollution and giving advice to industry.
(c) Conservatory of Coastal Areas and Lake Shores.
(d) National Agency for the Recovery and Disposal of Wastes, which carries out studies and participates in works of construction and in operations in this sector.
(e) Delegation for Land Use Planning and Regional Action (DATAR).

See also the decrees No.77–760 of 7 July 1977 and No.85–400 of 29 March 1985.

3.3.4   Delegation for land use planning and regional action (DATAR)

DATAR is subject to the Prime Minister. It is a special co-ordination and promotional organisation which, *inter alia*, co-ordinates land use planning and environmental protection. For example, it intervenes when planning problems arise which might adversely affect the environment or the suppression of nuisances. The first environmental action programme was prepared under the aegis of DATAR.

4. INTEGRATED SYSTEM OF CONTROL FOR CERTAIN CLASSIFIED INSTALLATIONS

4.1 This is a system under which all installations which may be dangerous, insanitary, noxious or noisy are classified. It is a comprehensive system of control over pollution from such installations, covering various forms of pollution. More than 400 types of installations are listed. There are two principal classes.

Installations for which a declaration is required

An installation falling within this class is subject to general regulations for the benefit of the neighbourhood and the protection of public health.
No express authorisation is needed. An application must be submitted to the local prefect, with a file giving details. If the prefect is satisfied that there will be compliance with the relevant regulations, he must send a receipt to the applicant, and operations may commence.

Installations for which express authorisation is required

An application must be submitted to the local prefect. A Circular of 28 October 1982 sets out the need for evidence of competence with two main requirements.
(a) There must have been a technico-ecomomic analysis to establish the conditions necessary for the protection of the environment. Measures to be adopted must be

based on the best available technology, within acceptable economic limits. (Circular of 2 February 1982.)

(b) A programme for the prevention and control of accidental pollution of air and water must be prepared. (Circular of 28 October 1982.)

There are also requirements concerning explosives, incineration of industrial waste, and risks of major accidents.

4.2 It is interesting to note how the English and French systems of integrated pollution control started from two very different standpoints, yet, facing much the same problems, have gradually become similar. This is surely what biologists would call 'convergent evolution'.

Appendix F

Federal Republic of Germany

1. TYPE OF CONSTITUTION

Germany is a true federation, comprising 16 Lander, which are the constituent 'states' in which the residue of legislative power resides. Each Land has its own legislature and executive, although their constitutions vary for historical reasons and because some are considerably larger than others.

Within each Land there are Kreis, which are district authorities, and Gemeinden, which are local authorities. Both have rights of self-government guaranteed by the constitution.

2. LEGISLATURE

2.1 Federal legislature

2.1.1 The federal legislature has only such powers of legislation as are granted by the constitution. The residue of legislative powers lies with the Lander. It is important to note also that members elected by the Lander sit in the Federal Council (Bundesrat) which serves as a second chamber for the federal legislature.

Federal legislative powers fall into four classes:

(a) Exclusive – can be passed only by the federal legislature. The only laws in this class which can have any effect on environmental protection and which have been passed to date concern federal railways and air traffic. It is also accepted that there is an unwritten competence to legislate on certain other matters, because of their very nature. Those matters include national planning.

(b) Concurrent – powers held concurrently with the Lander.
To avoid conflict, the Lander can legislate on subjects within this class only if the federal legislature has not exercised the power. The Constitution provides however, that federal legislation is needed
on matters over which there can be no effective regulation by an individual Land;
where legislation by a Land could affect adversely the interests of the nation or of other Lander;

for the purposes of uniformity of living conditions within the Lander, and for essential uniformity in certain other legal and economic matters.

The Constitution lists the following matters which fall within this class of concurrent legislation, and which can have effects on the environment:

civil claims by property owners for protection against pollution from gaseous emissions, noise and vibration;

certain regulations under the Penal Code, e.g. negligently causing serious injury or death, carelessly contaminating wells to the danger of the public;

pollution of air and water, pollution by noise and waste disposal, and pollution from road traffic;

unauthorised operation of installations;

protected areas;

serious dangers arising from toxic substances and other environmental hazards, trading in toxic substances;

federal immission control laws, and water regulations for industry;

building and operation of nuclear installations for peaceful purposes and protection against dangers arising therefrom, the disposal of radioactive substances and the unauthorised handling of nuclear materials;

promotion of agricultural and forestry production;

coastal protection and offshore fisheries;

shipping and waterways.

(c) Framework legislation.

Framework laws may be isssued in specified subjects which set standards for the whole nation, and which must be implemented by each Land. The subjects specified include:

hunting and the protection of the countryside with its fauna and flora as provided for under the Federal Nature Protection Law;

regional planning and water supply as provided for by the Federal Regional Planning and Water Supply Laws.

(d) Laws on Co-operation in Community Responsibilities.

Community responsibilities include those of the Lander to improve living conditions. The Federal Government contribution is mainly in planning and financing.

2.2   Lander

2.2.1   The environmental laws passed by the Lander concern waste disposal, immission control laws, and land use planning laws.

In addition the federal authorities have left to the Lander the passing of the Water Law, Mining Law and Neighbourhood Law.

In general, the Lander agree on a law, and it is then passed by each with only minor variations.

2.3   Administrative decrees

Administrative decrees and regulations are issued by the authorities. They are for internal use only, but have wider effects in practice. They ensure that laws are enforced uniformly, and establish discretionary guidelines. Decisions which depart from those guidelines may be found invalid.

Many of the administrative regulations need the consent of the Bundesrat. Environmentally, the most important are the TA Luft used to enforce the Federal Immission Control Law.

3. ADMINISTRATION

3.1 Federal government

There is no department of the Federal Government concerned solely with environmental protection. The various departments with their responsibilities concerning the environment are:

(a) Federal Minister of the Interior – responsible for:
  general environmental planning and legislation;
  water resources, air pollution, refuse treatment;
  noise reduction;
  safety of nuclear installations, and protection against radiation;
  international co-operation.
(b) Federal Economics Minister – responsible for:
  mineral resources and energy policy.
(c) Federal Minister of Food, Agriculture and Forestry – responsible for:
  plant and animal protection;
  hunting;
  protection of the natural environment;
  forest and timber resources;
  international fishing and agriculture policies.
(d) Federal Transport Minister – responsible for:
  road building and road traffic
  waterways and inland waterway traffic;
  shipping and air transport.
(e) Federal Minister for Regional Planning, Building and Urban Development – responsible for:
  town and country planning; building.
(f) Federal Minister for Research and Technology – responsible for:
  raw materials and production technology;
  biology, ecology, health.

3.2 Co-ordinating and advisory bodies

(a) Cabinet Committee on Environmental Issues
  Chaired by the Federal Chancellor, it includes 12 ministers with environmental responsibilities.
(b) Standing Committee of Departmental Heads for Environmental Issues
  Chaired by the Minister of the Interior, it includes departmental heads of 16 ministries including the Chancellor's Office.
(c) Conference of Environmental Ministers

Established for co-operation with the Lander, it brings together Federal and Land minister for consideration of environmental problems.

(d) Federal Environment Agency

The Agency provides scientific advice on environmental problems for federal ministers. It assists in environmental planning, and in the evaluation of environmental assessments. It engages in research and co-ordinates federal environmental research. In addition to advising ministers, it informs the general public on environmental problems.

(e) The Institute of Water, Soil and Air Hygiene of the Federal Department of Health.

Engages in research within its own fields of responsibility.

(f) Federal Hydrology Institute

Responsibilities which include water quality and water resource measurements, and the development of new monitoring techniques.

3.3   The lander

The Lander authorities enforce both their own laws and federal laws. The latter are enforced either on their own authority and under their own enabling legislation, or under powers delegated to them by the Federal Government. With the consent of the Bundesrat, the Federal Government can issue administrative regulations on enforcement.

3.4   Kreis

Kreis are districts or groups of Gemeinden, apart from some of the larger Gemeinden which remain independent. Kreis are responsible for activities which go beyond the areas of individual Gemeinden in their districts, or which exceed their financial or organisational capacity.

Kries have their own administrative powers, and powers delegated to them by the Federal Government and Lander.

3.5   Gemeinden

3.5.1   Gemeinden form the lowest tier of the administrative authorities. They have their own administrative powers, and powers delegated to them by the Lander and the Federal Government. In the exercise of their own powers, they are subject to the Land for the legality of their actions, but not the substance.

3.5.2   In general, they are responsible for local activities, including sewerage, sewage treatment, supervision of abattoirs, issuing building permits and the construction and maintenance of local roads. Certain other responsibilities are delegated to them by the Federal Government or the Land, including the supervision of special building projects in their areas.

3.6   Public corporations

There are various public corporations established by legislation, many with environmental responsibilities. In particular there are Water and Soil Associations and

Water Resources Associations, numbering about 16,000 and covering about 35 per cent of agricultural land.

The Water and Soil Associations have reponsibilities which include:

construction and maintenance of river banks;
regulation of water flow;
drainage of premises;
removal and treatment of effluents;
control of groundwater;
supply of water for drinking and other purposes.

3.7 Independent advisory councils

Independent advisory councils with responsibilities for environmental protection include:

(a) Council of Experts on Environmental Questions, formed to advise on the state of the environment in the Federal Republic. It has a duty to:
advise periodically on the existing state of the environment;
note existing trends;
note any unsuccessful developments, and suggest remedies.
(b) Advisory Council for Nature Protection and Countryside Conservation, established under the Federal Ministry of Food, Agriculture and Forestry.
(c) Federal Commissioner for Nature Protection, appointed under the Chancellor.
(d) Reactor Safety Commission, and the Commission for Protection from Radiation, under the Federal Minister of the Interior.
(e) Association of German Engineers (VDI). Through its Clean Air Commission and its Noise Reduction Commission it produces:
guidelines on monitoring techniques;
guidelines on limit values for many constituents of emmissions.
There are over 200 VDI guidelines. Although themselves not legally enforceable, they are often accepted as the enforceable standards where legislation demands the use of the best available technical means.
(f) German Institute for Standards has performed a similar service in developing German Industry Standards for industrial products.
(g) Committee for Nuclear Technology has likewise produced guidelines on technical standards used in licensing procedures.
(h) Technical Supervisory Associations (TUV), under the supervision of the Lander authorities, provide impartial and competent inspections of installations to ensure safety and compliance with regulations.
(i) The Waste Water Technical Association (ATV), and the German Association for Gas and Water (DVGW) have also developed technical standards, for use in effluent treatment and water supply respectively.

4. JUDICIARY

4.1 Judicial system

4.1.1 In the Federal Republic there is a system of courts including:

- courts with general jurisdiction over civil and criminal matters
- administrative courts
- social courts
- tax courts

The courts dealing with civil and criminal matters have four levels

- municipal
- district
- court of appeals
- Federal Supreme Court

The administrative courts are at three levels. Appeals may be made to them concerning actions by governmental authorities, including appeals against actions and orders of environmental authorities. Parties such as neighbours of polluting installations can challenge the issue of the operating permit. They may also claim compensation, but such claims will be made in the courts with general jurisdiction over civil matters.

4.2   Judicial powers concerning environmental matters

4.2.1   Civil actions

German civil rights are complicated both in themselves, and in relation to each other. The principal features are outlined below.

A person whose life, health, freedom, property or other right is illegally affected by the intentional or negligent action of another is entitled to compensation. Intention or negligence is presumed, leaving it to the defendant to prove otherwise if he can.

A person can also claim compensation if he has been injured as a result of a violation of laws to protect persons. Actions are available also to prevent violations of other rights and harmful interference.

4.2.2   An owner of premises can claim a prohibition on emissions to the atmosphere of gases, odours, steam, smoke, noise and vibrations, except where:

(a) the emissions do not significantly affect his property; or
(b) the adverse effect originates from the use of neighbouring property which is similar to other local uses, and it is impossible or not reasonably economic to prevent such effect;
(c) the interference is from a plant built and operated under a licence from the appropriate authority.

The property owner suffering the interference can demand that measures be taken to reduce the damaging effects. If that is not practicable, in technical or economic terms, he can then claim compensation.

4.2.3   The Environmental Liability Act of 1990 imposes on operators of certain installations strict liability to compensate persons for environmental damage.

4.3   Administrative law

4.3.1   There are three levels at which actions under administrative law can be taken – Administrative Court, Higher Administrative Court, Federal Administrative Court.

4.3.2   Action may be taken in those courts by a person whose rights have been harmed due to an administrative mistake.

It has not yet been generally established that an association can bring such actions, although it has been made possible for them to do so in Bremen.

4.4   Criminal law

Prosecutions for environmental damage are brought by the public prosecutor's office and other national prosecuting authorities. Private prosecutions are not permitted.

For certain offences such as those involving bodily harm, the public prosecutor will act only on application by the injured party. If an application is not successful, the injured party may start proceedings to force the public prosecutor to take action.

5. FORMS OF CONTROL

5.1   It is not possible in this brief appendix even to outline all the forms of control used. Only those which may be of particular relevance to the subject matter of this book, or otherwise of interest outside Germany, are referred to here.

5.2   Atmospheric pollution – emission and immission standards

5.2.1   In Germany there are two sets of standards by means of which protection from atmospheric pollution is given.

5.2.2   Emission standards

Emissions are what is discharged to the atmosphere. They may be gases, including matter in suspension, noise, vibrations, light, heat, ionising radiations any other phenomena.

Emission values are set by means of TA Luft. They are applied to all new works, but they can be enforced only if they can be met when applying known technical standards. For existing works, emission standards must be such that they can be achieved by economically feasible methods.

5.2.3   Immission standards

Immission standards are based on the rights of neighbours to be protected from pollution. Even where works can meet the highest technical standards, under administative law, neighbours can object to the grant of a licence if immission standards would be exceeded.

Immission values are listed in TA Luft. They are calculated to protect human health, but not plants or animals. Because of that limitation, the Lander Commission for Immission Control has stated that the Federal Immission Control Law must be taken into account. Under that law people, animals, plants and property are to be protected. Nevertheless, on an interpretation of Section 3 paragraph 1, damage to property is to be taken into account only in so far as it affects the general public or the neighbourhood.

5.3   Licences for stationary installations

A licence for a stationary installation must be granted if all the relevant legal obligations are satisfied. The authority then has no descretion to refuse a licence.

Those obligations are:

(a) The operator guarantees that the necessary legal obligations of the operator will be observed.
(b) Other public law regulations do not prevent the establishment and operation of the installation.
(c) There will be no harmful environmental effects, dangers, or serious nuisances or other serious disadvantages to the neighbourhood.
(d) Measures will be taken to ensure limitation of emissions in accordance with the latest technology.
(e) Wastes from the operation will be disposed of properly and harmlessly, or so far as is technically possible and economically feasible.
(f) Installations must meet any properly imposed technical requirement.
(g) Emission limits imposed will not be exceeded.
(h) The operator will monitor, or have monitored, both emissions and immissions.

5.4   Pollution control agents

5.4.1   Water protection agents

A person discharging more than 750 cubic metres of waste water per day must appoint one or more Waste Water Protection Agents. The control authority may require such appointments by other dischargers. The agents must be appointed by a written contracts.

An agent must monitor compliance with the applicable regulations and permit conditions. He must ensure that treatment plant is operating properly, and recommend measures for improvement. He must also aim to reduce effluent quantity, and encourage the adoption of cleaner operating processes.

An agent is answerable only to the discharger, to whom he must submit an annual report. It is never one of his functions to denounce the discharger.

5.4.2   Immission control officer

Where a stationary installation with discharges to the atmosphere requires a licence, the operator must appoint one or more Immission Control Officer. Those officers are equivalent in status and duties to the Water Protection Agents described in 5.4.1 above.

5.4.3   Waste disposal agents

There are requirements equivalent to those above for the appointment of Waste Disposal Agents in connection with the disposal of wastes on land.

5.4.4   In addition to making those appointments, the operator must provide the name of the member of the board of directors responsible for the discharge of the firm's environmental duties.

5.5   Effluent charges

5.5.1   The Waste Water Charging Law 1976 empowered the relevant authorities to impose effluent charges for dischargers to surface waters. A five year period was allowed to enable dischargers to install suitable waste water treatment plant.

5.5.2   Liability to pay those charges now arises from both the discharge of water polluted by their use, and from rainfall run-off. The charges are calculated according to quantity, and the presence of suspended solids, and oxidisable and toxic constituents. The fact that charges are paid will not justify any reduction of effluent standards. Charges are reduced by 50 per cent if legal minimum standards, or standards specified in the permit are met; and may be so reduced if the water supplied to the discharger was already polluted.

5.5.3   Where a local authority receives waste waters into its sewers, it may charge for the service, but itself will become liable to pay effluent charges for the ultimate discharge into the environment. It can, however, make it worthwhile for a company to discharge into public sewers rather than directly into the environment.

Appendix G

New Zealand

1. NEW ZEALAND ENVIRONMENT ACT

The New Zealand Environment Act 1986 established a new post of Parliamentary Commissioner for the Environment, and extended the powers of the Ombudsman to deal with environmental matters.

2. PARLIAMENTARY COMMISSIONER FOR THE ENVIRONMENT

2.1 Terms of appointment

2.1.1 The Act created the post of Parliamentary Commissioner for the Environment, who serves as an officer of Parliament. He is appointed by the Governor-General on the recommendation of the House of Representatives.

His term of office is for five years but is renewable. He is not to be a Member of Parliament, or of any local authority.

2.1.2 An important protection for him is that he may be removed or suspended only by the Governor-General on an address by the House of Representatives for disability, bankruptcy, neglect of duty or misconduct.

A further protection is that he is paid out of the Consolidated Account without further appropriation. Furthermore, his salary cannot be reduced during the continuance of his appointment.

2.1.3 He may appoint staff, incuding persons with expert knowledge, to assist him.

2.2 Functions

2.2.1 The functions of the Commissioner are:

(a) With the objective of maintaining and improving the quality of the environment, to review from time to time the system of agencies and processes established by the government to manage the allocation, use, and preservation of natural and physical resources, and to report the result to the House and such other bodies as he considers appropriate.

(b) Where he considers it necessary, to investigate the effectiveness of environmental planning and management by public authorities, and advise them on any remedial action he considers desirable.

(c) To investigate any matter by which, in his opinion, the environment has been or may be adversely affected, whether through natural causes or acts or omissions of any persons. To advise the appropriate persons or public authorities on preventive or remedial action, and to report to the House.

(d) At the request of the House or any of its select committees, to advise on any petition, Bill or other matter before it, which may have a significant effect on the environment.

(e) On a direction of the House, to enquire into any matter that has had or may have a substantial and damaging effect on the environment, and to report. For this purpose he is given special statutory powers, and the immunities and privileges of a District Court judge exercising a civil jurisdiction.

(f) To undertake and encourage the collection and dissemination of information relating to the environment.

(g) To encourage preventive measures and remedial actions for the protection of the environment.

2.2.2 In the performance of his functions, where he considers it appropriate, he shall have regard, in particular but not exclusively, to the following.

(a) The maintenance and restoration of ecosystems of importance, especially those supporting habitats of rare, threatened or endangered species of flora or fauna.

(b) Areas, landscapes, and structures of aesthetic, archaeological, cultural, historical, recreational, scenic, and scientific value.

(c) Land, water, sites, fishing grounds, or physical or cultural resources, or interests associated with such areas, which are part of the heritage of the tangata whenua, the local people or community, and which contribute to their well-being.

(d) Effects on communities of people of:
    (i) actual or proposed changes to natural and physical resources;
    (ii) the establishment or proposed establishment of new communities.

(e) Whether any proposals, policies or other matters within his area of responsibilities, are likely to:
    (i) result in or increase pollution; or
    (ii) result in the occurrence, or increase the chances of occurrence, of natural hazards or hazardous substances; or
    (iii) result in the introduction of species or genotypes not previously present in New Zealand, including its territorial sea; or
    (iv) have features, the environmental effects of which are not certain, and the potential impact of which is to warrant further investigation in order to determine the environmental impact of the proposal, policy or other matter; or
    (v) result in the accumulation or depletion of any natural or physical reasources in a way or at a rate that will prevent the renewal by natural processes, or will not enable an orderly transition to other materials.

(f) All reasonably foreseeable effects of any such proposal, policy or other matter on the environment, whether adverse or beneficial, short term or long term, direct or indirect, or cumulative.

(g) Alternative means or methods of implementing or providing for any such proposal, policy or matter in any or all of its aspects, including the consideration, where appropriate, of alternative sites.

2.3 Powers and rights

2.3.1 General power

The Commissioner has such powers as may be necessary to enable him to carry out his functions under the Act.

2.3.2 Particular powers etc

(a) He may from time to time require any person who in his opinion is able to give information on any matter which is being investigated or enquired into by him, to furnish such information and produce such documents which, in the opinion of the Commissioner relate to such matter, and which may be in the possession or under the control of that person.

(b) He may summon before him and examine on oath any person who in his opinion is able to give such information. He may administer the oath, and the law relating to perjury applies.

A person is not compelled to comply if he is bound to secrecy by any enactment, other than the State Services Act 1962 and the Official Information Act 1982, and his compliance would be a breach of secrecy under the enactment.

(c) In any proceedings relating to or arising from any consent or attempt to obtain consent, the Commissioner

(i) has a right to be present and heard for the purpose of calling evidence;

(ii) may examine, cross-examine and re-examine any witness;

(iii) may be represented by counsel, or any other duly authorised representative.

2.3.3 The Commissioner may, either generally or in respect of a particular matter, and subject to such conditions and restrictions as he thinks fit, delegate his functions to an officer or employee.

The power to delegate may not itself be delegated. Neither does it apply to certain powers specified in the Act, including the power to summon or require information of any person, (see 2.3.2(a) and (b)), act as a commission of enquiry, (see 2.2.1(e), or report to the House of Representatives.

Every delegation is revocable at will.

2.4 Duty to maintain secrecy

Except for the purposes of the administration of the Act, and the performance of any duties under the Act, the Commissioner and any person holding an office or appointment under him shall maintain secrecy in all matters which come to their knowledge in the performance of their functions and exercise of their powers under the Act.

2.5   Annual and other reports

The Commissioner shall report each year to the House of Representatives on the performance of his functions under the Act, and any other matter he thinks appropriate.

He may also submit reports to the House at any other times.

3.   OMBUDSMAN

The Environment Act 1986 also extended the functions of the Ombudsman, appointed under the Ombudsman Act 1975, to include environmental matters.

Appendix H

Examples of Existing Legislative Provisions

1. ENFORCEMENT AND IMPROVEMENT NOTICES

United Kingdom Environmental Protection Act 1990, Section 13

13. (1) If the enforcing authority is of the opinion that the person carrying on the prescribed process under an authorisation is contravening any condition of the authorisation, or is likely to contravene any such condition, the authority may serve on him a notice, ('an enforcement notice').
    (2) An enforcement notice shall
        (a) state that the authority is of the said opinion.
        (b) specify the matters constituting the contravention or the matters making it likely that the contravention will arise, as the case may be;
        (c) specify the steps that must be taken to remedy the contravention or to remedy the matters making it likely that the contravention will arise, as the case may be; and
        (d) specify the period within which those steps must be taken.
    (3) The Secretary of State may, if he thinks fit in relation to the carrying on by any person of a prescribed process, give to the enforcing authority directions as to whether the authority should exercise its powers under this section and as to the steps which are to be required to be taken under this section.

Ontario Environmental Protection Act, Sections 9–11

9. (1) A person responsible for a source of contaminant may submit to the Director a program to prevent or to reduce and control the addition to, emission or discharge into the natural environment of any contaminant from the source of contaminant.
    (2) When a program referred to in subsection (1) is submitted to the Director, the Director may, with the consent of the Minister, refer the program to the Environmental Council for its consideration and advice.
    (3) The Director may issue an approval to be known as a 'program approval', directed to the person who submitted the program.

10. The Director shall, in a program approval,
    (a)   set out the name of the person to whom the approval is directed;
    (b)   set out the location and nature of the source of contaminant;
    (c)   set out the details of the program; and
    (d)   approve the program.
11. Notwithstanding the issue of a program approval, when the Director is of the opinion, based on reasonable and probable grounds, that it is necessary or advisable for the protection or conservation of the natural environment, the prevention or control of an immediate danger to human life, the health of any person or to property, the Director may issue a stop order or control order directed to the person responsible
(For copies of the control and stop order provisions see below.)

Mauritius Environment Protection Act 1991, section 57

57. (1) Where he is of the opinion that a person is contravening, or is likely to contravene an environmental law, the Director may cause to be served on him a programme notice
    (a) stating the opinion of the Director;
    (b) specifying the matter constituting the contravention or the matter making it likely that the contravention will arise, as the case may be;
    (c) requesting the person to submit for his approval before a specified date a written programme of measures which the person intends to take to remedy the contravention or to eliminate the likelihood of a contravention.
  (2) The Director may
    (a) hold consultations with the person to determine the appropriate method of remedying the contravention or eliminating the likelihood of a contravention;
    (b) consult a technical advisory committee or the (Environmental Co-ordination) Committee;
    (c) request the person to submit additional information, proposal or research study.
  (3) On approving a programme of measures, the Director shall issue a programme approval stating
    (a) the notice issued under subsection (1);
    (b) the measures that shall be taken to remedy the contravention or eliminate the likelihood of a contravention; and
    (c) the period within which the measures shall be implemented.
  (4) The Director may
    (a) supervise and issue directions in respect of the implementation of the measures contained in the programme approval;
    (b) with the consent of the person, modify the programme approval;
    (c) at any time, revoke a programme approval.
  (5) No person shall be prosecuted for a contravention in respect of which a programme approval is in force.
  (6) Where
    (a) a person fails to comply with

      (i) a request in a notice under subsection (1);

      (ii) a programme approval issued under subsection (3);

      (iii) any direction issued under subsection (4); or

  (b) a programme approval is revoked under subsection (4);

the Director may issue an enforcement notice or a prohibition notice.

2. CONTROL, PROHIBITION AND STOP NOTICES AND ORDERS

United Kingdom Environmental Protection Act 1990, Sections 14 and 18

14. (1) If the enforcing authority is of the opinion, as respects the carrying on of a prescribed process under an authorisation, that the continuing to carry it on, or the continuing to carry it on in a particular manner, involves an imminent risk of serious pollution of the environment the authority shall serve a notice (a 'prohibition notice') on the person carrying on the process.

   (2) A prohibition notice may be served whether or not the manner of carrying on the process in question contravenes a condition of the authorisation and may relate to any aspects of the process, whether regulated by the conditions of the authorisation or not.

   (3) A prohibition notice shall

     (a) state the authority's opinion;

     (b) specify the risk involved in the process;

     (c) specify the steps that must be taken to remove it and the period within which they must be taken; and

     (d) direct that the authorisation shall, until the notice is withdrawn, wholly or to the extent specified in the notice cease to have effect to authorise the carrying on of the process;

       and where the direction applies to only part of the process it may impose conditions to be observed in carrying on the part which is authorised to be carried on.

   (4) The Secretary of State may, if he thinks fit in relation to the carrying on by any person of a prescribed process, give to the enforcing authority directions as to—

     (a) whether the authority should perform its duties under this section; and

     (b) the matters to be specified in any prohibition notice in pursuance of subsection (3) above which the authority is directed to issue.

   (5) The enforcing authority shall, as respects any prohibition notice it has issued to any person, by notice in writing served on that person withdraw the notice when it is satisfied that the steps required by the notice have been taken.

Section 18, set out below, is neither a prohibition notice nor a stop notice, but serves a similar purpose. It is therefore included here.

18. (1) Where, in the case of any article or substance found by him on any premises which he has power to enter, and inspector has reasonable cause to believe that, in the circumstances in which he finds it, the article or

substance is a cause of imminent danger of serious harm he may seize it and cause it to be rendered harmless (whether by destruction or otherwise).

(2) Before there is rendered harmless under this section
  (a) any article that forms part of a batch of similar articles; or
  (b) any substance,
the inspector shall, if it is practicable to do so, take a sample of it and give to a responsible person at the premises where the article or substance was found by him a portion of the sample marked in a manner sufficient to identify it.

(3) As soon as may be after any article or substance has been seized and rendered harmless under this section, the inspector shall prepare and sign a written report giving particulars of the circumstances in which the article or substance was seized and so dealt with by him, and shall
  (a) give a signed copy of the report to a responsible person at the premises where the article or substance was found by him; and
  (b) unless that person is the owner of the article or substance, also serve a signed copy of the report on the owner;
and if, where paragraph (b) above applies, the inspector cannot after reasonable inquiry ascertain the name or address of the owner, the copy may be served on him by giving it to the person to whom a copy was given under paragraph (a) above.

Ontario Environmental Protection Act, Sections 113 and 117

113. The Director may, where he is authorized by this Act to issue an order known as a 'control order', order the person to whom it is directed to do any one or more of the following, namely,

  (a) to limit or control the rate of addition, emission or discharge of the contaminant into the natural environment in accordance with the directions set out in the order;
  (b) to stop the addition, emission or discharge of the contaminant into the natural environment
    (i) permanently,
    (ii) for a specified period, or
    (iii) in the circumstances set out in the order;
  (c) to comply with any directions set out in the order relating to the manner in which the contaminant may be added, emitted or discharged into the natural environment;
  (d) to comply with any directions set out in the order relating to the procedures to be followed in the control or elimination of the addition, emission or discharge of the contaminant into the natural environment; and
  (e) to install, replace or alter any equipment or thing designed to control or eliminate the addition, emission or discharge of the contaminant into the natural environment.

Note Sections 114 and 115 relating to compliance, and to variation or revocation of an order.

117. The Director may, where he is authorized by this Act to issue an order known as a 'stop order', order the person to whom it is directed to immediately stop or cause the source of contaminant to stop adding to, emitting or discharging into the natural environment any contaminant either permanently or for a specific period of time.

118. A stop order shall be in writing and shall include written reasons for the order.

Note Section 119 on compliance and revocation.

Mauritius Environment Protection Act 1991, Section 59

59. (1) Where he is of the opinion that an enterprise or activity or the manner in which the enterprise or activity is carried on, involves an imminent risk of serious pollution to the environment, the Director may cause to be served on the person owning, or managing, or in charge of, or in control of the enterprise or activity a prohibition notice.

(2) A prohibition notice may be served whether or not
   (a) the enterprise or activity, or the manner in which the enterprise or activity is carried on, constituted a contravention of an environmental law;
   (b) there is in force in relation to that enterprise or activity, a licence, permit or approval issued under any environmental law or any other enactment.

(3) A prohibition notice shall
   (a) state the Director's opinion;
   (b) specify the risk of serious pollution involved as well as the way in which the enterprise, activity or the manner in which the enterprise or activity is carried on, is suspected to give rise to the risk;
   (c) specify the measures that shall be taken to remove the risk of pollution and the period within which they shall be implemented;
   (d) specify the enterprise or activity, or any aspect of the enterprise or activity that is prohibited, or specify any conditions in which the enterprise or activity may be carried on.

(4) A prohibition notice shall not be a bar to a prosecution for any offence, even if there are consultations with the person served with the notice.

(5) Any person who fails to comply with a prohibition notice, shall commit an offence.

3. FREEDOM OF INFORMATION

European Communities Directive 90/313/EEC on Freedom of Access to Information on the Environment

Article 1

The object of this Directive is to ensure freedom of access to, and dissemination of, information on the environment held by public authorities and to set out the basic terms and conditions on which such information should be made available.

Article 2

For the purposes of this Directive:

(a) 'information relating to the environment' shall mean any available information in written, visual, aural or data-base form on the state of water, air, soil, fauna, flora, land and natural sites, and on activities (including those which give rise to nuisances such as noise or measures adversely affecting, or likely so to affect these, and on activities or measures designed to protect these, including administrative measures and environmental management programmes;

(b) 'public authorities' shall mean any public administration at national, regional or local level with responsibilities, and possessing information, relating to the environment with the exception of bodies acting in a judicial or legislative capacity.

Article 3

1. Save as provided in this Article, Member States shall ensure that public authorities are required to make available information relating to the environment to any natural or legal person at his request and without his having to prove an interest.

   Member States shall define the practical arrangements under which such information is effectively made available.

2. Member States may provide for a request for such information to be refused where it affects:
   - the confidentiality of the proceedings of public authorities, international relations and national defence,
   - public security,
   - matters which are, or have been, *sub judice*, or under enquiry (including disciplinary enquiries), or which are the subject of preliminary investigation proceedings,
   - commercial and industrial condifentiality, including intellectual property,
   - the confidentiality of personal data and/or files,
   - material supplied by a third party without that party being under a legal obligation to do so,
   - material, the disclosure of which would make it more likely that the environment to which such material related would be damaged.

   Information held by public authorities shall be supplied in part where it is possible to separate out information on items concerning the interests referred to above.

3. a request for information may be refused where it would involve the supply of unfinished documents or data or internal communications, or where the request is manifestly unreasonable or formulated in too general a manner.

4. A public authority shall respond to a person requesting information as soon as possible and at the latest within two months. The reasons for a refusal to provide the information requested must be given.

Article 4

A person who considers that his request for information has been unreasonably refused or ignored, or has been inadequately answered by a public authority, may seek a judicial or administrative review of the decision in accordance with the relevant national legal system.

Article 5

Member States may make a charge for supplying the information, but such charge may not exceed a reasonable cost.

Article 6

Member States shall take the necessary steps to ensure that information relating to the environment held by bodies with public responsibilities for the environment and under the control of public authorities is made available on the same terms and conditions as those set out in Articles 3, 4 and 5 either via the competent public authority or directly by the body itself.

Article 7

Member States shall take the necessary steps to provide general information to the public on the state of environment by such means as the periodic publication of descriptive reports.

United States Freedom of Information Act

S.552

(a) Each agency shall make available to the public information as follows:
(1) Each agency shall separately state and currently publish in the Federal Register for the guidance of the public—
(A) descriptions of its central and field organization and the established places at which, employees (and in the case of a uniformed service, the members) from whom, and the methods whereby, the public may obtain information, make submittals or requests, or obtain decisions;
(B) statements of the general course and method by which its functions are channeled and determined, including the nature and requirements of all formal and informal procedures available;
(C) rules of procedure, descriptions of forms available or the places at which forms may be obtained, and instructions as to the scope and contents of all papers, reports, or examinations;
(D) substantive rules of general applicability adopted as authorized by law, and statements of general policy or interpretations of general applicability formulated and adopted by the agency; and
(E) each amendment, revision, or repeal of the foregoing.
Except to the extent that a person has actual and timely notice of the terms thereof, a person may not in any manner be required to resort to, or be adversely affected by, a matter required to be published in the

Federal Register and not so published. For the purpose of this paragraph, matter reasonably available to the class of persons affected thereby is deemed published in the Federal Register when incorporated by reference therein with the approval of the Director of the Federal Register.

(2) Each agency, in accordance with published rules, shall make available for public inspection and copying—

(A) final opinions, including concurring and dissenting opinions, as well as orders, made in the adjudication of cases;

(B) those statements of policy and interpretations which have been adopted by the agency and are not published in the Federal Register; and

(C) administrative staff manuals and instructions to staff that affect a member of the public;

unless the materials are promptly published and copies offered for sale. To the extent required to prevent a clearly unwarranted invasion of personal privacy, an agency may delete identifying details when it makes available or publishes an opinion, statement of policy, interpretation, or staff manual or instruction. However, in each case justification for the deletion shall be explained fully in writing. Each agency shall also maintain and make available for public inspection and copying current indexes providing identifying information for the public as to any matter issued, adopted, or promulgated after July 4, 1967, and required by this paragraph to be made available or published. Each agency shall promptly publish quarterly or more frequently, and distribute (by sale or otherwise) copies of each index or supplements thereto unless it determines by order published in the Federal Register that the publication would be unnecessary and impracticable, in which case the agency shall nonetheless provide copies of such index on request at a cost not to exceed the direct cost of duplication. A final order, opinion, statement of policy, interpretation, or staff manual or instruction that affects a member of the public may be relied on, used, or cited as precedent by an agency against a party other than the agency only if—

(i) it has been indexed and either made available or published as provided by this paragraph; or

(ii) the party has actual and timely notice of the terms thereof.

(3) Except with respect to the records made available under paragraphs (1) and (2) of this subsection, each agency, upon any request for records which (a) reasonably describes such records and (b) is made in accordance with published rules stating the time, place, fees (if any), and procedures to be followed, shall make the records promptly available for any person.

(4) (A) In order to carry out the provisions of this section, each agency shall promulgate regulations, pursuant to notice and receipt of public comment, specifying a uniform schedule of fees applicable to all constituent units of such agency. Such fees shall be limited to reasonable standard charges for document search and duplication and provide for recovery of only the direct costs of

such search and duplication. Documents shall be furnished without charge or at a reduced charge where the agency determines that waiver or reduction of the fee is in the public interest because furnishing the information can be considered as primarily benefiting the general public.

(B) On complaint, the district court of the United States in the district in which the complainant resides, or has his principal place of business, or in which the agency records are situated, or in the District of Columbia, has jurisdiction to enjoin the agency from withholding agency records and to order the production of any agency records improperly withheld from the complainant. . . .

(G) In the event of non-compliance with the order of the court, the district court may punish for contempt the responsible employee, and in the case of a uniformed service, the responsible member.

(6) (C) Any person making a request to any agency for records under paragraph (1), (2) or (3) of this subsection shall be deemed to have exhausted his administrative remedies with respect to such request if the agency fails to comply with the applicable time limit provisions of this paragraph. If the Government can show exceptional circumstances exist and that the agency is exercising due diligence in responding to the request, the court may retain jurisdiction and allow the agency additional time to complete the review of the records. Upon any determination by an agency to comply with a request for records, the records shall be made promptly available to such person making such request. Any notification of denial of any request for recouds under this subjection shall set forth the names and titles or positions of each person responsible for the denial of such request.

(b) This section does not apply to matters that are—

(1) (A) Specifically authorized under criteria established by an Executive order to be kept secret in the interest of national defense or foreign policy and (B) are in fact properly classified pursuant to such Executive order;

(2) related solely to the internal personnel rules and practices of an agency;

(3) specifically exempted from disclosure by statute (other than section 552b of this title), provided that such statute (A) requires that the matters be withheld from the public in such manner as to leave no discretion on the issue, or (B) establishes particular criteria for withholding or refers to particular types of matters to be withheld;

(4) trade secrets and commercial or financial information obtained from a person and privileged or confidential;

(5) inter-agency or intra-agency memorandums or letters which would not be available by law to a party other than as agency in litigation with the agency;

(6) personnel and medical files and similar files the disclosure of which would constitute a clearly unwarranted invasion of personal privacy;

(7) investigatory records compiled for law enforcement purposes, but only to the extent that the production of such records would (A) interfere

with enforcement proceedings, (B) deprive a person of a right to a fair
trial or an impartial adjudication, (C) constitute an unwarranted invasion of personal privacy, (D) disclose the identity of a confidential
source and, in the case of a record compiled by a criminal law
enforcement authority in the course of a criminal investigation, or by
an agency conducting a lawful national security intelligence investigation, confidential information furnished only by the confidential
source, (E) disclose investigative techniques and procedures, or (F)
endanger the life or physical safety of law enforcement personnel;

(8) contained in or related to examination, operating, or condition reports
prepared by, or on behalf of, or for the use of an agency responsible
for the regulation or supervision of financial institutions; or

(9) geological and geophysical information and data, including maps,
concerning wells.

Any reasonably segregable portion of a record shall be provided to any
person requesting such record after deletion of the portions which are
exempt under this subsection.

(c) This section does not authorize withholding of information or limit the
availability of records to the public, except as specifically stated in this
section. This section is not authority to withhold information from
Congress.

United Kingdom Control of Pollution Act 1974

94 (1) If a person discloses information relating to any trade secret used in
carrying on a particular undertaking and the information has been given to
him or obtained by him by virtue of this Act he shall, subject to the
following subsection, be guilty of an offence and liable on summary conviction to a fine not exceeding level 5 on the standard scale.

(2) a person shall not be guilty of an offence under the preceding subsection by
virtue of the disclosure of any information if

(a) the disclosure was made

(i)   in the performance of his duty, or

(ii) in pursuance of 79(1)(b) of this Act (arrangement by a local
authority for the publication of information on an air pollution
problem), or

(iii) with the consent in writing of a person having a right to disclose
the information; or

(b) the information is of a kind prescribed for the purposes of this
paragraph and, if regulations made for those purposes provided that
information of that kind may only be disclosed in pursuance of the
regulations to prescribed persons, the disclosure is to a prescribed
person.

United Kingdom Environmental Protection Act 1990

20 (1) It shall be the duty of each enforcing authority, as respects prescribed
processes for which it is the enforcing authority, to maintain, in accordance

with regulations made by the Secretary of State, a register containing prescribed particulars of or relating to—

(a) applications for authorisations made to that authority;
(b) the authorisations which have been granted by that authority or in
     respect of which the authority has functions under this Part;
(c) variation notices, enforcement notices and prohibition notices issued
     by that authority;
(d) revocations of authorisations effected by that authority;
(e) appeals under Section 15 above;
(f) convictions for such offences under section 23 below (general
     offences provision) as may be prescribed;
(g) information obtained or furnished in pursuance of the conditions of
     authorisations or under any provision of this Part;
(h) directions given to the authority under any provision of this Part by the
     Secretary of State; and
(i) such other matters relating to the carrying on of prescribed processes or
     any pollution of the environment caused thereby as may be prescribed;

but that duty is subject to sections 21 and 22 below.

(2)   Subject to subsection (4) below, (concerning port health
authorities) the register maintained by a local enforcing authority shall also contain
prescribed particulars of such information contained in any register maintained by
the chief inspector … as relates to the carrying on in the area of the authority of
prescribed processes in relation to which the chief inspector … has functions under
the Part; and the chief inspector … shall furnish each authority with the particulars
which are necessary to enable it to discharge its duty under this subsection.

(5) Where information of any description is excluded from any register by
     virtue of section 22 below, a statement shall be entered in the register
     indicating the existence of information of that description.
(7) It shall be the duty of each enforcing authority—
     (a) to ensure that the registers maintained by them under this section are
          available at all reasonable times for inspection by the public free of
          charge; and
     (b) to afford to members of the public facilities for obtaining copies of
          entries, on payment of reasonable charges.

21 (1) No information shall be included in a register maintained under section 20
        above if and so long as, in the opinion of the Secretary of State, the inclu-
        sion in the register of that information, or information of that description,
        would be contrary to the interests of national security.
   (2) The Secretary of State may, for the purpose of securing the exclusion from
        register of information to which subsection (1) above applies, give the
        enforcing authorities directions—
        (a) specifying information, or descriptions of information to be excluded
             from their registers, or
        (b) specifying descriptions of information to be referred to the Secretary
             of State for his determination;
        and no information referred to the Secretary of State in pursuance of
        paragraph(b) above shall be included in any such register until the
        Secretary of State determines that is should be so included.

(3) The enforcing authority shall notify the Secretary of State of any information it excludes from the register in pursuance of directions under subsection (2) above.

(4) A person may, as respects information which appears to him to be information to which subsection (1) above may apply, give a notice to the Secretary of State specifying the information and indicating its apparent nature; and, if he does so—

(a) he shall notify the enforcing authority that he has done so; and

(b) no information so notified to the Secretary of State shall be included in any such register until the Secretary of State has determined that it should be so included.

22 (1) No information relating to the affairs of any individual or business shall be included in a register maintained under section 20 above, without the consent of that individual or the person for the time being carrying on that business, if and so long as the information

(a) is, in relation to him, commercially confidential; and

(b) is not to be included in the register in pursuance of directions under subsection 7 below;

but information is not commercially confidential for the purpose of this section unless it is determined under this section to be so by the enforcing authority or, on appeal, by the Secretary of State.

(2) Where information is furnished to an enforcing authority for the purpose of

(a) an application for an authorisation or for the variation of an authorisation;

(b) complying with any condition of an authorisation; or

(c) complying with a notice under section 19 (2) above; (information a person is required by notice to give to an enforcing authority);

then, if the person furnishing it applies to the authority to have the information excluded from the register on the ground that it is commercially confidential (as regards himself or another person), the authority shall determine whether the information is or is not commercially confidential.

(3) A determination under subsection (2) above must be made within the period of fourteen days beginning with the date of the application and if the enforcing authority fails to make a determination within that period it shall be treated as having determined that the information is commercially confidential.

(4) Where it appears to an enforcing authority that any information (other than information furnished in circumstances within subsection (2) above) which has been obtained by the authority under or by virtue of any provision of this Part might be commercially confidential, the authority shall

(a) give to the person to whom or whose business it relates notice that the information is required to be included in the register unless excluded under this section; and

(b) give him a reasonable opportunity

(i) of objecting to the inclusion of the information on the ground that it is commercially confidential; and

(ii) of making representations to the authority for the purpose of justifying any such objection;

and, if any representations are made, the enforcing authority shall, having taken the representations into account, determine whether the information is or is not commercially confidential.

(5) Where, under subsection (2) or (4) above, an authority determines that information is not commercially confidential

(a) the information shall not be entered on the register until the end of the period of twenty-one days beginning with the date on which the determination is notified to the person concerned;

(b) that person may appeal to the Secretary of State against the decision,

and, where an appeal is brought in respect of any information, the information shall not be entered on the register pending the final termination or withdrawal of the appeal.

(7) The Secretary of State may give to the enforcing authorities directions as to specified information or descriptions of information, which the public interest requires to be included in registers maintained under Section 20 above notwithstanding that the information may be commercially confidential.

(11) Information is, for the purposes of any determination under this section, commercially confidential, in relation to any individual or person, if its being contained in the register would prejudice to an unreasonable degree the commercial interests of that individual or person.

United Kingdom Water Resources Act 1991

190(1) It shall be the duty of the Authority to maintain, in accordance with regulations made by the Secretary of State, registers containing prescribed particulars of—

(a) any notice of water quality objectives or other notices served under section 83 above (concerning water quality objectives);

(b) applications for consents under Chapter II of Part III of this Act;

(c) consents given under that Chapter and the conditions to which the consents are subject;

(d) certificates issued under paragraph 1 (7) of Schedule 10 to this Act;

(e) the following, that is to say—

(i) samples of water or effluent taken by the Authority for the purposes of any of the water pollution provisions of this Act;

(ii) information produced by analyses of those samples;

(iii) such information with respect to samples of water or effluent taken by any other person, and the analyses of those samples, as is acquired by the Authority from any person under arrangements made by the Authority for the purposes of any of those provisions; and

(iv) the steps taken in consequence of any such information as is mentioned in any of sub-paragraphs (i) or (iii) above; and

(f) any matter about which particulars are required to be kept in any register under section 20 of the Environmental Protection Act 1990 (particulars about authorisations for prescribed processes, etc) by the chief inspector under Part I of that Act.

(2) It shall be the duty of the Authority

(a) to secure that the contents of registers maintained by the Authority under this section are available, at all reasonable times, for inspection by the public free of charge; and

(b) to afford members of the public reasonable facilities for obtaining from the Authority, on payment of reasonable charges, copies of entries in any of the registers.

4. OBLIGATION TO CONSULT

United Kingdom Water Resources Act 1991

Schedule 10

1 (4) Where an application is made in accordance with this paragraph the Authority shall—

(a) publish notice of the application, at least once in each of two successive weeks, in a newspaper or newspapers circulating in

(i) the locality or localities in which the places are situated at which it is proposed in the application that the discharges should be made; and

(ii) the locality or localities appearing to the Authority to be in the vicinity of any controlled waters which the Authority considers likely to be affected by the proposed discharges;

(b) publish a copy of that notice in an edition of the *London Gazette* published no earlier than the day after the publication of the last of the notices to be published by virtue of paragraph (a) above;

(c) send a copy of the application to every local authority or water undertaker within whose area any of the proposed discharges is to occur;

(d) in the case of an application which relates to proposed discharges into coastal waters, relevant territorial waters or waters outside the seaward limits of relevant territorial waters, serve a copy of the application on the Secretary of State and on each of the Ministers.

2 (1) It shall be the duty of the Authority to consider any written representations or objections with respect to an application under paragraph 1 above which are made to it in the period of six weeks beginning with the day of the publication of notice of the application in the *London Gazette* and are not withdrawn.

3 (1) This paragraph applies where the Authority proposes to give its consent under paragraph 2 above on an application in respect of which such representations or objections as the Authority is required to consider under sub-paragraph (1) of that paragraph have been made.

(2) It shall be the duty of the Authority to serve notice of the proposal on every person who made any such representations or objection; and any such notice shall include a statement of the effect of sub-paragraph (3) below.

(3) Any person who made any such representations or objection may, within the period of 21 days beginning with the day on which the notice of the proposal is served on him, in the prescribed manner request the Secretary of State to give a direction under paragraph 4 (1) below in respect of the application.

(4) It shall be the duty of the Authority not to give its consent on the application before the end of the period of 21 days mentioned in sub-paragraph (3) above and, if within that period—

(a) a request is made under sub-paragraph (3) above in respect of the application; and

(b) the person who makes the request serves notice of it on the Authority, the Authority shall not give its consent on the application unless the Secretary of State has served notice on the Authority stating that he declined to comply with the request.

Index